✦ LITERACY AND RACIAL JUSTICE

LITERACY AND RACIAL JUSTICE

The Politics of Learning after *Brown v. Board of Education*

✦ CATHERINE PRENDERGAST

With a Foreword by Gloria Ladson-Billings

Southern Illinois University Press
Carbondale

Library of Congress Cataloging-in-Publication Data
Prendergast, Catherine, date.
    Literacy and racial justice : the politics of learning after Brown v. Board of
Education / Catherine Prendergast ; with a foreword by Gloria Ladson-Billings.
        p. cm.
    Includes bibliographical references (p.) and index.
1. African Americans—Education. 2. Literacy—United States. 3. Discrimination
in education—United States. I. Title.
LC2731 .P72 2003
371.829'96'073—dc21   2002154285
ISBN 0-8093-2524-1 (hardcover : alk. paper)
ISBN 0-8093-2525-X (pbk. : alk. paper)

Printed on recycled paper. ♻

The paper used in this publication meets the minimum requirements of American National Standard for Information Sciences—Permanence of Paper for
Printed Library Materials, ANSI Z39.48-1992. ∞

For my parents,
Kevin and Jane Prendergast

✦ CONTENTS

✦ FOREWORD

In May 1954, when the Supreme Court handed down the first *Brown v. Board of Education,* I was completing first grade in my neighborhood school in West Philadelphia, Pennsylvania. The decision barely caused a ripple in my community. Despite the fact that almost every child in my school was Black (there was one White family who attended the school), we were not considered a legally segregated school district. Unlike the schools in the South, Philadelphia did not maintain two separate school districts. People attended their neighborhood schools. Those neighborhoods just happened to be comprised of either all-Black or all-White families!

In May 1955, when the Court handed down *Brown II* (desegregate "with all deliberate speed"), I was giddy with the excitement of having skipped a semester of second grade. Sitting in third grade with students who were older and bigger was simultaneously exciting and frightening. Once again, all of the students were African Americans. We were all neighborhood kids who were oblivious to the legal and social changes the nation was experiencing. However, by late summer of 1955, that all would change.

In mid-August 1955, a fourteen-year-old Black boy named Emmett Till went to visit his relatives in the tiny rural community of Money, Mississippi. While there, Emmett pulled out some snapshots of White children and bragged to his cousins and their friends about the fact that he attended school with them. Buoyed by his peers' disbelief, young Till insisted that one of the White girls was his girlfriend. That inconceivable bit of information spurred one of the Mississippi boys to challenge Till to speak to a White woman in the local candy store. As the boys left the store, Emmett looked back and said, "Bye baby," to the woman. By the next day, Emmett Till was dead. In the dark of night, two White men came to Till's uncle's house and dragged him out into a car. The killers beat Till, shot him, tied his body to a turbine, and threw it into the river. When his body was discovered, it was so horribly bloated and deformed that he did not look human. Mamie Bradley, Emmett's mother, used her son's mutilated body to make a statement. Rather than a closed casket ceremony, which is typical when someone's death involves visible trauma to the body, Mrs. Bradley chose an open casket so that the world could see what the murderers did to her son.

Emmett Till's funeral in Chicago attracted media from across the nation. *Jet Magazine,* a weekly news and entertainment publication in the Black community, published a photograph of the mutilated Emmett Till. For weeks my sleep was disturbed by that image. Some time later, when the two men who had been arrested for Till's murder, Roy Bryant and W. J. Milam, were swiftly acquitted, the nightmares became a twenty-four-hour-a-day preoccupation. How could it be that two adults could kill a boy and not be punished? What about my own brother, who was just a year older than Emmett Till? My brother loved spending his summers in the South, visiting relatives. He loved swimming in the creek, stealing watermelons from some unsuspecting farmer's garden, eating the homemade pies, cakes, and biscuits my aunt baked. My brother was brash and city slick like Till. Would these same men kill my brother if he said the wrong thing? As a seven-year-old I had no way of understanding the impact of the *Brown* decisions. Instead, I could not get past the brutal, senseless murder of someone like my brother.

By 1976, some drastic changes had occurred in the United States. The civil rights movement had forced a number of legislative and social changes. Martin Luther King Jr. had pricked the moral conscience of the nation and mobilized its citizens to nonviolently demand equal rights for all. Also, a more militant group of Black people organized into the Black Panther Party, and the struggle for Black liberation prompted a sense of Black consciousness and pride. At the same time, the Supreme Court ruled in *Washington v. Davis* that the tests used to determine eligibility for the District of Columbia's police force were not discriminatory despite the fact that African Americans failed this test at twice the rate of their White counterparts. This ruling was a clear reversal of civil rights gains, but once again, the impact of this ruling was lost on me.

In 1976, I was a teacher in the same Philadelphia schools that I had attended. By this time, it was clear that schools in the North were as segregated (and often more so) as those in the South. Philadelphia was under a court order to desegregate, and Whites were fleeing to the northeast section of the city and surrounding suburbs. But the growing racial encapsulation of Blacks was not the major agenda item of the city. Philadelphia was in the midst of a multimillion-dollar bicentennial celebration. The city's downtown area was spruced up and on display for tourists, business travelers, and national conferences. The fact that almost 70 percent of the school children were African American and almost 70 percent of their teachers were White did not seem to faze the community. Two hundred years of nationhood had not produced much racial progress in the "Cradle of Liberty."

In 1978, the Supreme Court ruled on the *Bakke* decision, in which Alan Bakke claimed that he was a victim of discrimination in that he was denied admission because of a special admissions program to increase enrollment of students of color at the University of California at Davis Medical School. This time the Court's decision spoke directly to me. In the fall of 1978, I was entering graduate school at Stanford University, about three hours south of the University of California at Davis. Although I had excellent undergraduate grades, I had no doubt that the changing times (e.g., civil rights activity, increased demands for opportunity made by African Americans, and judicial redress) helped with my admission to the university. The *Bakke* decision was a vivid reminder that the door of opportunity for Blacks had been opened only a crack and that at any moment it could be slammed shut.

I recount these cases and their relevance to my life because as I read *Literacy and Racial Justice,* I am reminded of the ways that the law and literacy have been recruited to maintain a system of racial inequity and discrimination that is antithetical to the democratic principles that the nation alleges. Catherine Prendergast has woven together the legal cases and literacy policies to demonstrate the ways that the *system* of racism infiltrates every aspect of life in the nation.

Today, schools throughout the nation struggle to produce literate students—particularly literate African American, Latino, and Southeast Asian immigrant students. But the majority of work focusing on literacy places its emphasis on student deficiency. Little work examines teacher competence, and almost all work examines teacher attitudes and beliefs about the competency and worthiness of students of color. Instead, it seems that the early literacy community is stuck in debates about methodology—phonics versus whole language—and concerned less about the needs of students than the politics that surround the debates.

This volume uses critical race theory as a rubric for understanding the persistence of literacy failure among African American students. The book melds the "stories" of the law with the stories of literacy and produces a rich, textured analysis of why working on one has ramifications for the other. This style is elegantly showcased in the chapter that reexamines Shirley Brice Heath's classic, *Ways with Words*. It is a wonderful treatment of this scholar's work in that it places it in its historical, political, and social context in a way most readers could never do. It highlights the tensions and contradictions that scholars confront, and it fills in the empty spaces that emerge in our reading of texts.

Prendergast offers what I would call a "big" text—not big in the sense of length of book but big in the sense of scope and ideas. This work focuses on what literacy has come to mean in a society that is highly racialized and how ideologies of multiculturalism struggle to penetrate the rigidly established belief systems and accepted practices. It is big in its conception of the student as citizen. Current discourse around schools and students position students (and their families) as consumers or students as potential workers.

The concept of students (and their families) as consumers has emerged in the current conversations about school choice. Instead of seeing schools as public institutions at the center of democratic citizen formation, schools have become primarily means to economic success. The U.S. commitment to the ideology of the individual works against a concept of the social contract that requires us to give up some individual rights for the common good. Indeed, the notion of the common good seems to be slipping farther away from our consciousness. We are experiencing an unprecedented retreat from public spaces. We relegate "the public" to the poor and disenfranchised. Who travels on public transportation? Who lives in public housing? Who uses public health services? And, increasingly (at least in urban areas), who attends public schools?

If students and their families are seen as consumers, then schools have no need to focus on the broad social goals of citizenship. Instead, such a conception of students and their families necessitates narrowly focused boutique-like schools aimed at recruiting niche markets that ultimately reconstitute themselves as interest groups, not citizens. While there is a place for specialty schools, these schools cannot be allowed to subvert the civic mission of schools in a democracy.

The notion of schools as feeding the economic engine through the development of potential workers is also troubling. Students should leave school with enough knowledge and skills to participate in the economy. But work skills are not the only skills schools should offer to students. With increasing job specialization and multiple work lives, it is impossible for schools to offer some generic set of skills that meet changing marketplace demands. However, the office of citizen is one that we want all students to hold. It requires a broad understanding of the liberal arts and the cultivation of critical thinking and decision-making skills. Whether or not people ever work for a living (e.g., consider the independently wealthy, stay-at-home parents, and people with disabilities), they remain citizens. Their civic responsibilities are as important as those of any other citizen.

Prendergast has used literacy as a tableau for civic participation. In a high technology, global environment, citizens need a highly developed literacy. They need to know how to do more than decode and comprehend literal texts. They need to understand the ways that laws and judicial decisions impact their life chances and those of their wider communities. They need to understand the two-edge sword literacy represents—an opportunity for racial good, and a tool for racial injustice. They need, as Paulo Freire urged us, to read the word and the world. This volume represents an important step in making transparent the critical role that literacy has played (and continues to play) in structuring the existing social order. This is a big book because it will never allow the reader to envision civil rights rulings without envisioning literacy and envisioning literacy without envisioning its racial underpinnings.

This is an ambitious book that lives up to its promise. It moves deftly between theory and practice and destabilizes many notions that are taken for granted of what it means to be a literate U.S. citizen. It unearths the privilege and arrogance of both the legal and educational establishments and promotes expansive thinking in both arenas. It is a breath of fresh air in what has been a very stale atmosphere.

Gloria Ladson-Billings
University of Wisconsin–Madison

✦ ACKNOWLEDGMENTS

Numerous individuals and institutions made this book possible. My colleagues at the University of Illinois have been marvelous and encouraging, and I am especially grateful for the contributions and support of Nancy Abelmann, Dennis Baron, Teresa Bertram, Matti Bunzl, Dara Goldman, Philip Graham, Gail Hawisher, Debra Hawhee, Steve Lamos, Lisa Lampert, Martin Manalansan, Bill Maxwell, Peter Mortensen, Lori Newcomb, Paul Prior, and Zoreh Sullivan. The material in the following pages has been read and commented on by colleagues at other institutions who were generous with their time, intellect, and honesty. This book is better for having passed through the hands of Beth Daniell, John Duffy, Tom Fox, Rubén Gaztambide-Fernández, Cecilia Ford, Joseph Harris, Michael Heller, Gloria Ladson-Billings, Martin Nystrand, Jacqueline Jones Royster, and Keith Walters. I owe the greatest debt in this case to Deborah Brandt, a perennially encouraging and challenging reader. Karl Kageff and the editorial staff at Southern Illinois University Press have shown me how a model academic press operates, steering this book through its final stages with skill and engagement. It has been a pleasure to work with them.

I had a great deal of help collecting the research for this book. Jane Williams and Thomas Mills of the University of Illinois Law Library lent their expertise whenever I needed it and were undeterred by even the most niggling question. I am grateful for the timely assistance of Nicole Sulgit and Carrie LaManna, who collected some of the primary and secondary sources. A special thanks to Shirley Brice Heath for having the foresight to archive her materials, and for giving me permission to quote from them; I am indebted also to Ron Chepesiuk of the Winthrop University archives, who helped guide me through them.

Research involving texts is one enterprise. Research involving human beings is quite another and is entirely dependent upon the generosity and good will of the people who open themselves up in ways large and small. The courageous staff and students of High School X gave me a gift by letting me walk among them. They did so, I recognize, in part for their own purposes. I hope I have in some way honored those purposes in my portrait of them.

I have been blessed with friends, family, and colleagues who have provided companionship, warmth, insight, and ideas. With me throughout the years this book was in progress, they have left their imprint on the work—Greg Allen, Ali Benedek, Roman Benedek, Laurie Bergman, David Eng, Cathy Gale, Rebecca Holden, Michele Hong, Jami Moss, Sam Nelson, Carol Sickman-Garner, Pete Sickman-Garner, Deborah Siegel, Laura, Bobby, Wayne, and Joan. I would lastly like to thank John, for his sustaining love and patience.

A version of chapter 1 appeared as "The Economy of Literacy: How the Supreme Court Stalled the Civil Rights Movement," *Harvard Educational Review* 72:2 (summer 2002), pp. 206–229. Copyright © 2002 by the President and Fellows of Harvard College. All rights reserved. Reprinted with permission. Portions of chapter 2 appeared in "Race: The Absent Presence in Composition Studies," *College Composition and Communication* 50 (1998), pp. 36–53. Copyright © 1998 by the National Council of Teachers of English. Reprinted with permission. A version of chapter 3 appeared as "The Water in the Fishbowl: Historicizing *Ways with Words*," *Written Communication* 17 (2000), pp. 452–490. Copyright © 2000 by Sage Publications. Reprinted by permission of Sage Publications, Inc. I thank the editors and publishers of these journals for permission to reprint material here.

✦ LITERACY AND RACIAL JUSTICE

✦ INTRODUCTION: THE TANGLED HISTORY OF LITERACY AND RACIAL JUSTICE

"They can't take race out of this case," Thurgood Marshall argued before the Supreme Court of the United States of America in *Brown v. Board of Education* (1954) nearly fifty years ago. Marshall was responding to the opposing counsel's attempt to discuss segregation as the product of neutral statutes rather than as a manifestation of racism. Few today would question his assessment that racism was an intractable issue in *Brown*. Though less obvious, it has become apparent that literacy cannot be taken out of that case, either. For better and for worse, literacy following *Brown* became one of the most prominent battlegrounds on which struggles over what constituted racial discrimination and remedy were fought in the Supreme Court and in communities. As a result of the civil rights movement, literacy and racial justice have become intertwined in the American imagination to the extent that it is now difficult to invoke one without at least approaching the other. Debates over school choice, standardized testing, affirmative action, and reparations all exhibit the conceptual enmeshment of literacy and racial justice, as proponents on every side of these issues advance their position as finally offering the fulfillment of *Brown*'s promise to place all children on a level playing field. In the politics of learning

1

after *Brown,* it would seem that literacy and racial justice are virtually synonymous. But are they?

In this book, I examine the intersections, both historical and rhetorical, between literacy and racial justice in America in order to explain why national literacy initiatives, like standardized testing and school vouchers, are so often promoted as the means toward racial justice, yet why few of these initiatives as they are presently conceived are likely to provide that justice. I focus the investigation primarily on the post-*Brown* years, as it was the *Brown* decision that fixed the notion of education as the path to equal opportunity in the minds of Americans. Within this period, I isolate literacy projects—studies, resolutions, programs, and litigation strategies—that attempt to put into practice the energy for social change generated by the civil rights movement and examine how these projects struggle to redefine both literacy and racial justice. Each chapter documents moments in which people use their literacy to protest the persistence of racial injustice in post–civil rights America, and expose the insufficiency of present remedies to address that injustice. Each chapter, then, traces a period of civil rights growth and backlash.

If literacy has become the site of the struggle for racial justice since the civil rights movement, it is because it has been for so many years the site of racial injustice in America. Throughout American history, literacy has been managed and controlled in myriad ways to rationalize and ensure White domination. In many states, before the Civil War, enslaved African Americans were restricted by law from learning to read and write. After Reconstruction, literacy institutions were closed against freed African Americans, and new forms of deterrence emerged along with segregation to stymie African American efforts to use the literacy they had acquired to exercise their rights as citizens and acquire property and employment.[1] Up until the mid-twentieth century, literacy tests were used widely and often arbitrarily as a tool to disenfranchise African American voters and exclude immigrants configured as racially undesirable.

Although the civil rights movement is already remembered as a time when America's commitments to democracy and equality were challenged and found wanting, it might also be remembered specifically as a time when Americans demonstrated their investments in literacy, using the federal justice system to challenge White control of public education. African Americans like Herman Sweatt, George

McLaurin, and Oliver Brown brought suit against segregated institutions so that bit by bit, the legal struggle that would eventually challenge "separate but equal" could progress, albeit at a great price. Sweatt, who successfully challenged the University of Texas Law School to admit him in a 1950 Supreme Court case, suffered burned crosses and slashed tires once admitted; he eventually became ill and failed out. The petitioners in the *Briggs v. Eliot* case—one of the federal district court cases decided with *Brown*—were fired, denied credit, threatened, and driven out of the state (Patterson, 2001). The backlash against desegregation litigation suggests that many Whites, too, had an investment in literacy; they were willing to commit crimes large and small in order to maintain their exclusive franchise on better funded and more prestigious literacy institutions.

The civil rights movement with its legislative mandates for desegregation and voter rights was supposed to end the tradition in America of using literacy to maintain inequities along racial lines. A recent volley of threats to the gains of the civil rights movement, however, suggests that the United States in many ways is turning back the clock to pre-*Brown* days. The multiple legal challenges to affirmative action in higher education, the decline of busing culminating in the 1999 overturning of the historic 1971 *Swann v. Charlotte-Mecklenberg Board of Education* decision, and the general persistence of school segregation and educational inequity all witness the unfulfilled promises of *Brown* and subsequent antidiscrimination measures. In response to these events, legal and literacy scholars alike have begun to reassess the impact of the civil rights movement on education and racial justice today. Noting the loss of historically Black colleges and institutions, persistent racism in White dominated schools, and continued segregation, literacy scholars have called for investigation of some of the methods and motives of desegregation as it has occurred, or rather as it has failed to occur.[2] Legal scholars have charged that the reality of racism in the United States was never fully recognized in the rhetoric of *Brown* or in ensuing antidiscrimination measures, nor were the educational opportunities of African Americans as improved as they should have been as a result of litigation.[3] They find that although the decision in *Brown* helped fuel the civil rights movement, it failed to challenge fully White supremacy and left in its wake problematic notions of racism that would hamper attempts to seek legal remedy for years to come.

Given the tangled history of literacy and racial justice to date, I believe a combination of insights from legal studies and literacy studies might productively inform debates still circulating around reading, writing, and remedy. Court decisions have to a large extent sculpted education and attitudes toward literacy in the latter half of the twentieth century. Many of these same court decisions have also not uncoincidentally determined the shape and flow of the civil rights movement and public understanding of racism and remedy. As laws are proposed at the outset of the twenty-first century to promote increased literacy testing in schools nationwide as an avenue toward racial justice, and as challenges to affirmative action in higher education mount, this legal history is now more than ever crucial to probe. Decisions are now being made on the federal level that will affect the experiences with literacy of all children in public schools. However, with all the debate over issues of literacy and racial justice, certain fundamental questions crucial to the outcomes of these decisions have yet to be considered, specifically: How does the failure of the country to deliver on many of the promises of the civil rights struggle thus far affect how people understand, value, and invest in literacy, when questions of literacy and education were so much at the heart of that struggle? How do people use the literacy they have acquired to address the persistence of racial discrimination in the face of formal equal protection under the law? What kind of literacy instruction will serve the cause of racial justice in the post–civil rights era? These questions are vital because they bring into consideration how literacy initiatives, many of them conceived with abstract values in mind, might be received by those who are to benefit from them. These questions prompt us to investigate a history of racially discriminatory practices in America, and their impact on the present.

Current literacy policy tends not to consider these questions. Literacy policy tends to be based now, as it has been for some time, on what literacy researchers call the "ideology" of literacy, the flawed but rhetorically seductive and seemingly deathless argument that literacy will guarantee equality of opportunity, moral growth, and financial security and ensure the democratic participation of all individuals in society, regardless of other factors. Literacy scholars have worked through various methodological perspectives to challenge the ideology of literacy—which Harvey Graff (1979) has more pointedly called "the literacy myth"—and have inquired who benefits from proposing literacy as the answer to all social malaise. Studies have sought to demonstrate what literacy can and cannot accomplish, in many areas distinguishing those accomplishments that have been deemed literacy's to other agents, like schooling, class, or gender (e.g., Cook-Gumperz, 1986). Amid public cries of deficit and crisis, literacy research has shown that literacy rates have in fact escalated. While the nation pursues greater literacy standards, some have questioned who benefits from escalating literacy demands. Increasingly, scholars have found literacy to be a resource with potential, but by no means guarantees for individuals at the mercy of larger economic and social forces (Brandt, 2001; Graff, 1995; Street, 1984).

This scholarly concentration on the ideology of literacy has revealed how literacy requirements have often been used in the service of racial bigotry. An examination of the history of the use of literacy tests as a tool to exclude voters led Edward Stevens (1988), for example, to label such practices a testimony not only to the power of racial bigotry but to the power of the ideology of literacy as well (p. 66). Drawing on the history Stevens uncovers, I see an even stronger correlation between racial bigotry and the ideology of literacy; I argue that one of the key components of the ideology of literacy became the notion that literacy belongs to Whites. In colonial times, illiteracy was not considered a great barrier to political or social involvement as the main requirement for suffrage was that one own property and be White and male (E. Stevens, 1988). African Americans during this period were legally considered property, so the question of their voting rights seemed moot. In the 1820s and 1830s, suffrage in the North was extended to the nonpropertied class. Suddenly the concern emerged that free African Americans might themselves seek suffrage. As a result, segregation in the North was instituted widely, including in schools (Woodward, 1974). In the South, in the 1820s and 1830s, fear of slave rebellion grew as the abolition movement intensified, leading several states to institute restrictions on teaching those enslaved to read and write[4] (Cornelius, 1991).

The mid-nineteenth century witnessed the tremendous strength of the ideology of literacy as it supported the expansion of public schooling; this period also saw an increase in literacy restrictions on voting as nativism and fears of advancement of racialized groups grew. White identity was perceived to be challenged by the influx of southern European, Jewish, and Middle Eastern immigrants of what was determined to be ambiguous racial stock. As Stevens (1988) documents, in the 1850s, both Connecticut and Massachusetts had instituted literacy tests for voting registration, and New York had begun to ponder how it could use literacy tests to restrict undesirable groups without also disenfranchising favored groups. Following Reconstruction, literacy test requirements for voter registration were instituted in several states across the South as well. In 1896, the year the Supreme Court decided *Plessy v. Ferguson,* giving constitutional approval to "separate but equal," Louisiana had 127,263 registered African American voters. Four years later, in 1900, due in part to literacy tests, there were only 5,354 registered African American voters (E. Stevens, 1988, p. 74). Widespread use of literacy tests as a tool to disenfranchise African Americans and immigrants with fewer opportunities to acquire literacy was recorded as late as 1965, when Congress debated the Voting Rights Act.

In the area of voter enfranchisement, literacy functioned as a replacement for property, as a means to preserve certain privileges of citizenship for Whites; when property in and of itself no longer signified reliably as a means to distinguish those who were considered White from those configured as non-White, literacy was brought to serve as the distinguishing factor. The particular attribute of literacy tests that made them useful to White supremacists is that their outcomes could be easily manipulated and standards arbitrarily enforced to maintain racial distinctions (Litwack, 1998; MacLeod, 1991). Literacy, then, could be made to serve as a distinguishing trait, whether an applicant could read and write or not. Making explicit how literacy and race became interchangeable, Deborah Brandt (2001) points out, "Throughout recent history, literacy has often served as a stand-in for skin color in the ongoing attempts to subordinate African Americans" (p. 106).

In immigration restriction, the ideology of literacy functioned similarly, nativists arguing literacy tests could serve as a replacement for racial quotas, so sure were they of the correlation between literacy and whiteness. The "ideology of literacy" was broadly invoked in the United States to configure as non-White and therefore inadmissible any groups considered a threat to the unity of White identity. Of course, there were other forces behind literacy's spread seemingly unrelated to racial bigotry; the growth of mass public schooling was supported in large measure by Protestant Evangelicalism as many Christians felt it a moral imperative that people be able to read the Bible for themselves. Yet, as David Wallace Adams (1988) points out in his study of Native American boarding schools in the late-nineteenth and early-twentieth centuries, Protestantism alone does not explain the dual emphasis on valuing personal property and distinguishing the civilized from the barbaric in the curriculum of these schools, nor does it explain the purpose of Native American schooling in the context of the White project to grab Native American land. Adams offers that many Whites construed literacy as a form of property they could exchange with Native Americans for territory. Effectively, then, the nation was built in part by giving Native Americans "civilization" in the form of literacy in exchange for America.

Literacy and Racial Justice: The Politics of Learning after Brown v. Board of Education argues that the ideology of literacy has been sustained primarily as a response to perceived threats to White property interests, White privilege, the maintenance of "White" identity, or the conception of America as a White nation. Mainly I demonstrate through historical study how literacy has been accepted as White property in crucial contexts that helped shape the country, including pivotal congressional hearings and Supreme Court cases. I am aided in this enterprise by legal studies that record how White identity itself functions as property in American culture and in court. As legal analysts have observed, although the end of slavery changed the legal status of many African Americans from property to citizens, it also provoked the recognition in the courts that "holders" of White identity possess valuable property (Harris, 1993). This recognition of White identity as having property value is not strictly analogous to the situation in slavery in which a formal system of rules was established to govern the ownership and sale of those enslaved. Contracts are not drawn up to govern the loan or sale of White identity in the way that they were drawn up during slavery to regulate the loan or sale of human beings. A cultural belief in the value of White identity, however, persisted past the Emancipation Proclamation, embodied in those who make and enforce the law. Judicial decisions, legislation, and economic arrangements have been greatly affected by this cultural belief. What I highlight here are the judicial decisions, legislation, and economic arrangements that have been specifically affected by a belief that literacy is White property. In identifying where literacy has been recognized as White property, I use the concept of property in its broader definition, as quality, trait, or attribute. Recognizing that literacy has been often regarded as a White trait, something that Whites possess naturally, rather than as a White privilege, I maintain, more accurately reveals why many Whites—including those recently contesting affirmative action in educational settings—have acted as if something has been taken away from them when the goods of literacy are redistributed.

What they had to lose, it would seem, is White identity itself. Beginning in the nineteenth century, literacy abilities were frequently imagined as parsed to different races, and literacy tests for immigration and naturalization were advocated under a potent racial rubric. These literacy tests were offered as the most efficient means to identify those who were of the most pure specimens of the White race. Later, throughout the civil rights movement, many Whites increasingly invested in literacy to retain a sense of inviolable White community. As social and economic pressures forced the breaking of Jim Crow laws in employment in the 1960s and 1970s, for example, and African Americans and Whites in certain areas of the country faced each other in the same jobs for the first time, some Whites looked to literacy to catapult them into a job where they would not have to work with African Americans. Scholarship has suggested that literacy demands have escalated and shifted as the result of expanding capitalism in the last fifty years;[5] I argue that the escalation and shift that has been charted cannot be considered in isolation from how the dynamics of race shape people's conceptions of their place in the economic, cultural, and political order.

A general belief in the value of literacy is not in and of itself a form of violence or oppression. The notion that literacy can, under the right circumstances and in accordance with other factors, provide opportunities was employed by many through the civil rights movement and continues to be employed to challenge White supremacy. But because literacy also continued to be operationally defined as White property in national forums, like the federal courts, many civil rights inspired efforts to promote literacy for disenfranchised groups have, as a rule, not enjoyed systemic support. Grass roots movements have had to do literacy work at great personal cost, often through unpaid effort, and are left scrambling for ways to make up for gaps in the system. Bob Moses's "Algebra Project" serves as one example of this phenomenon. The Algebra Project was started through Moses's volunteer efforts to combat the effects of math tracking in the schools. Schools resisted the program so strongly that Moses found himself drawing on his vast experience fighting for voter rights in the South during the civil rights movement, just to get the Algebra Project launched (Moses, 2001). As the following chapters detail, the assumption of literacy as White property in crucial contexts has meant that a burden has been placed upon people of color to create and sustain alternative literacy institutions and programs like the Algebra Project, or to show evidence of literacy again and again to mainstream organizations.

To what extent literacy scholarship has taken up part of this burden and how it might avoid increasing it is examined here as well. It might not be an overstatement to say that the study of literacy is itself a by-product of the civil rights movement, as attempts to date academic interest in literacy across various fields have been unable to place its origin much before the 1960s.[6] Material reasons in part account for this. The War on Poverty waged by the Johnson administration led to unprecedented federal funding of literacy research, often directed toward evaluating the success of literacy programs such as Head Start.[7] The general theoretical climate of literacy research also evidences the challenges to White supremacy that the civil rights movement brought. To defeat cognitive deficit explanations of variation in literacy achievement, researchers have shown the unrecognized proficiencies of people who fail according to official literacy standards and have identified as culturally normed literacy practices previously considered universal. By now a near consensus among literacy scholars has emerged that literacy is a context-specific phenomenon characterized by a range of cultural practices around the use of print, rather than a universal and quantifiable cognitive skill. Literacy researchers have drawn on cultural anthropology and historical archives to move toward a conception of culturally situated, shifting, and multiple "literacies" and away from a conception of a single, normative literacy, even while state and federal legislatures in adopting standardized testing pursue the opposite course. Reflecting the ethos of the civil rights movement, research has called for tolerance of cultural variation in literacy practices.[8]

Perhaps the most crucial legacy of culturally sensitive conceptions of literacy is that they have helped many argue against essentially racist, faux-genetic explanations of the scholastic performance of African American and Latina/o students. Racist explanations for achievement gaps were prominent at the height of the civil rights movement as part of the backlash against civil rights initiatives. Most infamously, Arthur Jensen's (1969) "How Much Can We Boost IQ and Scholastic Achievement?" argued that compensatory education programs undertaken by the government would be of no avail because African Americans were enslaved by their genes.[9] Unfortunately, deficit theories of literacy achievement have resurfaced in the last decade, most notably with the publication of Richard Herrnstein and Charles Murray's (1994) *The Bell Curve.*[10] The appearance of research in the 1990s arguing that African Americans are inferior to Whites suggests most obviously that racism and bigotry persist in public and academic communities alike. But this reiteration of deficit research also suggests that the current multicultural explanations for differences in literacy achievement have not succeeded in revealing in their entirety the most deeply held assumptions about literacy, and the most deeply felt attachments that develop through literacy. I depart, then, from the current trend in literacy research of emphasizing the multiplicity of local, situated, and often marginalized literacy practices and their cultural distinctness from mainstream literacy practices. Valuable as this orientation has heretofore been, it leaves scholars without the necessary foothold to discuss the impact of national forces and events on literacy development.

As others have argued and I too will maintain, literacy acquisition and development are not processes involving autonomous relationships to texts (Street, 1984). People acquire and develop literacy through relationships with institutions and with other people. Institutions that promote literacy tend to serve several functions, as religious institutions, community organizations, or markers of identity. Consider small towns and large universities that deck themselves out in school colors for the big game. Consider the bumper stickers that identify a car owner's child as an honors student. Consider dating agencies that match up people who can prove they are alumni of elite colleges. How people experience literacy development becomes bound up with how they perceive their own identity, and the identity of others. Although a full examination of these attachments is beyond the scope of this work, in the following chapters, I seek to illuminate the ways literacy has become bound up with racial identity in critical contexts, hence, how literacy has become racialized.

I begin this investigation where the civil rights movement got a critical push in the courts, with *Brown v. Board of Education.* Breaking with prevailing wisdom that holds up the *Brown* decision as an unalloyed condemnation of White supremacy, in Chapter 1, I argue that the conception of literacy informing *Brown* and two subsequent crucial civil rights era Supreme Court decisions, *Washington v. Davis* (1976) and *The Regents of the University of California v. Bakke* (1978), was a conception of literacy as White property. Examination of these cases demonstrates that as the majority of the justices became increasingly fixated on what remedy might cost Whites, the rhetoric of declining literacy standards was brought to slow the progress of the civil rights movement. Analysis of these cases reveals that legal racial justice remedies in this country have been governed by what I call the economy of literacy as White property: Once African Americans were granted relief in one literacy environment—public high school, for example—that environment was subsequently perceived to have lowered in its value. This economy rather than recognition of past discrimination has dominated debates over racial justice in the last twenty-five years.

This chapter also explains why affirmative action debates have been so fraught. The landmark affirmative action case, *The Regents of the University of California v. Bakke,* in which Bakke, a White man, charged he was discriminated against by a special admissions program at the University of California at Davis Medical School, was a poorly prepared, poorly argued, and poorly decided case. I argue that the counsel for the regents, and some of the Supreme Court justices, acted primarily out of their desire to preserve the credibility of their own literacy institutions. A tangled but nevertheless influential decision resulted that promoted Harvard's admissions policy as the model for affirmative action; this decision did little then, to promote the constitutionality of affirmative action. In suggesting as I do in the process of making this argument that the Supreme Court justices were influenced by personal and cultural investments in their own literacy institutions, my analysis both builds on and contributes to burgeoning research in law that questions the neutrality of the justice system. Scholars like Anthony Amsterdam and Jerome Bruner (2000) have argued that judges, like lay people, are influenced by cultural stories and affected by biases. The intellectual and political movement in law titled by its members "critical race theory" also guides my discussion as it examines how cultural stories about race affect legal decisions as much or more than constitutional principles[11] (Crenshaw, Gotanda, Peller, & Thomas, 1995; Delgado, 1995a). Critical race theory's critique of the legal and political deployment of the principles of neutrality and colorblindness, and its analysis of how racism operates as the norm, rather than as an aberration from the norm in the United States, inform each chapter.

Critical race theory also serves another function in this investigation, however, as it provides a site to examine the aftermath of the Supreme Court decisions discussed in Chapter 1. Critical race theorists write of the tokenism and glass ceilings they experience as law professors of color in academic settings decades after *Brown* and *Bakke*. Their lives chart the period of civil rights struggle and backlash, yet their response to this backlash is not primarily a new litigation strategy but rather a new rhetoric of racial justice, one that exposes the courts as having done little to prevent an atmosphere in which literacy instruction is still too often instruction in the value of White identity. Chapter 2 examines how critical race theorists attempt to exit the economy of literacy as White property by rejecting the discourses of litigation and mainstream legal scholarship that they find have perpetuated rather than exposed the cultural myths that informed *Brown;* instead of looking to the law, they craft a textually controversial, self-consciously "storied" rhetoric within their writing to reveal the enduring nature of the equation between literacy and Whiteness and undo the cultural belief that colorblindness has been achieved informing debates over literacy.

Chapter 3 develops the study of the aftermath of *Brown* further by examining the halting pace of desegregation in a region of South Carolina in the late 1960s and early 1970s. Shirley Brice Heath's influential study of literacy practices during desegregation, *Ways with Words* (1983), provides a window into how the national mandate to desegregate public schools affected the lives of people in specific locales. *Ways* begins by asserting this federal action as the exigence motivating the study of literacy practices in African American and White communities in the Piedmont region from 1968 to 1977. Desegregation histories of this area show that in the communities Heath studied, however, desegregation was slow to be enforced and was continually countered as many Whites invested in literacy instruction elsewhere as a mode through which to assert a separate "White" identity. This rereading of *Ways* as a chronicle of the failure of desegregation to secure lasting educational equity revises traditional, ahistorical readings of the text—readings that identify the problems in the schools after desegregation as resulting from a clash of cultural values between White and African American communities. These readings directly reflect, however, the historical context that determined greatly the story Heath was able to tell. Heath's field notes and letters reveal that the strained racial relations that were both the historical context of and impetus for *Ways* also functioned as constraints on her research as she tried to negotiate existing stereotypes characterizing discourse on race; they further reveal a taboo on discussing race relations in operation both in the communities Heath studied and scholarly communities she was hoping to address. This chapter concludes that the story Heath told as a result of these taboos obscured that the problems African American children encountered in predominantly White schools were primarily caused not by the African American and White communities' inability to understand one another but rather by the shared understanding of White privilege.

Why revisit Heath's study? I do so because there is no more comprehensive study of literacy in communities in the midst of desegregation. It is not possible to travel into the past to collect the kind of data Heath was able to collect. Although textual documents and oral histories exist from the period Heath studied, these can give only evidence of written literacy practices or provide retrospective accounts of oral and written literacy practices. Heath has provided an invaluable and unduplicated resource for others to draw upon in studying the period. But there is another reason to look again at *Ways with Words*. *Ways* remains after two decades a pivotal study, one cited in nearly all subsequent research on cultural variation in literacy. It has influenced a generation of literacy teachers and scholars internationally. Heath's correspondence and the local desegregation histories I draw upon help explain the forces that shaped the text and, therefore, a great deal of literacy scholarship and teaching in the last quarter century.

While Heath was working on problems of African American and White communication in the communities and public schools of South Carolina, the national organization of the Conference on College Composition and Communication (CCCC) was concerned with reports of problems on the college level nationally. The use of what was commonly called Black English in the classroom had become a critical point of controversy. *The Students' Right to Their Own Language* resolution that the CCCC passed in 1974 was one of many efforts made by literacy teachers and scholars to embrace the project of racial justice in their work. Such efforts were strongly affected in the 1980s, however, as the federal government sought to reverse the influence of the civil rights movement on education and curriculum. Chapter 4 examines this period of backlash through the figure of Ronald Reagan, revealing his investments in literacy as he sought to purge "minority issues" from literacy and language teaching. Reagan, like some of the Supreme Court justices profiled in the first chapter, imagined public education as having deteriorated since *Brown v. Board of Education;* he saw in private and parochial institutions a return to "old fashioned" literacy basics, and a refuge from civil rights agendas. Yet while Reagan nostalgically envisioned literacy purified from race and held up the experience of immigrants to back up this vision of literacy, the history of immigration and naturalization demonstrates that during that period of time romanticized by Reagan, literacy and immigration were both highly racialized. From the late 1800s through President Truman's administration, debates in immigration policy hearings revolved around the use of literacy tests, and literacy was often a focal point of naturalization court cases in which one's White identity had to be proven prior to naturalization. Ideologies of literacy therefore played a role in enforcing a conception of America as a White nation.

The cost of the history reviewed in the first four chapters on literacy instruction today is uncovered in Chapter 5, which moves the discussion of literacy and racial justice further toward the present. In this chapter, I address explicitly the question of what kind of literacy instruction can serve the cause of racial justice in the post–civil rights era through a portrait of "High School X," an alternative public secondary school that has attempted since its inception in 1971 to put the ethos of racial justice into practice.[12] HSX's efforts to promote racial justice have included active recruitment of students of color, student-enforced antiharassment policies, and a required class on the topic of racial discrimination designed by an African American teacher who had been in the 1960s the first to integrate her high school in Mississippi. In this chapter, I draw on oral histories of the school's founders and teachers, archival research, and classroom observation to present a school offering many positive models for reimagining education in the service of racial justice. But this account also reveals continuing tensions between integrationism and separatism as paths to racial justice, and tensions between groups claiming protection in the post–civil rights era; these tensions played themselves out repeatedly in curriculum, classroom dynamics, and literacy practices. I observed that despite (and in many ways because of) the multicultural curriculum, the invitation to take ownership in a majority White school was more difficult for some of the African American students to accept.

The complications to the enterprise of literacy presented by a legacy of racial strife best show themselves in this study of High School X. In fact, while presented last in this volume, my study of HSX was where the central questions motivating my research first evolved. It became clear to me while at HSX, for example, that the history of legalized segregation that kept African American students out of mainstream educational institutions affected HSX's ability to both define itself as an alternative to traditional education and attract and retain African American students. Furthermore, the pedagogical goals of fostering "student ownership," espoused by so much literacy research and by this school, are complicated by a history in which some have been allowed to "own" literacy while others have been discouraged from such ownership.

In the conclusion, I broaden my discussion of the politics of learning in the present day by reviewing current literacy initiatives intended to fulfill the promise of *Brown,* including those promoting school choice and school testing. Afflicted by the same historical amnesia hobbling previous literacy initiatives, the current proposals, I find, are based on the same abstract ideologies of literacy that have failed to bring racial justice in the past. Many of these recent proposals rest on assumptions about literacy and race relations having no support in American history, and no support in the following pages. What the following pages do contain, however, are several key moments, in 1968, 1971, and 1990, of protest to a history of valuing literacy as White property, including protests over White domination of literacy in public schools, elite private colleges, and professional organizations. The purpose of *Literacy and Racial Justice* is to recognize and engage with these protests, as they contain the vital information that literacy in the American context has too long been treated as a mark that must be achieved by individuals before reparations for the past might be considered. A literacy that creates rather than threatens unity in this country, I maintain, will be one that takes this insight, and its mandate to confront and end a history of injustice, to heart.

1 ✦ THE ECONOMY OF LITERACY: HOW THE SUPREME COURT STALLED THE CIVIL RIGHTS MOVEMENT

Until the middle of the twentieth century, the dominant U.S. educational policy was to use whatever means possible, including the force of law, to restrict access to literacy for African Americans and to preserve it for Whites. Throughout much of the nineteenth century, these restrictions included making it a crime to teach enslaved people to read or write and providing only a second-class education to the newly freed (Cornelius, 1991). Until the mid-twentieth century, segregation continued to deny equal education to African Americans, restricting their access to literacy institutions well after passage of the Fourteenth Amendment had mandated equal protection under the law for all citizens. Reviewing this history, Anderson (1988) remarked that it has been an American tradition rather than an aberration to provide unequal education to Whites and African Americans. Ostensibly, the United States Supreme Court's 1954 decision in *Brown v. Board of Education* was intended to end this tradition by discontinuing segregation in schools. However, it did not. Observing that students of color and White students in the 1990s were in many ways more segregated than they were before the civil rights movement and the legal order to desegregate, Ladson-Billings and Tate (1995) have called for a reexamination of *Brown*.

At stake in *Brown* was the question of whether or not segregated public education violated the Equal Protection Clause of the Fourteenth Amendment. As part of its effort to define "equal protection," the Court also took up the task of defining the importance of education. In this, the Court thought on a grand scale; the rationale in *Brown* for ending legalized segregation rested on defining public education as the precursor to good citizenship, cultural values, professional preparation, and even normalcy, a "right which must be made available to all on equal terms":

> Today, education is perhaps the most important function of state and local governments. . . . It is the very foundation of good citizenship. Today it is a principal instrument in awakening the child to cultural values, in preparing him for later professional training, and in helping him adjust normally to his environment. In these days it is doubtful that any child may reasonably be expected to succeed in life if he is denied the opportunity of an education. Such an opportunity, where the state has undertaken to provide it, is a right which must be made available for all on equal terms. (*Brown*, 1954, p. 493)

This language in the *Brown* decision linking public education to citizenship, opportunity, professionalism, and undefined normalcy is representative of what Cook-Gumperz (1986) has identified as the late-twentieth century's "ideology of literacy" (p. 33). According to Cook-Gumperz, as the twentieth century progressed, schooling came to be seen more and more as the principle vehicle for ensuring both "social stability and economic advancement" and the transformation of individuals into "members of the wider society" (pp. 33–34). At the same time, Cook-Gumperz maintains, literacy, conceptually conjoined to mass schooling, came to be seen as both a basic human right and the building block of modern society. In order to render what in the 1950s was seen as a potentially volatile decision with broad social implications, the Court supported its decision in *Brown* largely on this ideology of literacy. The repeated use of "today" in the Court's language emphasizes the modern imperative of schooling. As the twentieth century drew to a close, however, literacy scholars began to point out flaws in the governing ideology of literacy, demonstrating through cross-cultural and historical study that literacy and education do not necessarily result in the opportunities imagined. Further, Cook-Gumperz (1986) argues that the notion that mass schooling provides a kind of functional literacy, which in turn provides equal opportunity, has the effect of blaming individuals for the social stratification that modern schooling, with ranking devices like tracking, actually facilitates.

Scholars have also observed that the designation of literacy and education as "rights" is more rhetorical than real. Though the *Brown* decision initiated desegregation by determining that an education free of segregation and inequality is a right, this right has proven to be all too fungible in practice, as has been documented (Kozol, 1991; Ladson-Billings & Tate, 1995). Considering these persistent racial inequities in education, a 1988 conference entitled The Right to Literacy, sponsored by the Modern Language Association, spawned a volume of essays explicitly questioning the notion of literacy as a right. In this volume, the editors suggest that formulating literacy in terms of rights is inevitably problematic because literacy "is not in itself a panacea for social inequity" or a way to "grant more influence or power to those who have been disempowered by their race" (Lunsford, Moglen, & Slevin, 1990, p. 2).

It is no accident that literacy scholars began to wrestle with the rhetorical enmeshment of rights, equal opportunity, education, and literacy in the late 1980s, following a period of diminished government enforcement of civil rights laws against discrimination in housing, education, and employment (Lipsitz, 1998). In response to this same governmental neglect, critical race theorists—predominantly legal scholars of color—have come to consider rights and equal opportunity to be ultimately race dependent (e.g., Bell, 1992a; Crenshaw et al., 1995; Delgado, 1995a; Williams, 1991). They argue that civil rights, intended to ensure life and liberty, have generally been sacrificed for property rights, intended to protect ownership. Further, they argue White identity has been recognized in the courts as having property value. Harris (1993) explains:

> [W]hiteness . . . meets the functional criteria of property. Specifically, the law has accorded "holders" of Whiteness the same privileges and benefits accorded holders of other types of property. The liberal view of property is that it includes the exclusive rights of possession, use, and disposition. (p. 1731)

Bell (1987) points out that the property value of White identity was established when a fundamental contradiction presented by the Declaration of Independence—that all men were created equal and are entitled to liberty, except those enslaved—was resolved by labeling African Americans as property. Harris demonstrates that the property value of White identity was reinforced in the 1896 Supreme Court case *Plessy v. Ferguson,* which established the "separate but equal" doctrine that *Brown* would later overturn. Plessy argued that in being barred from a White streetcar, he had been denied the reputation of being White and thus its pecuniary value (Harris, 1993, p. 1747). The Court decided that Plessy did not meet Louisiana's legal criteria for being White and thus was not deprived of property (*Plessy v. Ferguson,* 1896).

As Lamos (2000) points out, critical race theorists reveal not only the property value given to White identity but also the complicity of the justice system in maintaining education as White property. Harris (1993), for example, extends her discussion of White property to suggest that legal challenges to affirmative action in educational settings are predicated on the notions of White entitlement to education. Bell (1980a, 1992a, 1992b) offers his critique of the race-dependent nature of rights in part through a review of desegregation litigation. The analysis of critical race theorists reminds us that major cases defining public and legal notions of racism also dealt with education and literacy. *Brown,* a case most obviously about education, resulted in defining racism as school segregation. Because it was such a high-profile case that mobilized mass interests, *Brown* ensured that ideologies of literacy would continue to inform legal definitions of racial discrimination and remedy.

A subsequent pivotal antidiscrimination case, *Washington v. Davis* (1976), defined racial discrimination as being necessarily intentional. Although on the surface an employment discrimination case, at issue in *Washington* was a Washington, D.C., police force written entrance exam, which African American applicants failed at twice the rate of Whites. The question of racial bias in literacy testing was therefore discussed at great length in the oral arguments before the Supreme Court. During these arguments, the justices reinforced the rhetoric of "literacy crisis" that defined public discourse on literacy during the mid- to late-1970s (Graff, 1979). I argue that this rhetoric provided fertile ground for subsequent challenges to affirmative action. The decision in *Washington,* for example, informed one of the most prominent and legally significant cases over racial justice and literacy, *Regents of the University of California v. Bakke,* which was argued in 1977 and decided in 1978.

Alan Bakke, rejected twice by the University of California at Davis Medical School, charged that as a White man he was discriminated against by the school's affirmative action policies. As I will argue, the majority of the Court in this case seemed more concerned with upholding certain conceptions of literacy standards than with ensuring the equality of education that had eluded the country even after *Brown*.

For many observers, *Brown* and *Bakke* bookend the legal struggle for civil rights in the Supreme Court, the first case holding the great promise that the later case definitively showed to be unfulfilled. However, looking at the conceptions of literacy informing these cases, I argue that the continuities between the two are as important to consider as the discontinuities. Despite the lofty prose equating education with equal opportunity, the ideologies of literacy informing these crucial decisions were consistent with the maintenance of education as White property. Through the *Brown* decision, the Court formulated education as a specifically racialized attribute. The arguments, the decision, and the remedies proffered in *Brown* constructed equal education as the opportunity to be educated among Whites. Encoded, then, in the ideology of literacy that *Brown* presented was a privileging of White identity. This privileging remained consistent throughout *Washington* and *Bakke*. Examination of the records of these cases, the justices' decision, the counsels' arguments, and the expert witnesses' testimony demonstrates that the definition of literacy as White property that had preceded *Brown* survived in it and subsequently survived through *Bakke*. These cases were unable to condemn fully the caste system of segregation and unable to remedy sufficiently inequities in educational resources. Instead, they continued rather than reversed the equation between Whiteness and literacy that had occurred for centuries by reinforcing the cultural belief in literacy as White property.

How these cases racialized notions of literacy is significant in understanding a period of struggle to improve the material conditions of the lives of African Americans. The *Brown* decision represents a moment when the NAACP's legal defense team, hemmed in by White supremacy, had little choice but to use the master's tools—bigotry—to attack the master's house—legalized segregation (Tushnet, 1994). A historically sensitive analysis of *Brown* reveals the constraints under which Marshall and his team of NAACP lawyers labored, and the ability of White supremacists to thwart even the most pressing moral imperative—to remove legalized segregation, the country's most visible symbol of White supremacy. Although problematic, the ideology of literacy advanced in and emerging from *Brown* played a great role in generating energy for all kinds of demands that eventually had little to do with literacy. It has not, however, assured equality of education, as Carter (1980), one of the chief architects of the NAACP's strategy in *Brown,* has noted. The absence of equality in education after *Brown* has prompted investigation into the cultural climate surrounding the decision. Bell (1980a) argues, for example, that the Court's desire to placate Whites ultimately took precedence in the decision over the well-being of African American schoolchildren. Dudziak (1988/1995) suggests that from the beginning, the Court and the nation sought to eliminate only those signs of oppression that were causing the nation economic and political harm. She argues that segregation was a weakness the United States could ill afford during its Cold War efforts to expand its influence in countries where people of color were in the majority. The mixture of interests and motives leading up to *Brown* suggests that a lukewarm attack on segregation might have been all the country and the Court were willing to embrace at that time.

By the late 1970s, the Court's commitment to racial justice had cooled even further. While Justice Marshall was disturbed by the slow progress of actual change and the laissez-faire attitude of his colleagues, the oral arguments of the *Washington* and *Bakke* cases suggest that many of the justices were disturbed by the demands for actual change generated by the civil rights movement. The rhetoric of "literacy crisis" served to slow the progress of the civil rights movement even further as the discussion about improving the conditions of African American lives was displaced by laments over declining literacy standards. The public education that had been the gold standard of literacy as equal opportunity in *Brown* was denigrated in *Washington* and *Bakke*. I argue that this denigration occurred because people of color were perceived to have unrestricted access to public education. In the economy of literacy as White property, once previously segregated racialized groups were granted relief in one literacy environment, that environment was denigrated to lower its value.[1]

To show this gradual denigration, I begin with a discussion of the faith in public education the *Brown* decision reflected—a faith based in the notion that desegregated public schools would be mostly White. In the oral argument of *Washington,* justices no longer had that faith and would question the value of a public high school education for professional advancement or even minimal literacy attainment. The following year, the *Bakke* decision would reveal a further rejection of public education in a more subtle form, as the most influential opinion in that case—that of Justice Powell— would employ Harvard's admissions policy to de-legitimize and, in fact, render unconstitutional the University of California at Davis Medical School affirmative action admissions policy. This unfortunate decision would make all subsequent affirmative action programs vulnerable to continual challenge, thereby affecting students' experience with literacy nationally to this day.

Brown: *Equal Education in an Unequal Society*

Mark V. Tushnet, who clerked for Thurgood Marshall in the 1970s, observed that Marshall's stories describing successful civil rights litigation embodied the Trickster figure of African American oral tradition, illustrating how to use a racist system against itself. According to Tushnet, Marshall told a story about Whites who got a court injunction against the local African American church forbidding the church to use property that had been donated to it for a cemetery. The church was allowed to keep the land, however, and eventually a developer offered to buy it:

> "After some brief negotiations, the church agreed to sell the land at a price that not only would allow it to purchase land for a cemetery anywhere in the city, but also would pay off the mortgage, repair the building, and generally do just about anything else it wanted." Marshall would conclude this story with its moral "Thank God for prejudice." (Tushnet, 1994, p. 4)

Tushnet uses this anecdote to explain that the original strategy of civil rights litigation to desegregate schools was to "work within a racist system to combat racism" (p. 3). The fight to end segregation, he points out, began by relying indirectly on *Plessy v. Ferguson* and its establishment of "separate but equal," not by disputing it. Tushnet's analysis suggests the degree to which the NAACP's lawyers depended on the available strategies within a racist system to arrive at *Brown,* a watershed moment of the civil rights struggle in the courts.

Brown v. Board of Education refers to the four school segregation cases from Delaware, Kansas, South Carolina, and Virginia that the Supreme Court considered as a body. Two decisions, customarily known as *Brown I* and *Brown II,* were handed down by the Court. *Brown I* refers to the May 17, 1954, decision in which segregated schools were found to be unconstitutional. On May 31, 1955, *Brown II* ordered the dismantling of segregated education "with all deliberate speed." By condemning segregation, the first decision rendered a critical moral statement, although, as I will show, it did so in terms that would prove problematic. The second decision, many have argued, fell just short of retracting the previous condemnation of segregation and certainly sapped the decision of a good deal of practical effectiveness (Lawrence, 1980; Patterson, 2001). To understand why *Brown* turned out as it did, it is necessary to examine the strategies for implementing school desegregation leading up to *Brown* that suggest the climate of racial assumptions in which the NAACP's lawyers were forced to negotiate.

In the late 1920s and early 1930s, the NAACP legal team's strategy was to bring about the end of segregation by default. They argued for equities in funding, physical structures, and faculty between African American and White schools, which they felt could not possibly be satisfied. This attack on inequities in educational funding did not include a direct attack on segregation as unconstitutional because it was feared that a direct push at overturning segregation's legal support, *Plessy,* might result in the decision being upheld. Instead, their arguments alleged violation of civil rights by showing gross disparities in educational resources available to African Americans and Whites, indirectly relying on *Plessy*'s separate but equal clause—though they never directly called on *Plessy* for support (Tushnet, 1994). Graduate and professional schools became obvious targets for this strategy because almost none of these schools in the southern states served African Americans. Over time, cases evolved from arguing the inadequacies of physical facilities and faculty to arguing the inadequacies of intangible attributes of the curriculum. The NAACP argued, for example, that the ability to associate in extracurricular activities and engage in social networks comprised a professional education as much as the official curriculum (Patterson, 2001). Once education could be articulated as a matter of both tangible and intangible factors, including unrestricted social interaction, it only remained to argue that the act of segregation itself was the source of harm (Whitman, 1993).

By the 1950s, the national climate had changed significantly enough to make overturning *Plessy* less the impossible goal it had seemed in the 1930s. As the United States sought to expand its influence internationally at the beginning of the Cold War, it faced scrutiny for its hypocrisies at home. Newspapers in Asia and Africa carried stories condemning segregation as a failure of the United States to support democracy on its own soil (Dudziak, 1988/1995). African American veterans of World War II were less patient with the second-class citizenship that the country they had risked their lives defending was offering them. Meanwhile, businesses and industries within the United States were finding the cost of maintaining segregated facilities or hiring only White workers in southern cities increasingly burdensome. Thurgood Marshall and others began to see that an attack on segregated education at all levels, and even a challenge to segregation itself as unconstitutional, might have greater support. By 1950, Marshall had begun to make it clear to those who sought improvement in segregated facilities that the NAACP would not involve itself in pursuing cases along those lines. He began the push to overturn *Plessy,* sculpting with Robert Carter a controversial approach based on proving that segregated schools caused African American children psychological harm (Tushnet, 1994).

The most compelling arguments supporting this approach were those presented by social scientists, including Kenneth Clark of the City College of New York. His now famous research measured the effects of segregation on children's psychological health by asking African American children in segregated and nonsegregated schools questions about their feelings toward Black and White dolls (Clark, 1950). Using Clark's findings, the NAACP advanced the argument that no segregated school could ever be considered equal because segregation itself fosters feelings of inferiority that impede learning. This argument was the most influential expert evidence supporting the condemnation of separate but equal education in *Brown I.* Although the argument was controversial at the time, both in and outside of the NAACP, it might have been attractive to a Supreme Court looking not to offend Whites. The argument of psychological harm, as construed in *Brown I,* provided the grounds for overturning separate but equal without challenging White supremacy.

In fact, the argument relied on White supremacy as its foundation. The testimony of David Krech, a professor of psychology at the University of California and an expert witness for the plaintiffs in the South Carolina case, affirms White supremacy even as it decries segregation by citing the "inadequate education we build into the Negro" as the reason for White superiority:

> I would say that most white people have cause to be prejudiced against the Negro, because the Negro in most cases is indeed inferior to the white man, because the white man has made him [that] through the practice of legal segregation. . . . [A]s a consequence of inadequate education we build into the Negro the very characteristic, not only intellectual, but also personality characteristics, which we then use to justify prejudice. (Whitman, 1993, pp. 63–64)

Krech's excuse for White prejudice is an example of using bigotry to fight bigotry. The pathologizing of African American children represented by the testimony of Krech and others proved to be an intractable part of understanding the harm of segregation. In their decision, the Court quoted the following language from the district court decision of the Kansas case (*Brown*, 1951), which alleges even cognitive deficiency in African American children as a result of segregation:

> Segregation of white and colored children in public schools has a detrimental effect upon the colored children. The impact is greater when it has the sanction of the law; for the policy of separating the races is usually interpreted as denoting the inferiority of the Negro group. A sense of inferiority affects the motivation of the child to learn. Segregation with the sanction of law, therefore has a tendency to [retard] the educational and mental development of the Negro children and to deprive them of some of the benefits they would receive in a racial[ly] integrated school system.[2] (*Brown*, 1954, p. 494)

According to critical race theorists, many of the problems with the *Brown* decision are rooted in the Court's problematic normalizing of a segregated society (Lawrence, 1980). Lawrence (1980) argues that the Court's reasoning was flawed because it failed to acknowledge that the only purpose of segregation was to denote White superiority. With a sideways acknowledgement of the harm of segregation, the *Brown I* decision overturned *Plessy* while at the same time leaving the property value of Whiteness that *Plessy* established intact (Bell, 1987; Harris, 1993).

The assumption of the value of White identity informed the educational expert's testimony for the NAACP's legal defense in the *Brown* trial, as well. Picking up on the arguments over equity in intangible elements of the curriculum, which had succeeded in the graduate and professional school cases, Hugh Speer, professor of education at the University of Kansas City, argued that African American children were harmed by being denied the opportunity to associate with White people—a vital part of the curriculum in what he termed our multicultural society:

> The more heterogeneous the group in which the children participate, the better [they] can function in our multi-cultural and multi-group society. For example, if the colored children are denied the experience in school of associating with white children, who represent 90% of our national society in which these colored children must live, then the colored child's curriculum is being greatly curtailed. (Whitman, 1993, p. 71)

Speer's argument assumed that students of color would remain a minority in a society overwhelmingly dominated by Whites. The argument neglected the various legal and cultural machinations that operate to maintain that ratio.[3] Additionally, it assumed that participation in a heterogeneous group in school necessarily meant better functioning in a heterogeneous society. Yet at the time Speer made his remarks, there was no indication that an end to segregation in educational settings would mean an end to segregation in all areas. In order to be credible, Speer's argument had to sidestep the actual nature of the national society in which this education takes place, including the limitations placed on heterogeneity by Jim Crow laws and northern residential segregation. Similarly, in order to be accepted, the NAACP had to limit its attack on racism to educational segregation in the South (R. Carter, 1980). Regardless of the assumptions underlying Speer's argument, accepting it means believing that a setting devoid of White children becomes by default an educationally poorer setting, a reasoning that confirms the value of being White.

If, despite its shortcomings, the Court's decision in *Brown I* impressed the country as a firm condemnation of segregation, the effect of that condemnation was quickly muted by *Brown II.* Threats of a radical and even violent reaction to desegregation hung over the entire proceedings of *Brown I,* from considering the verdict to devising the remedy. In 1951, for example, former Supreme Court Justice James Byrnes became governor of South Carolina and announced that his state would abolish public schooling before it would desegregate (Patterson, 2001; Tushnet, 1994). Muse (1964) records that, in contrast, the initial southern reaction to *Brown II* was relief—a feeling that the Court had come to its senses. The qualification of "with all deliberate speed," as well as lack of clarity as to whether *Brown I* outlawed segregation or merely race-based school assignment, led to the virtual unenforceability of the desegregation mandate in the face of resistance. Considering the Court's failure to act decisively, Lawrence (1980) suggests that after *Brown II,* the country continues to experience de jure, or legal, segregation as what is popularly imagined as de facto, or actual, segregation has been sanctioned by law through purposeful neglect.

Bell (1987) argues that the racial balance remedy proposed by *Brown II* inevitably failed African American schoolchildren because it failed to improve education, and as a former attorney for the NAACP, he regrets that the pursuit of equality of resources was so readily abandoned by the legal defense team. He writes:

> The racial-balance goal can be met only in schools where whites are in the majority and retain control. The quality of schooling black children receive is determined by what whites (they of the group who caused the harm in the first place) are willing to provide—which, as we should not be surprised to learn, is not very much. (p. 116)

Faced with the loss of control over the schools, many in the African American community wondered about the wisdom of the approach taken in the *Brown* case. There were petitions to maintain all-African American schools, a move the integrationists saw as a betrayal (Bell, 1980a). Many African American teachers in Topeka, Kansas, opposed the *Brown* suit from the very beginning, fearing that they would be replaced by White teachers in integrated schools (Whitman, 1993). Their fears turned out to be well founded. In the first eleven years after desegregation, over thirty thousand African American teachers were dismissed; many of those who weren't dismissed were relocated to desegregated schools where they were marginalized and poorly treated (Foster, 1997). Black principals and administrators were demoted as well (Bell, 1987).

The decision in *Brown* and the remedy of desegregation changed the way racism was expressed and discussed in the United States. However, ending legalized segregation and ending discrimination would prove to be two different challenges. Bell (1992a) describes the situation faced by people of color:

> Racial bias in the pre-*Brown* era was stark, open, unalloyed with hypocrisy and blank-faced lies. . . . Today, because bias is masked in unofficial practices and "neutral" standards, we must wrestle with the question whether race or some individual failing has cost us the job, denied us the promotion, or prompted our being rejected as tenants for an apartment. (p. 6)

According to many critical race theorists, the decision in *Brown* actually made fighting these forms of discrimination a more difficult task (Freeman, 1980, 1995; Lawrence, 1980). First, it problematically defined discrimination narrowly as segregation (Lawrence, 1980). Second, by establishing educational opportunity as an end in itself, rather than concerning itself with equality of result, it gave no provisions for improving the conditions of schools that were underfunded and made efforts to remedy educational inequity difficult to pursue in any terms other than racial balancing. Lastly, as Freeman (1980, 1995) observes, *Brown* laid the groundwork for subsequent challenges to antidiscrimination legislation by bolstering many doctrinal abstractions—chiefly equal opportunity, legal neutrality, and color blindness. These abstractions serve to dehistoricize the concept of racial discrimination. Freeman (1995) argues that the failure to consider discrimination in the history of race relations in the United States opened the door for later reversals of the gains of the civil rights movement. In short, the ideologies of literacy supporting the *Brown* decision may have propelled the Court to condemn segregation, but the goal of ensuring equality of education remained elusive, and the true character of racial discrimination remained unrecognized.

Washington: *Invoking the "Literacy Crisis"*

Washington v. Davis (1976) is generally acknowledged as one of those later reversals of the gains of the civil rights movement. The case dealt a near fatal blow to antidiscrimination legislation by narrowly defining racism as necessarily intentional, effectively invalidating the notion of unequal outcomes as racism. Although an employment discrimination case, questions of reading and writing ability were debated at great length to determine the validity of a charge of racial bias in literacy testing. The Court called into question whether a high school education was sufficient to prepare people for professional training. In this case, applicants who were denied admittance to the District of Columbia's Metropolitan Police Department alleged that Test 21, a written test that African American applicants failed at twice the rate of White applicants, discriminated against African Americans. The city argued that verbal ability was needed to enforce the law and that Test 21 was predictive of performance on the Recruit School training test taken during the training period. The Court sided with the city by ruling that Test 21 "serves the neutral and legitimate purpose of requiring all applicants to meet a uniform minimum standard of literacy" (*Washington v. Davis,* 1976, p. 255). However, as Justice Brennan, joined by Justice Marshall, noted in his dissent, the Court never examined the training test to determine how it might be related to job performance. The city's argument that Test 21 was predictive of success on the training test was unsupported by proof of any correlation between Test 21 and "performance of the job of being a police officer" (*Washington v. Davis,* 1976, p. 267). Justice Brennan argued that the burden of proof should fall not on those attempting to prove discrimination but on the city to establish the usefulness of the test.

Justice Brennan's dissension, while too strict in its interpretive framework to challenge directly the notion that literacy can be characterized as a uniform minimum standard, does call into question the notion of transferability of literacy skills from one task to another that undergirds the decision of the majority. Since then, literacy scholars have conducted research that has challenged this notion more directly. Ethnographic investigations, including Scribner and Cole's (1981/1988) study of the Vai people of Liberia, Heath's (1983) study of working-class communities in the Carolina Piedmont, and Street's (1984) study of literacy practices in Iran, revealed the multifaceted nature of literacy in practice. These studies all concluded that the abilities to read, write, and memorize are highly contextual and task dependent with limited transferability to new contexts and tasks, and hence it is not possible to speak of a single, normative literacy. Historical studies of literacy by Cook-Gumperz (1986) and Graff (1979, 1995) challenged the notion of literacy as an abstract and neutral set of skills consistent over time and place. As a field, literacy scholars have come to a near consensus that acultural conceptions of literacy, such as those that the city argued in *Washington* and that were accepted by the Supreme Court, are flawed. Of course, these ethnographic and historical literacy studies were not available at the time the Court was deliberating. However, other expert conceptions of literacy as context dependent were available—for example, studies that measured the construct validity of the entrance test to the need of the job—and their relevance was debated in the case.

In listening to the oral arguments, it becomes clear that members of the Court were concerned that "expert" testimony might replace the "commonsense" notion that police officers need to have reading and writing skills.[4] The counsel for the city, David Sutton, appealed to these commonsense notions of literacy in arguing that verbal ability was necessary to learn basic tools of the police trade. He argued that police work takes place in an evolving legal context that requires basic understanding of the components of criminal offenses, the laws of arrest, search, and seizure, and elements of report writing. He referred to Test 21, a general test given to many civil servants—not just police officers—as "a straightforward test of verbal ability" (*Complete Oral Arguments,* 1980, p. 8). Justice Stevens asked repeatedly if any of the counsels were contending that verbal ability was not necessary for the job of being a police officer[5] (p. 32). Counsel for the respondents in this case, Richard Sobol, argued in return that the city had not met its burden under the Equal Protection Clause of the Fourteenth Amendment to the Constitution to establish proof that Test 21 was not an excessive test of verbal ability. He offered the *Washington Post* crossword puzzle as an example of a test of verbal ability and asked whether it was an appropriate test of verbal ability for this situation. He further asked why the requirement of a high school diploma, which all applicants had to meet in order to fill out an application, was not considered enough evidence of verbal ability. In order to prove appropriateness, he maintained, a "construct validation" study, as he termed it—that is, a study measuring a trait (in this case, verbal ability) against an analysis of the actual tasks of the job—needed to be conducted (*Complete Oral Arguments,* 1980, p. 58). Although such a test was routine in employment discrimination cases, it was not conducted in this case, nor were any experts brought in to testify to the complexity of reading and writing tasks on the job.

The actual content of Test 21 was not invoked as part of this debate over its appropriateness, though perhaps it should have been, as its appropriateness as a test of the kind of verbal ability police officers might need on the job is far from self-evident. The test is made up of several kinds of questions, including analogy (e.g.,

"GARDEN is related to FLOWER as LAKE is related to a) pool b) river c) beach d) cottage e) fish"); vocabulary (e.g., "CRISP means most nearly a) broken b) frosty c) brittle d) burnt e) dry"); and reading comprehension (e.g.:

> "The practical skill of primivite [*sic*] man became, in time quite admirable in the treatment of certain kinds of disease and even more so in surgery. Examples of his accomplishments may be seen today among primitive tribes, and, together with prehistoric remains, testify to the status of medicine before history was written." The quotation best supports the statement that primitive man a) lacked knowledge of surgery b) exhibited more skill in medicine than in surgery c) was not easily affected by disease d) developed a definite skill in dealing with physical ailments e) buried complete records of his ability. (Brief for Petitioner, 1975, p. 209ff.)

The argument could have been made that it is not clear how these questions might pertain particularly to the job of a police officer, rather than the job of an archeologist, gardener, or fry cook. Almost indefensible as job related questions are the many questions testing knowledge of idioms, highly culturally bound expressions (e.g.:

> The saying "To believe a thing impossible is a way to make it so" means most nearly a) It is unwise to begin what is beyond one's ability. b) The only way to prove a thing can be done is to do it. c) We can do whatever we think we can do. d) What is easy to obtain is not worth having. e) Lack of confidence leads to failure. (Brief for Petitioner, 1975, p. 261)

Even granting that the test should measure a minimum standard of literacy, and that a minimum standard is necessary for police officers, it might have been worth pursuing the question of how each of these questions (including those with spelling errors) contributes to such a standard, and in what way, if only to push the issue of how a minimum standard of literacy might actually be defined. By not engaging in such scrutiny, members of the Court by default accepted Sutton's characterization of the test as "straightforward." They showed themselves to be unconcerned with the issue of what might actually be on the test and, by extension, unconcerned with the question of what literacy itself might be.

Though Sobol argued that expert notions might have revealed literacy to be context dependent, even he appeared unable to treat literacy contextually. Instead, both the attorneys and the justices often discussed literacy in quantitative rather than qualitative terms. Sobol focused on "how much" rather than "what kind" of verbal ability was deemed necessary for the job of being a police officer. The conception of literacy as a quantifiable skill in the *Washington* case was in many ways what allowed literacy to be positioned as endangered by antidiscrimination legislation. Sutton, counsel for the petitioner, played on fears of declining literacy standards. In response, Sobol argued that forcing employers to meet the burden of proof for their literacy requirements did not involve lowering standards if discriminatory effects were in evidence. He protested Sutton's approach: "There is an underlying current in the briefs in this case that there is something about the *Griggs* test which requires putting incompetents in jobs"[6] (*Complete Oral Arguments*, 1980, p. 60). However, in his rebuttal, Sutton strengthened the rhetoric of declining standards by charging that Sobol would have the department "tap the ocean's depths" (p. 82) to determine the lowest workable cutoff score for the test. One justice remarked that "the problem is we live in an age if one can believe what he hears and reads, that many high school graduates don't have high school educations" (p. 83). Another justice offered that Test 21 could be seen as a necessary measure to sort out the part of the high school crop without a high school education. These comments echoed an earlier remark by Justice Rehnquist, who offered: "Test 21 obviously adds something since many high school diplomates failed it" (p. 63). This remark reinforced the necessity of the test and the inadequacy of a high school education, as well as the notion that literacy skills could be measured in terms of an amount.

After lamenting the precipitous decline in educational standards, Sutton, speaking directly to Justice Marshall, argued for the Metropolitan Police Department's record of equal opportunity employment, pointing out that the African American population of the Metropolitan Police Department had spiraled to 41 percent. Justice Marshall responded, comparing the current state of the department now to its state in 1866: "I don't get anything out of how much it's grown. The question is, is it constitutional now?" (*Complete Oral Arguments*, 1980, p. 84). Sutton maintained that the test had no adverse impact and that the Metropolitan Police Department had complied with the Civil Rights Act. He repeatedly argued that the police department could do no more than they had already done to increase African American presence on the force and therefore no redress of potential racial imbalance should be imposed, and no back pay could be demanded. At this point, Sutton invoked the various remedies demanded since the Civil Rights Act to remedy discrimination, and on that note the argument closed.

Following the rhetoric of declining standards with the discussion of remedy was significant. In *Washington,* a high school diploma had ceased to be sufficient for professional advancement in the minds of many of the justices, and it had ceased to be the bearer of equal opportunity it was thought to be when the Court decided *Brown.* Here, knowledge and literacy were separated from the act of getting a public education, whereas in *Brown,* these had all been conflated. In *Washington,* the arguments did not center on the relevance of public education but rather on its irrelevance. Ironically, once African Americans were nominally granted remedy in the form of admittance to formerly all-White schools in *Brown,* the value of that education diminished in the eyes of the members of the Court. This ideological shift in the value of public education only mirrored the physical shifting of the populations in the schools, as "White flight" had become a feature of the post-*Brown* era.[7]

The racializing of education that was reinforced through demographic shifts and court decisions is significant for thinking about a cultural view of literacy. In analyzing the *Washington* case, Lawrence (1987) focuses not on literacy primarily but on the acultural conception of racism in the case. Nevertheless, his conclusions inevitably lead him to discuss literacy. He suggests that had racism been understood as a systemic and pervasive feature in U.S. culture, rather than as an aberrant act of intention, the outcome of the decision might have been different. The Court might have considered that the test did not measure features of communication at which African American applicants might excel. For example, African American police might be better skilled at communicating in their own neighborhoods, where White police had been seen as an invading military presence. Lawrence argues that by failing to account for the socially pervasive influence of racism, the decision reinforced the cultural myth that Whites are more intelligent than African Americans. He points out that the more the test can be seen as neutral, the more the lower performance of African Americans becomes a confirmation of this myth.

Lawrence (1987) further discusses the significance of the case being about the job of a police officer. Police officers are representatives of state authority, and in a systemically racist country, authority is vested in White people. Whites, from employees of the civil service commission to Supreme Court justices, he suggests, were uncomfortable and unaccustomed to seeing African Americans in positions of authority. It became necessary, then, to rationalize, however unconsciously, a way to legitimize an overwhelming White presence in authority positions.

Conceptions of literacy as White property, I argue, were put in service of this rationalization. The problem with the decision in *Washington* was not simply that it held up literacy to be abstract and neutral rather than socially situated but that it did not take into account the economics of literacy as White property as part of the social situation. Test 21 failed in numerous ways. It failed to provide equal opportunity by not measuring people with culturally appropriate standards; in other words, it failed to test communicative skills that African Americans might have that Whites might not. Additionally, Test 21 failed to take into account the historically unequal education African Americans and Whites received prior to the test. Test 21 only succeeded in confirming the equation of literacy and Whiteness already established and entrenched in the minds of the White majority to rationalize the exclusion of African Americans from authority positions.

Lawrence's explanation of the justices' decision becomes even more plausible because the justices not only were presented with no evidence establishing Test 21's relationship to job performance but also were presented with evidence from a study appended to the brief filed for the petitioner that there was little to no relationship. Passing Test 21 had a "positive but low relationship to job performances" for White officers, but for African American officers, "Test 21 . . . does not predict differences in on-the-job performance" (Brief for Petitioner, 1975, p. 99). This study, conducted by the Standards Division of the U.S. Civil Service Commission, correlated job performance ratings with performance on Test 21 and the Recruit School's training test.[8] The city was forced to argue that Test 21 was predictive of success on the training test, because that was all the test could predict. Therefore, as Justice Brennan noted in his dissent, the argument that Test 21 was predictive of success on the training test was irrelevant because all officers were tutored until they passed the training test. In the particular cultural context in which it appeared, Test 21 actually had no purpose except as a replacement of legalized segregation.

In terms of the civil rights movement, the result of the *Washington v. Davis* decision was disastrous, coming at the moment when it was most crucial to recognize the systemic nature of racism keeping people of color members of a perpetual underclass. The Court reinforced the notion of racial discrimination as the discrete "faults" of "atomistic individuals whose actions are outside of and apart from the social fabric without historical continuity" (Freeman, 1995, p. 30). This conception of racism is the one that Freeman (1995) identifies as most hampering antidiscrimination efforts. I would argue that it has similarly hampered efforts to provide equality of education as a remedy for historic discrimination. In the oral argument to the *Washington* case, Justice Marshall attempted to revive the goal of providing equal education by asking Sutton, "Suppose the high schools of this area are very low. Would anything be done about that?" (*Complete Oral Arguments*, 1980, p. 83). Sutton dodged the implication of societal responsibility to provide decent education to all citizens, arguing that it had no relationship to the right of a community to a "competent police force" (p. 84). The issue of providing equality of education was not pursued, as the discussion in the end was dominated by Sutton's contention that no discrimination existed that needed to be addressed. The notion that it was the responsibility of the state to provide equality of education was further eroded in *Regents of the University of California v. Bakke*, the case the Supreme Court heard a year after *Washington*.

Bakke: "Well, I come from Harvard . . ."

Alan Bakke, a White applicant to the University of California at Davis Medical School who had been rejected twice, charged that a special admissions program with sixteen seats set aside for minority students instituted by faculty to improve minority recruitment was discriminatory. The *Bakke* case generated intense public interest, with more than 130 organizations filing *amicus* briefs[9] (Gormley, 1997). *Bakke* differed significantly from *Brown* and *Washington* in that the interests of groups of color were not represented in the case itself, even though the outcome stood to affect greatly the fate of admissions programs geared at redressing past discrimination. Recognizing the potential significance of the case, several groups of color petitioned the regents not to bring their appeal to the U.S. Supreme Court because the record had been so poorly prepared; in fact, the poor quality of the record had been noted by some of the justices of the Court in their internal memos (H. Ball, 2000). No attempt had been made to document the history of discrimination in California state schools, and no attempt had been made to challenge the criteria for admission—grades and the MCAT (Bell, 1992b). Additionally, the University of California at Davis claimed that Bakke would have been admitted if he had not been White, even though the medical school had rejected other White applicants with higher scores (Selmi, 1999). This problematic claim placed the African American and Chicano/a students served by the special admissions program in an unfavorable light. In a memo to Justice Marshall dated September 13, 1977, law clerk Ellen Silberman pointed out that the case was an "unfortunate one" on which to base the fate of affirmative action (H. Ball, 2000). If heard by the Supreme Court, Silberman observed, the case could end any legal attempts to pull people of color in general and African Americans in particular "out of the lowest occupations and into the mainstream of America" (H. Ball, 2000, p. 91).

The overall tone of Sutton's final words in *Washington*, which suggested that the civil rights movement had gone too far, characterized the discussion of discrimination and remedy in the oral arguments in *Bakke*. Here, the members of the Court took a more active role in invoking the "slippery slope" of a remedy's costs to Whites by asking how many minorities in the medical school would be enough to ensure diversity. Justice Rehnquist asked, "What if the UCD had decided that . . . they would set aside 50 seats, until that balance were redressed and the minority population of doctors equaled that of the population as a whole" (H. Ball, 2000, p. 93). Justice Powell also asked whether the number of seats should be related to the population. At this, the regents' counsel, Archibald Cox, whose job it was to defend the special admissions program, balked, suggesting that

> as the number gets higher, the finding of invidiousness increases and social purposes are diminished. . . . I think one of the things which causes all of us concern about these programs is the danger they will give rise to some notion of group entitlement to numbers, regardless either of the ability of the individual or of their potential contribution in society. (H. Ball, 2000, p. 93)

In using the term *invidiousness*, Cox made reference to the new understanding of racism forged in the *Washington v. Davis* decision, which determined that "disproportionate impact is not irrelevant, but it is not the sole touchstone of invidious discrimination" (*Washington v. Davis,* 1976, p. 242). After Justice Stevens pressed the issue, Cox later defined invidious discrimination as "classifying a person as inferior" (H. Ball, 2000, p. 94). However, Cox was unable to explain what test would differentiate the case of fifty set-aside seats from the case of sixteen, given that the motivation was the same. Cox's argument suggests that the mere presence of more people of color in the educational environment is cause not only to question their qualifications and their utility to society but also to investigate whether Whites had been stigmatized or classified as inferior in an effort to meet that goal. His argument also creates a damning equation—the greater the quotient of racialized others, the greater burden those individuals have to produce evidence of their literacy and social usefulness. Certainly such sentiments poorly represent the cause of racial justice if redressing racism in the social fabric of the nation is to be taken seriously.

Derrick Bell, in analyzing *Bakke,* suggested that the poor arguing of the issues in the case meant that they were "treated more like a law school exam or an exercise in moral philosophy than a matter of paramount importance to Black citizens still striving for real citizenship in all these years" (1992b, p. 651). Yet I believe that the manner in which the case was argued illustrates that the matters involved, far from being trivial, were of paramount importance to many Whites as well, in terms of maintaining the investment in literacy as White property in the face of perceived threat. At stake in the case, even if not directly challenged, were the standards used to judge literacy attainment as racially and culturally neutral—standards whose arbitrary nature had not been examined even in the face of a racially disparate impact.[10] The chairman of the admissions committee testified that everyone admitted to Davis's medical school, regardless of whether they were admitted under the special admissions program with lower cutoff scores or the regular admissions program, was qualified. The performance of students of color at the medical school was shown to be satisfactory or better than White students, suggesting that admission test scores do not accurately predict performance.

Bell (1992b) suggests that had groups of color been represented in the case, the neutrality of literacy standards would certainly have been called into question. From the standpoint of people of color, generating information on discrimination in California schools or questioning the neutrality of the scores would have been crucial. He argues that the people who were arguing both sides of this case had benefited from those standards and had everything to lose by questioning their legitimacy and neutrality. Rather than question the legitimacy of standards, Cox and some members of the Supreme Court took advantage of their shared connections to elite literacy institutions to identify those institutions as maintaining the standards under threat. They were invested in doing so because their reputations were in part tied to the reputation of Harvard University—the literacy institution to which they were affiliated or from which they had received degrees.

These investments in the standards of their own literacy institutions were evident in seemingly incidental aspects of the oral argument and the decision. For example, Justice Blackmun asked Cox whether the special admissions policy might be viewed in the same way as an athletic scholarship, since attracting students demonstrating athletic prowess is the aim of most institutions. Cox responded with a chuckle, "Well, I come from Harvard, sir. I don't know whether it's our aim, but we don't do very well." General laughter enveloped the courtroom. Justice Blackmun remarked, "I can remember the time when you did"[11] (Kurland & Casper, 1978, p. 628). Identifying the cronyism that marked the argument of *Bakke*, Dreyfuss and Lawrence (1979) observe that this exchange restored "the special kinship of those on the bench and the attorney for the university in this lament for Harvard football and their common interest in preserving the quality of higher education. One exception to the laughter was Justice Thurgood Marshall"[12] (p. 184).

In his biography of Cox, Gormley (1997) writes that the purpose of this joke was strategic. Cox had planned to liken the special admissions program to athletic scholarships, but the regents of the University of California had asked him not to because they felt such a comparison would trivialize special admissions. Gormley maintains that Cox used the joke to get the Court off the topic, and in that way it worked. But the fact that the joke worked is nonetheless significant in understanding how investments in literacy institutions played a role in the argument and decision of the case. Cox, as an alum and one of the most prominent members of the Harvard Law School faculty, embodied Harvard as an institution and was in a position to invoke its literacy value. Since one-third of the Court had received degrees from Harvard and thus shared an investment in the institution, it is not surprising that the joke worked. Although the motive of Cox's comment may have been to put himself in a position to argue the case the way the regents wanted, the effect was a subtle elevation of Harvard. In having failed to ensure athletic success—in having only questionably even sought athletic success—Harvard could be seen as having literacy standards unclouded by other criteria.

Harvard's appearance in the case was ultimately more than incidental. Harvard College's admissions program was in the appendix to the opinion of Justice Powell in the decision. Powell, another Harvard Law School alum, found Harvard's undergraduate admissions policy, in which race is taken into account along with other criteria, laudable even though he found Davis's special admissions program of set-asides unsupportable. Justices Brennan, White, Marshall, and Blackmun pointed out in their dissenting opinion that there was no distinction between Davis's and Harvard's programs in constitutional terms. However, a distinction existed for the counsel and for some of the justices based on the recognition of Harvard as the pinnacle of literacy attainment. Most problematic, Harvard moved from being the bearer of standards to being the determiner of constitutionality. Introducing Harvard as a model is significant because it shows that Harvard's admissions policies trumped the formulations of the writers of the Fourteenth Amendment and the convention of legal precedent. In *Bakke,* Harvard, and not the Constitution, was invoked to legitimate affirmative action, with the result that the notion of "quota" became anathema to the considerations of racial justice remedy, and Alan Bakke was admitted to the University of California at Davis Medical School.

Several opinions were written for *Bakke,* but Justice Powell's opinion, trumpeting Harvard's admissions policy, was to become effectively the law of the land for universities looking to avoid challenge to their affirmative action programs. However, challenges to affirmative action were not put to rest by *Bakke.* As a result of *Bakke's* formulations, which deny remedy where clear past discrimination by particular institutions on particular people of color cannot be proven, or where particular Whites not related to the discriminatory policies might be harmed, *Bakke* left affirmative action vulnerable (Bell, 1992b). Justice Marshall attempted during the oral argument to redirect the discussion away from the focus on harm to Whites toward a discussion of the lives of the people affirmative action was intended to benefit. During an exchange with Colvin, the counsel for Alan Bakke, on the issue of the constitutionality of "set-aside seats" as a remedy for historic discrimination, Justice Marshall charged, "You are talking about your client's rights. Don't these underprivileged people have some rights?" (H. Ball, 2000, p. 97).

Justice Marshall wrote his own opinion to *Bakke,* in which he asserted the continuing effects of racism in the social fabric of the nation and suggested the importance of literacy institutions in placing individuals in influential and prosperous positions:

> It is because of a legacy of unequal treatment that we now must permit the institutions of this society to give consideration to race in making decisions about who will hold the positions of influence, affluence, and prestige in America. . . . I do not believe that anyone can truly look into America's past and still find that a remedy for that past is impermissible. (*Bakke,* 1978, p. 402)

Meanwhile, the director of admissions at Harvard Law School and the dean of admissions at Harvard College reacted to the announcement of the *Bakke* decision by denying that they gave minority students any preference in the admissions process (Nadel, 1978). The *Harvard Law Record* reported that while Cox had advanced "the Davis position favoring quotas in his Supreme Court brief and oral argument, he would vote against quotas at Harvard" (Nadel, 1978, p. 4).

The Economy of Literacy as White Property

Bakke and *Washington,* both products of the late 1970s, were decided in a vastly different national climate than the one that surrounded *Brown.* By the 1970s, opposition to busing was intense. Public support for many civil rights measures had eroded, and the Supreme Court itself was more conservative. Residential segregation had increased in many areas. In its most literal sense, the property value of White identity is revealed in a story told by critical race theorist Patricia Williams (1997) about her attempts to buy a house in a virtually all-White neighborhood. Her financial matters were conducted over the phone because the house was in another state. Her loan was approved immediately, but when she received the paperwork from the bank, she noticed that the loan officer had checked off that she was "White" on the Fair Housing form. She amended the form, checking off "Black," and returned it to the bank:

> Suddenly the deal came to a screeching halt. The bank wanted more money as a down payment, they wanted me to pay more points, they wanted to raise the rate of interest. Suddenly I found myself facing great resistance and much more debt. (p. 40)

The reason the bank gave for wanting more money was that property values in the area had started to decline. Williams was puzzled, as prices there had remained stable since World War II. Finally, after a conversation with her real estate agent, she understood that *she* was the cause of falling prices, the start of the "tipping point" when Whites would begin to move out.

The *Washington* and *Bakke* cases reveal that literacy is governed by a similar economy. When African American applicants are admitted, whether to a high school or the police force or a medical school, literacy standards are perceived to be falling or in peril of falling. Frequently, when this perception of declining standards has occurred, many Whites simply go elsewhere, to attend other schools or take other jobs. The case in *Bakke* is interesting because it is more difficult to go "up" from such a distinguished place as the University of California at Davis Medical School. By fleeing to Harvard as the model and bearer of literacy standards, Justice Powell enacted a kind of White flight, away from the public toward the private sphere. The public education that had meant so much to the Supreme Court justices of the *Brown* decision as a means to equal opportunity is case by case denigrated until it is almost as devalued as the active pursuit of racial justice. Once remedy is granted in one literacy environment, that literacy environment is denigrated to devalue its worth. This is the economy of literacy as White property, an economy that served the White majority in the Supreme Court in its efforts to bring the course of racial justice to a halt.

2 ✦ *BAKKE'S* LEGACY: THE NEW RHETORIC OF RACIAL JUSTICE

Two months after the Supreme Court delivered their decision in *Bakke,* a group of predominately African American legal scholars held a conference at Harvard Law School to debate whether African Americans truly had won the *Brown* decision. They questioned the long-term impact of *Brown* on educational equity, antidiscrimination legislation, and poverty. This conference signaled that many of the people who had been litigating for years to see the promise of *Brown* enforced were growing frustrated with the progress of racial justice, even seeing *Brown* as having caused no interruption to the history of judicial denial of racial discrimination. Charles Lawrence, for example, remarked, "'The messages of *Plessy* and *Bakke* are basically the same: Blacks have no right to an end to segregation because the only injury is a figment of their imaginations'" (Hanifin, 1978).

Charles Lawrence, Derrick Bell, Alan Freeman, and some of the other scholars at the conference were the early inspirations behind a movement, later known as critical race theory, which would continue through the next few decades to reassess the gains of the civil rights movement in the courts. Critical race theory would also attempt to revive the flagging struggle for racial justice in the post-*Bakke* era and would do so by simultaneously embracing and announcing a rhetorical shift. Starting in the late 1980s, their publications turned away from strict analysis of the foundational civil rights cases; they began to address the exclusion they experienced in their own jobs and lives, and their rhetoric became marked by less moderate tone and more personal stance. Charles Lawrence's (1987) analysis of the *Washington v. Davis* case, for example, began with an unusual rhetorical move for that venue and time, an anecdote from childhood in which Lawrence recalls the form racism takes in integrated, even "progressive" educational settings in the North. As introduction to his analysis, he writes:

> It is 1948. I am sitting in a kindergarten classroom at the Dalton School, a fashionable and progressive New York City private school. My parents, both products of a segregated Mississippi school system, have come to New York to attend graduate and professional school. They have enrolled me and my sisters here at Dalton to avoid sending us to the public school in our neighborhood where the vast majority of the students are black and poor. They want us to escape the ravages of segregation.
>
> It is circle time in the five-year old group, and the teacher is reading us a book. As she reads, she passes the book around the circle so that each of us can see the illustrations. The book's title is *Little Black Sambo*. . . . I have heard the teacher read the "comical" text describing Sambo's plight and have heard the laughter of my classmates. . . . I do not have the words to articulate my feelings—words like "stereotype" and "stigma" that might help cathart the shame and place it outside of me where it began. But I am slowly realizing that, as the only black child in the circle, I have some kinship with the tragic and ugly hero of this story—that my classmates are laughing at me as well as him. (p. 317)

Lawrence uses this anecdote to illustrate why it is problematic for the courts to demand proof of conscious intent in discrimination cases. Certainly, he suggests, the teacher did not intend to be racist. He concludes that since so much of racism in this society is unconscious—the norm rather than a deviation from the norm—there is no language with which to expose and punish it given a legal system that demands proof of conscious intent.

But this scene also reveals how sites of literacy acquisition become as well sites of awakening children to cultural values (as *Brown* suggested), though in this event the cultural value being taught is the value of White identity. To demonstrate that this cultural value is confirmed throughout the educational process and not merely during the years of primary literacy acquisition, Lawrence goes on to recall a college companion's comment that he didn't even think of Lawrence as a Negro (p. 318). The acquisition of both primary and advanced literacy is portrayed as inseparable for Lawrence from the process of learning about the cultural value of being White—a form of discrimination the courts, focused on issues of intentional discrimination and acts of segregation, do not recognize.

Lawrence's departure from traditional precedent-based argument in this analysis is representative of an attempt in critical race theory to reveal both the insufficiency of antidiscrimination legislation and the personal costs of that insufficiency on their own lives and the lives of other people of color. As people of color who have attained the highest levels of education, critical race theorists themselves should be post–civil rights literacy success stories. Many critical race theorists point out that they are the beneficiaries of the end of segregation and the institution of affirmative action measures. As a qualification to their having "made it," however, critical race theorists write about the effect racism continues to have on their professional and personal lives. Thus critical race theory evolved from a scholarly enterprise into a political movement to address the marginal status of faculty of color within law schools. Around the country, law professors of color began to question the limits of the equalizing power of the educational system as they experienced tokenism, prejudicial slights from students and colleagues, and exclusion from mainstream legal scholarship circles. Their own experiences were mimicking the dwindling returns of the civil rights struggle as a whole. As Richard Delgado describes the death of the old racial justice rhetoric following *Bakke:* "Old approaches—filing amicus briefs, marching, coining new litigation strategies, writing articles in legal and popular journals exhorting our fellow citizens to exercise moral leadership in the search for racial justice—were yielding smaller and smaller returns" (1995a, p. xiii). Having seen through their experience as civil rights advocates that discrimination alters rather than disappears when Whites and African Americans are legally afforded the same rights and processes, many critical race theorists began to identify flaws in the ideologies of color blindness, incremental change, and equal opportunity—ideologies that undergirded much of the civil rights approach but which have as often served to mask racism as challenge it.

At the core of critical race theorists' exploration of the limited reach of the civil rights movement is a reconsideration of the utility of the concept of "rights." Critical race theory gained momentum in the mid-1980s by distinguishing itself from critical legal studies, a movement identifying the instability of concepts foundational to the law and liberalism, such as rights.[1] Prominent members of the critical legal studies movement referred to rights as hallucinations (Gabel & Kennedy, 1984, pp. 34–35). Yet the sweeping nature of this critique of rights would be challenged by many scholars of color at the 1986 Critical Legal Studies conference and in subsequent law review articles. Kimberlé Crenshaw, for example, argues that because critical legal studies held that all people consent to their oppression (without acknowledging that in the case of people of color, coercion perhaps more accurately explains the causes of oppression), the movement, like mainstream legal scholarship, "seldom speaks to or about Black people" (1988, p. 1356). She argues further that in rejecting rights discourse wholesale, critical legal scholars fail to "appreciate fully the transformative significance of the civil rights movement in mobilizing Black Americans and generating new demands" (p. 1356). Patricia Williams (1991) similarly argues that the nature of rights is less illusory than alchemical: "To say that blacks never fully believed in rights is true. Yet it is also true that blacks believed in them so much and so hard that we gave them life where there was none before" (p. 163). Mari Matsuda (1987) also points out that rights are both crucial and problematic, as people of color are in the contradictory position of having to believe simultaneously that they have a right to participate equally in society, and that rights are whatever people in power say they are (p. 339).

The doctrine of "color blindness" also falls under review. Richard Delgado's analysis of civil rights scholarship, "The Imperial Scholar: Reflections on a Review of Civil Rights Literature"—described by Derrick Bell as "an intellectual hand grenade, tossed over the wall of the establishment as a form of academic protest"[2]— charges that a number of mainstream, White, male civil rights scholars have ignored work by scholars of color, leading to a marginalization of such work in civil rights discourse. What is needed in the law is not more color blindness, Delgado argues, but more race consciousness, more awareness that race still signifies. Other critical race theorists who begin to connect racial discrimination in the legal profession to broader cultural practices of discrimination echo

Delgado's call. Questioning the neutrality of the justice system, they observe that while "the law" may be color blind, people who make the law are not and cannot be, and those people are overwhelmingly White. They suggest further that the precedent-based reasoning of legal argumentation ensures the weight of decisions made before men and women of color were in the profession of law, even where people of color may currently be occupying the bench. As the legal system and the words that sustain it become more and more implicated in the maintenance of inequity, critical race theorists craft a new rhetoric that makes use of allegory, parody, and fantasy to demonstrate the limits not only of integration but of the literacy they have acquired in integrated settings as well.

Significantly, critical race theorists have often been noted (and often faulted) not so much for their arguments—*what* they are saying—as for their departures from standard legal discourse—*how* they are saying. Responses to their work suggest the crucial place rhetoric occupies in their project, and in the entire justice system. Bell identifies the counterculture writing of critical race theorists as a form of protest, suggesting that the new rhetoric in the struggle for racial justice is not one of direct moral confrontation and appeal to abstract principles but rather one of indirect, stylized irony or personal anecdote dramatizing the contradictions and ambiguities faced by people of color in the United States. Critical race theorists' deliberately dissonant rhetorical stance also confronts the racialized atmosphere of the academy and signals the ways in which they continue to be outsiders. The forms their literacy practices take are therefore important to their scholarship, as they are the mechanisms by which authors of color counter stories that the culture propagates and the courts recognize about the post–civil rights United States, stories suggesting that the civil rights movement was sufficient to eradicate racism, or even that it went too far in giving people of color opportunities to acquire literacy.[3] The writing of critical race theorists necessarily, then, investigates the highly racialized nature of mainstream literacy acquisition. In the following pages, I focus on the textually controversial work of Derrick Bell and Patricia Williams, as they of all critical race theorists are most known for the range of rhetorical strategies they draw upon to reveal education in this country to be an education in the privileges of Whiteness.

It has been said of critical race theory that it offers no hope, that its challenges to the legal apparatus leave nothing to build on, and no path to pursue except one toward a paralytic despair. Critical race theory does not indeed generate a clear mandate for legal action, but I would suggest that the expectation that it should misses what it could offer. Clearly critical race theorists, in pointing out how the value of White identity has historically been recognized by the courts, are not angling for the creation of new laws to redistribute White identity more evenly. What emerges out of critical race theory, I suggest, is not primarily a litigation strategy but a rhetorical strategy to revive the struggle for racial justice. Critical race theorists do not so much dismiss the notions of rights, justice, property, and literacy so much as try to generate public debate over how these concepts, rendered meaningless by historical misuse, should best be invested with meaning. That search for meaning could be the *Bakke* decision's best, if unintended, legacy.

Bell

In 1969, student protests fueled by the assassination of Martin Luther King sparked minority recruitment efforts at Harvard Law School, resulting in the hiring of the school's first full-time African American professor, Derrick Bell. In 1990, Bell took a year of leave without pay to protest the law school's failure to hire or tenure a woman of color. One year of protest leave stretched to two, and subsequently, Bell's appointment was terminated under the standing university policy that faculty can take no more than two years of leave. In 1992, Bell, the first African American full-time professor ever hired by Harvard Law School, became one of the few members of the faculty ever to be fired by Harvard Law School.

Bell (1994) writes of this experience as one of many protests he has made against institutions' reluctance to fully commit themselves to amending discriminatory practices. In 1959, he quit a job with the Civil Rights Division of the Justice Department when he was asked to give up his NAACP membership, considered by the department to be a conflict of interest. From there he was hired by Thurgood Marshall and became one of five lawyers on the NAACP's Legal Defense Fund team fighting court battles to desegregate schools in the South. Later, as Deputy Director of Civil Rights at what used to be the Department of Health, Education and Welfare, Bell found himself frustrated with the department's slow implementation of Title VI of the 1964 Civil Rights Act (which bans discrimination in institutions that receive federal funding). He left that position, too. Shortly thereafter, he became one of the first in the legal profession of those formerly committed to goals of desegregation to question school integration as the singular way to ameliorate the effects of racial discrimination on African Americans.

Bell's departures were not limited to leaving various positions. He is also known for his departures from the standard form of legal analysis based on case law and precedent. He is quite forward in his rejection of the literacy practices valued by the mainstream legal community and makes the inadequacy of those practices one of the subjects of his work. In introducing two of his books, *And We Are Not Saved* and *Faces at the Bottom of the Well,* for example, Bell calls his use of fantasy as essential to the construction of his critique of racial inequities as the use of logical argumentation. He writes in *Saved,* "In order to appraise the contradictions and inconsistencies that pervade the all too real world of racial oppression, I have chosen in this book the tools not only of reason but of unreason, of fantasy" (1987, p. 5). He has elsewhere observed that stories have the added benefit of creating a comfortable distance between the writer, the reader, and the material—a kind of safety zone in which to approach a charged topic like racism.[4] Most of these stories dramatize in a general way the fundamental irrationality of the United States having been founded on principles of freedom and justice for all while only providing freedom for a few. His stories, then, are less "fantastic" in many ways than reality; Bell writes that he uses untrue stories "to explore situations that are real enough but, in their many and contradictory dimensions, defy understanding" (1987, p. 6).

Bell's stories are radical and satirical critiques of liberalism and integration; to create the safety zone between himself and the reader, he places the strongest of these critiques in the mouth of the fictional Geneva Crenshaw, a female African American lawyer who becomes the "author" of Bell's stories (Bell, 1995a). The stories in both *Faces* and *Saved* are punctuated with dialogue between the first-person narrator—an African American male lawyer with the traditional, integrationist, civil rights approach—and Geneva Crenshaw. In these dialogues, the narrator (whom Bell refers to as himself) serves as a foil: "In many stories, I'm the traditional, integration-oriented civil rights lawyer and she's the one who's prodding me to get with it"[5] (qtd. in Goldberg, 1992, p. 57). In "The Chronicle of the Sacrificed Black School Children," for example, Geneva chides Bell for thinking that school integration would solve everything. The chronicle begins with the sudden disappearance of all Black school children in a city that "had resisted meaningful school desegregation for so long that it was now possible to learn from the experience of other districts that integrating schools would not automatically insulate poor black children from the risks of ghetto life" (1987, p. 103). In the story, the town makes no move to recover the lost children until the superintendent of schools realizes how much money the White community would lose by not integrating.

In *Faces at the Bottom of the Well,* his second collection of chronicles, Bell focuses more on his own experiences with racism in academic settings, exploring the issue of tokenism in higher education settings; "A Law Professor's Protest" features Harvard University, where he had maintained he was too long the only African American professor. In the chronicle, the president of Harvard and all of the institution's 169 African American full-time professionals (representing less than 2 percent of Harvard's full-time professionals) die in a fiery explosion; only then do people realize how meager Harvard's minority recruitment efforts had been. This fictional incident was the substance of the actual Final Affirmative Action Report that the Association of Black Faculty and Administrators at Harvard submitted to the president in 1988. In discussing the unusual report and the administration's reaction with Geneva, Bell comments that the exclusion that kept W. E. B. Du Bois at the margins of Harvard persisted through Bell's own time at Harvard, despite antidiscrimination laws. This exclusion, he observes, is aided by the valuing of certain standardized forms of scholarship over others:

> Actually, tenure may be a more important barrier than overt racism, though the two are clearly linked. . . . Even outstanding scholarship can, if performed in a nontraditional format, disqualify a candidate seeking a position or promotion. Narrow measures of excellence harm many candidates, but tend to exclude disproportionately blacks and other people of color whose approach, voice or conclusions may depart radically from the usual forms. (Bell, 1992a, pp. 139–140)

Bell's stories continually dramatize the failure of measures such as integration and affirmative action to secure lasting retribution for the harm done African Americans. "The Racial Preference Licensing Act," not quite a modest proposal, suggests an alternative to these measures, one that relies on ameliorating the material conditions of African American lives not by attempting to curtail discrimination but by accepting its existence. The fictional president of the United States in "Licensing Act" puts into effect a new law meant to redress the unenforceable civil rights laws by allowing Whites to discriminate against African Americans if they pay stiff licensing fees, the proceeds of which will benefit African Americans. The benefits of the bill include relieving African Americans of the burden of having to divine when they are being discriminated against. The story suggests that economic disincentives placed on discrimination will be more effective in the long run than attempts to legislate against racism, and economic reparations paid to African Americans more useful in the long run than easily ignored legislation; "Licensing Act" illustrates Bell's thesis that Whites as a group have only ever given concessions to African Americans as a group when they stood to gain materially from that concession, or at best did not stand to give up anything they already have. Acknowledging history, Bell implies, one would have to be a lunatic to believe that one could legislate discrimination out of existence, or even educate it out of existence by an appeal to moral principles.

Bell's departures from argumentation based upon case precedent have not always been appreciated by more politically conservative legal scholars. In her review of *Faces,* Abigail Thernstrom, a staunch opponent of affirmative action, suggested that storytelling "relieves Bell of the necessity of making logical arguments sustained by evidence" (1992, p. 59). Bell's chronicles in *Faces* and *Saved,* however, are neither all story nor all argument. Bell suggests that the generic ambiguity of *Faces* led to a demi-erasure of the book:

> *Faces* fell in the cracks of media coverage. It was not a Black conservative book, in which case, you know, it would have shot to the top of the best seller list. . . . The reviewers weren't sure what to do with it. . . . Nor was it a Black pathology book, "ooh, I started off as the child of a fifteen year old drug-ridden mother who prostituted herself even the day after I was born.". . . It didn't fit into that category. And it wasn't a Black militant book, "I hate all white people." That also sells very well. (Bell, 1995a)

Bell here suggests that there are acceptable and unacceptable stories for African American authors to tell about racism, generic conventions to be followed or flaunted. African American authors speaking or writing within a validated genre are perceived to have more authority; should a work fall between genres, it hazards the charge of unintelligibility. Richard Delgado (1995b), too, notes that "agony tales" (tales of African American pathology) are very popular, but tales that actually critique the mainstream in a way that is difficult to dismiss—and he cites Bell's work as an example—tend to receive the most resistance from mainstream readers and are not absorbed into the literature (p. 207). Delgado and Bell suggest that the problem isn't that critical race theorists are telling stories but that they are telling different stories, stories that challenge the "naturalness" of White privilege, exposing those mechanisms that have bolstered the notion of literacy as White property.

Williams

Bell's protest over Harvard Law School's failure to tenure a woman of color made the national news. Patricia Williams (1991) writes that she was watching the *MacNeil/Lehrer News Hour* when it reported the story, and that this very news item was the exigence motivating her to write about the interstices between legal practice, and the ideal of justice.

Patricia Williams, like Bell, writes outside the lines of conventional legal discourse in order to counteract the irrational denial of the reality of racism. In textualizing this irrationality, however, Williams borrows devices from fiction but doesn't completely fictionalize, choosing instead to cull more directly from the world around her. Her exploration of color blind ideology is sparked, for example, by her son's experience in nursery school. Three separate teachers assure her that her son is color blind though a visit to an ophthalmologist shows his vision to be perfect:

> As it turned out, my son did not misidentify color. He resisted identifying color at all. "I don't know," he would say when asked what color the grass was; or, most peculiarly, "It makes no difference." This latter remark, this assertion of the greenness of the grass making no difference, was such a precociously cynical retort, that I began to suspect some social complication in which he was somehow invested. (1997, p. 3)

Williams soon learns that the teachers at the predominantly White school her son attended had been teaching students that color makes no difference. She also learns that they had been doing so because the children had been debating whether African American children could play "good guys."

The teachers in this situation were certainly well meaning, Williams offers. Nevertheless, she suggests that the denial of social tensions, even if unintentional, "leaves those in my son's position pulled between the clarity of their own experience and the often alienating terms in which they must seek social acceptance" (p. 4). Her son's attempts to adjust his communicative practices to reflect this denial ironically place him in a situation where he is pathologized and ushered swiftly into the world of remediation.

Williams's story about her son and his nursery school is significantly reminiscent of Charles Lawrence's story of discrimination in his own kindergarten classroom; in both cases, literacy acquisition is intricately bound up with the process of learning White privilege. Williams is often careful to point out that her experiences are not unique; her writing, then, could be read as allegorical rather than autobiographical. Like Bell and Delgado, who argue that telling stories is nothing new, Williams's allegories confront other allegories, specifically, those collective cultural myths that place people of color into certain readily resonant, archetypal positions. Demonstrating in "Notes from a Small World" how pervasive racism continues its impact even after acquisition of advanced literacy, Williams allegorizes the experience of Everyblackwomanlawyer. After getting in touch with the nine other Black women in her graduating class at Harvard Law School, Williams finds that they have all endured similar experiences: a sense of isolation while in law school followed by hyper-attention in some circumstances and absolute dismissal in others—race, in particular, being one characteristic prone to appear and disappear. As one of her colleagues remarks:

> I was anointed, no doubt about it, but always in a way that attributed my accomplishments to me as a woman but not to my race. So in fact what you do well will reflect well on you, but only as an individual. And what you do poorly—well that's when what you do will be dumped on the whole race. (qtd. in Williams, 1996, p. 90)

It is thus that successful women of color, Williams observes, are regarded as isolated abnormalities rather than as part of the larger cultural picture; any mistake that is made further confirms the cultural myth that African Americans are undeserving of their positions. Through this myth advanced literacy remains the property of Whites in the minds of many Americans, including teachers, legislators, researchers, and judges, and the world of Black female lawyers remains a small one.

By 1991, when Williams wrote her crossover book, *The Alchemy of Race and Rights,* no African American women lawyers had a permanent job at her alma mater, Harvard Law School. She begins her book with this observation, and adds—making clear the burden of assumed literacy deficit placed on African Americans by the construction of literacy as White property—that the reason is "because we're all too stupid." She continues, "To be fair, what Associate Dean Louis Kaplow actually said was that Harvard would have to 'lower its standards,' which of course Harvard simply cannot do" (1991, p. 5). She also notes that the morning she sees this on the news she is very depressed, in her "old terry bathrobe . . . trying to decide if she is stupid or crazy" (p. 4). Critics of *Alchemy* have suggested that she might be both and have mused that perhaps Williams is unhinged, or playing at being unhinged, but that either way her style is at odds with her credibility. It has been charged that her inclusion of "personal irrelevancies" invites readers to dismiss her (Jost, 1991). Williams has been accused of self-indulgence, paranoia, and—perhaps worse—"methodological non-chalance" and "principled genre-blurring" (Rieder, 1991, p. 41). "Genre-bashing, is more like it," as Williams has defined it.[6]

But what can this genre-bashing reveal? In Williams's work, it exposes the interested parties hiding behind authorized genres who make up those institutions the nation has invested with great power. In her pseudo-ethnography of the Clarence Thomas/Anita Hill hearings entitled "A Rare Case Study of Muleheadedness and Men, or How to Try an Unruly Black Witch, with Excerpts from the Heretical Testimony of Four Women, Known to Be Hysterics, Speaking in Their Own Voices, as Translated for This Publication by Brothers Hatch, Simpson, DeConcini and Specter,"[7] Williams combines and then bashes the genres of congressional hearings, anthropological field notes, and multiple choice tests; although the thrust of the essay as a whole is to turn what was popularly mythologized as a "high-tech lynching" into what from a different perspective seems more like a witch hunt, the complicity of all these textual forms and the institutions that support them (courts, universities, schools) in perpetuating the cultural myths of "the other" is also highlighted. In "Muleheadedness," Williams uses the language in which cultural myths are disseminated against itself. She puts the senators into the position of ultimate authorship not so much to hide but rather to dramatize the distortions unauthorized voices undergo when ventriloquized through authorized mouths. In dramatizing these distortions, Williams carries both the myths about African American women and the language that sustains them to their illogical extreme in order to undo them. The result is much like Bell's stories, a "fantasy" that is all too real. "Exhibit C," for example, is the witch's "confession." It is here that Williams most forcefully mocks the notion that equal opportunity has been achieved in academic settings:

> I'm a witch. Now I know this may be a little hard to comprehend, but I can prove it. First of all, I'm a black female law professor, a status so miraculous that that alone should convince you of my powers. The statistical probability of such a creature existing is about the same as that for mermaids and the Loch Ness monster, with the Loch Ness monster having a slight edge. (1992, p. 165)

Continuing in the mock confessional vein, Williams connects the plight of Black female law professors to African American women in general by listing her specific "powers":

> [I]f I have a baby, I tend to have a population explosion; if I move into a neighborhood, I come as the forward phalanx of an invading army; if I have an opinion, it is attributed to "you people." So you can see I have powers. (p. 167)

One of the major "finds," then, of Williams's archeological digs at the collective myths of the culture is that African American women have never needed to do anything to be perceived of as lying, crazy, hysterical, or even monstrous, short of open their mouths—and sometimes not even that. The problem Williams unearths is not that she is telling stories or even that she is telling different stories but that she, an African American woman, is the teller.

Literacy Practices as Protest

It is worth observing that critical race theorists, even though they are teachers themselves, do not articulate pedagogical imperatives advocating that students take up the rhetoric they have forged to continue the struggle for racial justice. Even as they embark on deconstructions of legal discourse, they are mindful that their positions as tenured law professors have allowed them this opportunity. Patricia Williams acknowledges that in her own teaching, she recognizes that students have to pass the bar (interview). Richard

Delgado's fictional law professor in *The Rodrigo Chronicles* is continually counseling the hot-headed radical legal student Rodrigo to hold off on his embrace of narrative until he achieves tenure. Critical race theorists generally acknowledge that one has to get into that position of being a respected jurist before one's pronouncements and justifications for departing from the rule of law can themselves become law, and that position is one that not many people of color, and particularly not many women of color, occupy. They are cognizant of their own positions and cognizant that those positions authorize them to speak to a certain extent.[8]

However, the limits of professional position given the economy of literacy as White property are documented in the critical race theory literature as well. Derrick Bell notes that his attempts to conform were not sufficient to negate a culture schooled in White privilege: "I soon discovered that, whatever my willingness to conform, my tenured status did not entitle me to admission to the Law School's inner circles" (Bell, 1994, p. 38). Patricia Williams has also remarked that no matter what level she attains professionally, she is marked as an African American female and dismissed as "unreliable, untrustworthy, hostile, angry, powerless, irrational and probably destitute" (1991, p. 147). She connects her experience to the experience of African American children in integrated schools by footnoting the following observation from Leon Litwack (1986): "Whatever else they learned in school, black children came to understand, as their parents had, that their color marked them as inferior in the eyes of whites, no matter how they conducted themselves" (qtd. in Williams, 1991, p. 249). Thus Williams connects the plight of faculty of color in law schools to the plight of children of color at all literacy levels.

Although many critical race theorists have argued that whenever there is the presence of others, those who had previously been excluded, the system changes, they also recognize that the token integration that has occurred in higher education has been insufficient. Guinier, Fine, Balin, Bartow, and Stachel's study of socialization in law school, for example, concludes that because the law school's model of the ideal lawyer is based on the role and technique of lawyering when there were no women or people of color in the profession, it is not simply enough to add women and people of color and stir (1994, p. 67). Without significant changes to the profession and pedagogy, Guinier et al. argue, women and people of color will continue to wind up on the bottom. With recent estimates that more than half of African American students who enroll at predominately White institutions of higher learning never see graduation, concerns about equality of results become all the more salient.[9] These studies reveal the limits of integration attempted without confrontation of the cultural belief in literacy as White property. Collectively, they serve as a means for continued problematizing of assimilationist teaching, putting flesh on Victor Villanueva's (1998) assertion that the sensibility that dominates American discourse on literacy always only validates a limited form of inclusion. As I will discuss in greater detail in subsequent chapters, American discourse on literacy has historically done even worse, that is, worked to legitimate racial exclusion.

This point is not lost on Williams and Bell, yet their work also auspiciously suggests the potential literacy has to be revalued and used for rhetorical action. As Mari Matsuda (1996) observes, critical race theorists continue to write because they are "cynically hopeful" that what they write and how they write furthers the movement toward racial justice. Remarking on the efficacy of language and literacy as a medium to inspire change, Bell has offered:

> [M]ost critical race theorists are committed to a program of scholarly resistance, and most hope scholarly resistance will lay the groundwork for wide-scale resistance. . . . We believe that standards and institutions created by and fortifying white power ought to be resisted. (Bell, 1995b, p. 900)

This resistance should be located well within traditions of resistance to White privilege. In identifying Bell and Williams strongly as members of a particular intellectual movement, there is always the peril of reducing their work, of lumping together authors with different purposes under one heading. It is perhaps more crucial, however, to avoid encouraging the kind of depoliticization Hanchard (1996) observes is the fate of many Black intellectuals who have been read in isolation from larger political movements. Bell and Williams both not only align themselves openly with other critical race theorists but also continually refer to larger political struggles within their work. Bell's casebook, *Race, Racism and the American Law,* for example, opens with a dedication to the Black athletes of the 1968 Olympics who protested racism. Accompanying the dedication is a drawing of a photograph of two of the athletes, John Carlos and Tommie Smith, who on the victory platform raised their arms in a Black Power salute while the National Anthem was played. The end of Bell's dedication invokes "all those who throughout America's history have risked its wrath to protest its faults" (1992b, p. vi).

Long before Bell, Williams, Lawrence, and Harris protested the assumptions of literacy as White property inherent in the remedy of *Brown,* Malcolm X condemned the *Brown* decision as implying the inferiority of African Americans. Before Malcolm X and the civil rights movement pointed out inconsistencies of American democracy, African Americans had protested the inconsistencies presented by the Declaration of Independence.[10] The critical race theory movement, then, might be seen as an extension of previous efforts to use literacy in unauthorized and difficult to measure ways to resist the privileging of White identity; the long history of these efforts indicates that the privileging of White identity in this country is not ephemeral, about to disappear in a generation or two, as doctrines of incremental assimilation like the melting pot model would suggest. Struggles to redefine purposeful literacy continue to remain at the center of the resistance. Pre-*Brown,* African Americans attempted to pursue both literacy and racial justice by seeking entrance into Jim Crow institutions where they knew they would not be allowed. This strategic move called attention to their position as outsiders and put them in a position to use the courts to challenge state law and, through that process, become heard. Similarly, post-*Brown,* critical race theorists position themselves rhetorically as outsiders in their scholarship to show that the advanced literacy they have acquired still does not in and of itself constitute racial justice.

3 ✦ DESEGREGATION COMES TO THE PIEDMONT: LOCATING *WAYS WITH WORDS*

The debate over the effects of the *Brown* decision on education and racial justice spread far beyond the courts and legal scholarship circles. This chapter directs its attention toward the community members, teachers, and literacy scholars who all had their own stake in the aftermath of *Brown,* sometimes joining their interests in concert, and sometimes opposing one another as they grappled with the implications, and pace, of racial integration in the schools. Public and scholarly interest attended the question of how desegregation might affect learning in the classroom and daily life in communities. Literacy research as a result burgeoned in the late 1960s and early 1970s, furthering the association in the American mind between literacy and issues of racial justice.

Here I examine this growing association by focusing on communities in the Carolina Piedmont, and on one literacy researcher's attempts to document the effects of desegregation during a critical period that revealed not only the promise of *Brown* but also all the unanswered questions *Brown* left for those who would be most affected by it. Perhaps the most pressing question of how literacy instruction should change after desegregation is brought to light in Shirley Brice Heath's *Ways with Words* (1983), one of the most influential literacy studies published in the last few decades. The goal of the text was to give teachers a way to navigate the changing circumstances brought by desegregation, so that they might better educate all children in the schools. Reporting on a period from 1968 to the late 1970s, *Ways* documents the literacy practices of working-class African American students in what Heath dubs "Trackton" and working-class White students in nearby "Roadville" and examines how these practices conflicted with the literacy practices validated at schools run by middle-class townspeople Heath identifies as "mainstreamers." Heath's conclusion, that the problems students encountered learning together after desegregation in the mainstream school were due to a clash of cultures, as well as to the failure of teachers to understand and value the uses of literacy children brought with them from their home communities, continues to influence both teacher training and literacy research.

Yet *Ways* has within its analytical structure a lacuna around the topic of race that renders the most revealing conclusions about the impact of *Brown* on literacy out of reach, and the central insight about how a volatile racial climate affects learning, moot. *Ways* is a study of racial desegregation, and yet puzzlingly race is hardly mentioned in the book. In her prologue, Heath steers the reader away from considering race, explaining that even though the people of Roadville are White and the people of Trackton Black, the middle-class townspeople, regardless of their race, have more in common with each other than with the people of either Roadville or Trackton. She writes: "Therefore, any reader who tries to explain the community contrasts in this book on the basis of race will miss the central point of the focus on culture as learned behavior and on language habits as part of that shared learning" (p. 11). Further downplaying the racial differences between the communities, the book concludes at one point, "Neither community's ways with the written word prepares it for the school's ways" (p. 235). Given this conclusion, most recently I have come to wonder, Does it matter that I remember Roadville as a White community and Trackton as a Black one? And if so, why does it matter?

If one reads *Ways* as it has traditionally been read, it does not matter greatly. What has mattered and what *Ways* has become known for is its use of ethnographic methods to arrive at a redefinition of literacy. Heath successfully employed the stories of her subjects to counter prevailing stories about literacy and orality in the scholarly community—particularly the notion that groups of people could be described as either oral or literate and the attendant notions that literacy could be considered an evolutionary step beyond orality, or that a class-neutral literacy could be achieved and was a desirable goal. Heath demonstrated that the communities she studied could only be defined as both oral and literate and crucially put a class identification on the kind of literacy valued by mainstream schools. In identifying powerful "narratives of literacy" that have shaped research and by extension pedagogy, Beth Daniell succinctly sums up the historical significance and continuing impact of *Ways:*

> Heath's stories of literacy in three different communities argue that it is more useful to regard orality and literacy not as a single continuum, but rather as two continua, two traditions, that meet, intersect, and cross in specific human situations. Heath's Carolina study remains the single most comprehensive project on literacy carried out in the United States. (1999, p. 398)

Daniell reminds us that cultural explanations of literacy have existed since the oral/literate dichotomy was constructed by theorists generalizing about entire civilizations. Heath's innovation was to define subcommunities based on the sociolinguistic conception of "speech communities" as important units of analysis. Yet these smaller units of analysis have not prevented *Ways* from acquiring its own epic and allegorical characteristics, a phenomenon Heath notes herself, somewhat regretfully, in reflections on the study years later.[1] The scholarly reception of *Ways* has contributed to making it a kind of grand narrative by divorcing its implications from any particular space or time: Rarely is *Ways* cited without mention of its innovations to understandings of literacy in general. Often the names Roadville and Trackton are brought up in these citations, or else reference is made to "working-class Black and White communities" and how their literacy practices vary from middle-class or school literacy practices. Sometimes the specific literacy practices of one of the communities is referred to—usually Trackton, infrequently Roadville—but almost never invoked is the specific historical context in which those practices were situated.

And yet, Heath herself in the opening lines of *Ways* situates these practices in place and time as she identifies the purpose of her study:

> In the late 1960s, school desegregation in the southern United States became a legislative mandate and a fact of daily life. Academic questions about how children talk when they come to school and what educators should know and do about oral and written language were echoed in practical pleas of teachers who asked: "What do I do in my classroom on Monday morning?" (p. 1)

These first lines of *Ways* introduce Heath's study as one that takes as its problem the legislative mandate to desegregate and the accompanying dislocations and confusions brought to the lives of teachers and students. As with the category race, Heath submerges discussion of desegregation through the bulk of the text, a move that might partially explain why racial desegregation is rarely mentioned in references to *Ways*. There is an irony to these decontextualized references, however, when one considers that perhaps the biggest insight of Heath's research is that to understand an utterance you have to understand something of the local situation from which the speaker came. Reading *Ways* against the backdrop of what I will be arguing is relevant local history, however, provides essential context to understanding the impact of *Brown* on the lives of the people Heath studied.

My desire to fill in the lacuna presented by *Ways* with relevant historical context took me to the archives of Heath's research, housed at the Dacus Library of Winthrop University. Included with memorabilia, newspaper articles, teaching materials, student papers, and drafts of publications is a bulk of correspondence Heath kept up about her research in the communities of Roadville and Trackton.[2] The detailed correspondence Heath conducted with colleagues in which she reflects on the development of her research not only provides a window into the controversies that developed as the sociolinguistic study of literacy evolved but also reveals that whether or not to highlight the race of the Trackton community was a matter of concern to Heath. It seems that the Heath of 1974 would have liked to foreground race more strongly in her analysis, but she was encouraged not to do so. What emerges from reading Heath's letters about the researching of *Ways* is a portrait of an ethnographer trying to negotiate existing stereotypes and raw tensions in the scholarly and public discourse on race while attempting to adhere to the tenets of the ethnographic approach of the 1970s. Even more significantly, however, the letters and other primary documents from the time reveal the myriad forms that resistance to desegregation took—literacy tests were put in place to deny movement of pupils to other schools; curricular innovations that would address issues important to African Americans were thwarted; hostile teachers often awaited the few African Americans who did manage to make the move. All of these conditions rendered African Americans in a poor position to accept the ostensible invitation extended by *Brown* for their children to attend majority White schools.

In a rare departure from decontextualized readings of *Ways*, Tom Fox suggests the relevance of a history of racial conflict to understanding the communities Heath studied: "While Heath is right to defend against simplistic generalizations on the basis of race, the enormous influence of the history of enslavement in the U.S. must profoundly influence the performance of black students in mainstream schools" (1990, p. 73). Fox makes a crucial connection here between Heath's avoidance of race and her ability to place the lives of her African American subjects in a particular historical context. Fox does not comment on the influence of that history on Whites as well, yet *Ways* itself suggests that it had one. Introduced as one of many examples of Roadville's citizens' mixed feelings about the mill, the recent desegregation is an undeniable part of this man's construction of his dissatisfactory economic situation:

> When the niggers (pause) uh, the blacks, you know, started comin' in, I knew that wasn't for me. I wasn't ever gonna work for no nigger—my granddaddy'd roll over in his grave if I did. Blacks takin' up the jobs now, ain't no chance for whites to move up, and I gotta have me a feelin' I can be my own boss for some things. I began lookin' for me a way out, and that's when this friend tol' me 'bout the tech school in Alberta. (p. 39)

This Roadville dweller's mention of his grandfather is significant because it speaks to what critical race theorist Charles Lawrence would call "the institution of segregation"— the cultural custom of segregation used in different ways around the nation to assert White supremacy (1980, p. 50). Given that this man is willing to leave the area rather than face the threat of working for African Americans, it seems that the institution of segregation defines much of his culture. Racism, inseparable here from class aspiration, is the very impetus driving him toward greater literate and professional development, out of the mill and toward the technical school. Heath acknowledges as much in her epilogue to *Ways*, citing that young adults of Roadville have not been allowed to forget that their parents did not come face-to-face with blacks in the mills, schools, or in their home communities until this past decade. Part of their urgency to move ahead and away from any association with the textile mills is their desire to find jobs in which they will not have to compete with blacks. (p. 362)

That the very presence of African Americans in their workplace is a sign to the working-class Whites of Roadville that they belong elsewhere makes problematic any conception of a natural racial and linguistic border between the two communities and makes necessary an investigation of how racism and the institution of segregation shape literacy.

The Roadville man's comment also reveals the almost immeasurable brevity of the period between de jure and what has commonly but contestedly been called de facto segregation.[3] The institution of segregation has survived in some form the Emancipation Proclamation, *Brown v. Board of Education,* Title VI of the Civil Rights Act, federally mandated busing, and countless other legislative and judicial civil rights measures occurring before and throughout the period of time Heath was conducting her research. Its continuing vitality is documented by Heath as she looks back upon *Ways* ten years after publication and writes that while the children of Roadville have left the Piedmont and have for the most part gone on to higher forms of education, the Trackton children have not experienced such mobility; instead many of them have been forced to go on public assistance as jobs at the mill evaporated. For the children of Trackton in the early 1980s, "the bottom fell out of the textile industry in the South and unemployment soared. . . . Drugs, violence, education failures, and major health problems plague their lives" (1993, p. 257). Heath remarks of these changes, "[T]he point here is that while some get ahead, others fall behind" (p. 261). The "some" here is specifically White working-class women, many of whom became teachers in the schools during a period when many African American teachers were losing their jobs. But the "others," the Trackton residents, were hardest hit by the mill closing, as they were last hired and therefore first fired. The fate of the Trackton residents reveals the limited range of the civil rights movement. Trackton residents were last hired and therefore first fired as a direct result of the institution of segregation; the unequal effect on Whites and African Americans of the economic changes of the 1980s had quite a bit to do with the Reagan administration's active moves to maintain the institution by dismantling the federal structures meant to enforce civil rights. The history of the communities Heath studied suggests that race is crucial to understanding the fate of these communities and how they were or were not in a position to cash in on their literacy. This history also suggests that race and class have been co-constructing, and that racism is a component of the national, rather than merely local, culture.

What *Brown* was to accomplish in and of itself, it apparently did not accomplish for the people of Trackton. Now more than thirty years after Heath began her research in the late 1960s, attempts at school integration are being abandoned not only in the Piedmont but also nationally. Revisiting *Ways* can help shed light on the cultural causes of this abandonment. *Ways* is a rare text; it documents a crucial era of post-*Brown* education reform employing an ethnographic perspective rarely used to address the topic at that point, and the nostalgia for segregation on the part of some of the subjects of the study is all too palpable in its record. I suggest that *Ways* could most fruitfully be read now not as chronicle of separate but equal unraced communities but as evidence of the persistence of prejudice, a story that suggests the failure of the arguments in favor of desegregation to broker lasting reforms toward equity, and as a story that reveals the different and racialized meanings literacy acquires in response to historical shifts.

Because they share desegregation as a problem space, yet differ in that they continuously foreground race and racism as sense-making categories, many of the legal analyses reviewed in the previous chapters inform this rereading of *Ways*. Critical race theorists have argued that since racism is deeply ingrained in American society—in the past, present, and for the easily foreseeable future—racism is a part of any American's culture, and no explanation of culture in America can be complete without considering its force. Through *Ways*, we again see how desegregation forced many Whites to invest in new modes to assert a separate "White" identity; *Ways*, like the post-*Brown* Supreme Court decisions *Washington* and *Bakke*, demonstrates how literacy becomes one of those new modes. The context of the civil rights movement and desegregation is therefore central not only to a richer understanding of *Ways* but also to understanding how many Whites have maintained their investments in literacy. Retelling the story of *Ways* within such a context will not contradict the cultural approach to understanding literacy that

Heath's work helped to promote, but it will, I hope, enhance it, encouraging literacy researchers toward an understanding of culture and literacy that accounts for the impact of racial discrimination on speakers, writers, communities, and texts.

Heath has acknowledged that in researching *Ways*, she was affected by the "fishbowl" dilemma that faces many ethnographers—"the difficulties (and hazards) of flipping ourselves out of the waters in which we must swim to survive" (1993, p. 258). Her letters and field notes reveal that the strained racial relations that were both the historical context of and impetus for *Ways*—what might be viewed as the water in the fishbowl—also functioned as constraints on Heath's use of race as a category to make sense of her data. Not using race, however, came at a price. The color blind rhetoric *Ways* embraced, if only by default, obscured that the obstacles faced by African American students new to predominately White schools were caused not by the African American and White communities' mutual misunderstandings but rather by their shared understanding of the institution of segregation and the privileges granted to White identity. Excerpts from Heath's letters and papers of her students suggest that part of this shared understanding is a taboo prohibiting mention of both the institution of segregation and the privileges of Whiteness. Because I believe this is a taboo that has led to the historically amnesiac readings of *Ways* discussed at the beginning of this chapter, I am appropriating the metaphor of the fishbowl and calling upon her letters to reveal the water that is still all too present around the readers of *Ways*, past and present.

Race and Sociolinguistics under Construction

As the opening lines to *Ways* suggest, Heath's research was originally driven by practical and pressing concerns. In the early 1970s, she was teaching at Winthrop University, which developed from a teaching college. In November 1974, she wrote to Herman Blake, a sociologist in the University of California system, that she had been studying a nearby African American community for five years to help her graduate students, mostly teachers returning to school to get a master's degree.[4] She writes that the goal of this informal research in the African American community was initially to introduce "specific aspects of enculturation to teachers in classes here at Winthrop." Rejecting mainstream studies of African American populations in urban areas as impertinent to the demographic her

65

own students would face as teachers, she used her anthropological training, acquired at Columbia University, where she had gotten her doctorate, to gather data about language practices of an African American community in the local rural area. She writes to Blake that whereas for the first five years she studied the community that would become "Trackton" she had had no intention of extending her audience past the teachers in her classrooms, by 1974 she had begun to consider the implications of her research for researchers as well as educators. The letter indicates that with this planned larger audience came concerns, however, about how to present the work in the context of existing research on African American students' language:

November 11, 1974

I mentioned my work in the Black community here in Rock Hill over the past five years. Initially I had no intention of extending the knowledge I gained from participating in the community beyond introducing specific aspects of enculturation to teachers in my classes here at Winthrop. I had worked in urban communities in New York and felt that conclusions drawn from my work there should not be transferred here without confirmation from direct participant observation here. In addition, since virtually all of my graduate students since 1970 have been teachers upgrading their certificates or working toward Masters' degrees, I felt the desperate need to be able to share with them something concrete in the way of enculturation patterns that would conflict with school expectations. Textbooks in Education courses generalized from mainstream research, reported isolated studies of "lower class Black children," or offered general conclusions from communities in urban areas. Quite frankly, I reject all of these for teachers in this locale. Teachers who come to Winthrop are primarily rural teachers; they do not teach many mainstream children as they are characterized in textbooks. Their students, Black, White, and Indian come from closed or semi-closed communities which have few enculturation patterns in common with the children characterized as "lower class" or urban in research reports. For these reasons, I have observed in several communities, visited schools scattered through the surrounding area, and, within the past few months, have begun to question my original intention not to extend the results of my research beyond my classes here at Winthrop.

The quotes around *lower class Black children* indicate Heath's awareness of and distaste for a stereotype that pervaded much research in sociology and anthropology on Black urban communities.

Carol Stack, an anthropologist researching Black urban communities at the same time as Heath was gathering data for *Ways*, observed in 1974 that long-standing racism in the social and behavioral sciences was only beginning to fall under investigation; Stack suggests that from the 1930s through the 1970s, sociological research reinforced stereotypes of African American families living in poverty as deviant and broken, adding that these biases led to few attempts to view these families "as they actually are, recognizing the interpretations black people have of their own cultural patterns" (1974, p. 22). As Stack describes, local cultural behaviors are subsumed under the heading "culture of poverty"—a distortion that she strived to correct, as did Heath, through ethnographic approaches aimed at describing African American communities in emic terms.

Heath's letters indicate that she was aware of these biases within the disciplinary communities she intended to address and that attempts to move beyond them motivated her work and her approach. She ends the description of her project in her letter to Blake with a series of quoted phrases, indicating her goal to move the field of anthropology away from stereotyped portrayals of "others":

November 11, 1974

Diane Lewis' "perspectivistic" anthropology is for me a challenge to urge other anthropologists interested in both community studies and education to place more emphasis in their publications on the interplay among communities and between all of these and mainstream institution than on uniquenesses which can be generalized to "others" and used as further "verification" of "what's wrong with those 'disadvantaged,' 'culturally different,' etc.?"

"Culture of poverty" discourse was not merely a scholarly matter but pervaded the local community Heath lived and worked in as well. When Pat Nichols, a graduate student in California (originally from South Carolina) and frequent correspondent of Heath's, asked Heath why, in an interview with the university alumnae magazine, she had taken a stance against teaching Black English directly, Heath responded by explaining that she had to modify her approach and rhetoric in the face of those who viewed Black Americans only as "poor" rather than as possessing their own distinct culture. She writes of the "uproar" caused by the confrontation of "culture of poverty" discourse merely implied in the title of a proposed course on "Language and Culture Among Black Americans":

November 23, 1973

I had been asked by the Education School to offer a course on Language and Culture Among Black Americans for the undergraduates going into teaching. You cannot imagine the uproar such a thought caused for many people; it seems they did not feel there could be anything distinctive about Black Americans' language or culture—unless it was caused by the fact that most of them "are poor." This will help you understand why in the Winthrop Alumnae Magazine, I low-keyed the Black English readers, but I insisted on the degree of interference between Black English and Standard English.

The final text of *Ways* further evidences Heath's attempts to combat "culture of poverty" discourse by describing the communities as she felt they would describe themselves. She writes, for example, "Trackton residents are not poor, and do not consider themselves so" (p. 53). A letter written to Nichols in October 1974, however, reveals a less emic view of the economic condition of the African American community—an economic condition that seems somewhat harsher than it is described in the final text of *Ways*—and reveals as well some conflict between Heath's attachment to the community and her position as ethnographer. This last statement, "Sometimes I'm very concerned about how one ever 'objectively' does work in a community," suggests a perceived need to adhere to the tenets of ethnographic practice circa 1974 in which objectivity was thought by many to be attainable and desirable:

October 8, 1974

The cold cold days of the past two weeks brought the news that several families could not buy coal, and one other had no furnace, and a new one would be $450.00 for them. I have been there as frequently as possible, if for no other reason than the fact that my presence seems to give an outlet for "someone to talk to." In addition, the kids are so dependent on me now for any break in the increasingly dreary routine of their lives that I feel under constant pressure to be there. Sometimes I'm very concerned about how one ever "objectively" does work in a community!

The classic dilemma posed by the ethnography of communication is inherent in the need to negotiate contradictory impulses; the directive to describe a culture on its own terms as it would describe itself often runs into conflict with terms, frameworks, and methods brought to make sense of the data. Publication places further pressure on the ethnographer to describe the data in such a way that its validity will be accepted by the disciplinary community; etic frameworks compete with emic frameworks, then, at all stages of the research, though the goal is for emic frameworks to win out.[5] In the next few months in letters to Nichols, Heath increasingly describes the interactions of the African American community in terms of the sociolinguistic work she was reading at the time—most notably the work of Bernstein, Labov, Halliday, and Hymes. Sociolinguistic terms such as *register, function,* and *context* occur frequently in her descriptions of language use. She writes to Nichols, for example, of the usefulness of Bernstein's work to her understanding of what goes wrong when the children of the community go to school, suggesting *context* as a crucial axis upon which clashes between working-class and school discourse are delineated.

Basil Bernstein's formulation of elaborated and restricted codes, and his tying of these codes to middle-class and working-class communities in England, informed greatly Heath's understanding of the differences between contextualized and decontextualized language practices in the African American community and the mainstream (school) community. Bernstein (1975) determined that an "elaborated code" oriented children towards the significance of relatively context independent meanings in speech and writing, whereas a "restricted code" oriented children toward a more context dependent use of language. Bernstein argues that the invisible pedagogy of the middle-class school presupposes middle-class conceptions of educational time and space and an elaborated code of communication.[6] Exposing this invisible pedagogy seems to be the goal of Heath's discussion in part 2 of *Ways* of how time, space, and language are managed in school. Papers written by her students in her classes at the university further indicate that teaching recognition of elaborated and restricted codes was part of her pedagogical approach to reeducating teachers in the mainstream community. Her letters also reflect her growing conception of the differences between the African American community and mainstream community as differences in contextual orientation. In a November 1974 letter to Nichols, Heath thanks Nichols for "sending the Bernstein volume with the very relevant article"; she writes of one child's low performance on a school report card, "I am sure context is the clue."

November 11, 1974

Many thanks for sending the Bernstein volume with the very relevant article. I have read it and ordered a personal copy, so I am returning your book. It was very helpful and is certainly confirmed in the community everyday, as I hear mothers give orders to children. . . . [The two year old's] mother never points out single items for him to identify; i.e., she does not say "that is a school bus." She will often say something in response to what he says, and he will take what she says and alter it and repeat it. . . . Report cards came out last week, and the first grader was reported to be "doing very slow work; off to a slow start." I was dismayed, since I know what she can do, and I am wondering whether or not I should go see the teacher. I am sure context is the clue. The child has been bringing her reading home this week and her mother (following the example of what she has seen me do with the neighborhood children) has been drilling her, and she can now read several pages.

Heath's mention here that one of the mothers began following her example of drilling the child for schoolwork and her wondering whether or not to "go see the teacher" indicate not only that Heath advocated building communicative bridges between school and home to resolve issues of language difference but also that she was such a bridge herself, serving increasingly as broker between the mainstream schools and the African American community to build mutual comprehension of literacy practices. She tries to mediate as well between the community and White mainstream business people in the town. She writes in this letter to Nichols: "I have also decided to take the 6 year old to the eye doctor, since there is a strong possibility she cannot see well. I had hesitated to do so, since I am not sure she can communicate with the eye dr. (a man with whom I can't communicate either)."

A week and a half later Heath writes to Nichols again of her decision to go forward with her plan to take the six-year-old to the eye doctor and reaffirms her understanding of the child as "contextually oriented": "I figured checking the eyes was one shot I could try before I try to deal directly with the teacher. This is the 6 year old whom I have worked with over the past few years, and I know she is not slow! She is just contextually oriented!" It seems that at this point, understanding the importance of the relationship of context to language in a designated culture provided Heath a way of countering racist cognitive deficit explanations of African American community members' failures to achieve according to main-stream standards. Episodes like the visit to the eye doctor, detailed in the letter below, reinforce her belief in the importance of context. Yet as the visit to the eye doctor also reveals, members of the mainstream community remained invested in tying language use to decreased cognitive ability. The doctor questions the child's capacity for "cerebration":

November 26, 1974

I took the community six year old back to the eye dr. yesterday, and I had a perfect example of the importance of certain critical vocabulary items, for which there is no contextual equivalent that we know of. The dr. put the machine in front of her eyes and kept turning and changing the lenses through which she was looking, and he asked "is this better, or is this better?" She had no understanding of what he meant, so he tried "is this clearer?" again, no understanding. I tried every concrete contextualized equivalent I could think of, but I am not at all sure I ever came up with the "truth." We are trying glasses for six weeks, but he is not at all sure it will work. His comment to me "there is so little cerebration there, we may never be able to tell" I countered with my conviction that there was potential there—it was up to us to find ways of getting it revealed!

Given the biases in sociological and behavioral research on Black families and the similar biases in the community where Heath worked and lived, it is perhaps not surprising that when in February 1975 Heath sent an abstract of her research to Joan Rubin, an editor of a journal with whom Heath had a previous working relationship, she did not mention the race of the community in it. In a cover letter, she justifies this decision by making reference to her "fear of the Bernstein pitfall." "The Bernstein pitfall" refers to the theoretical faux pas of drawing on Bernstein that Heath had been warned of by readers of her earlier work; in fact Rubin had previously written in a letter dated February 10, 1975, the phrase "Beware the Bernstein pitfall!!!" to Heath without explaining what the exact nature of the pitfall was. Rubin's comment alludes to interpretations of Bernstein's research by American linguists around the time Heath was writing; Bernstein found himself answering charges from both left- and right-wing scholars that his work was based in a denigrating deficit model that would lower teachers' expectations of working-class (and African American) students and give rise to drills and skills pedagogy (Bernstein, 1971, p. 19). The most notable of these critiques came from William Labov, who in counter-ing Arthur Jensen's work suggested that the notion that lower-class African American children have no language at all derives from Bernstein's views filtered through biases against working-class chil-dren (Labov, 1972, p. 204).

Although Heath thought of these readings of Bernstein as dis-torted, she seemed to see in obscuring the race of the subjects of her study a way to avoid the substance of the "pitfall"—that is, a way to avoid reinforcing cognitive and genetic deficit theories of African American scholastic achievement—while at the same time providing data that might challenge such theories. In her letter to Rubin, Heath points out that her "progress report" does not men-tion "the fact that the community is Black." Heath announces in this letter a further attempt to displace race as a significant category as she introduces a comparison between the language practices of a Black community and a "similar" White community. The aspect of the community that is most significant, she argues, is not the race of its occupants but that it is "closed and therefore totally depen-dent on internal culture":

> February 14, 1975
>
> Enclosed you will find an initial summary of the research from the local community which I mentioned to you in my last letter. You will note that the fact that the community is Black is not mentioned in the "progress report," which I am sending to you. . . . After the NYAS Conference, I began to think that my fear of the Bernstein pitfall should perhaps not keep me from testing the views of a few colleagues. I sent a brief abstract (again not identifying the fact that the residents of the community are Black) to the Stanford Child Language Research Reports. . . . It seems to me that the fact that the community is closed and therefore totally dependent on its internal culture (and the pas-sive reception of TV) is the crucial factor for understanding the lan-guage development. I have similar data on a closed White Southern Appalachian migrant mill town (over a much shorter period of field-work), and many of the features related to parent-child relations in language development are similar to those in the community described in the abstract.

In a letter to Nichols dated the next day, Heath further rumi-nates on the decision to obscure the race of the community and argues even more forcefully that the essential attribute of the lan-guage context is that the community is "closed":

February 15, 1975

At any rate, I hope you don't think my not referring to the community as Black was too tricky. It really is my firm conviction that the closed nature of the community is the crucial factor in the language development context, not the race of the speakers. Admittedly, the community is (maybe is puts the case too firmly [handwritten]) closed because of the race of the speakers, but it seems to me there are many examples of communities which are closed because of cultural factors also. (How do you feel about the definition of closed? [handwritten]).

Interestingly, questioning "why" the community is closed is not as important here as that it is closed. In this letter, Heath acknowledges the fact of segregation and acknowledges that the community is closed because of the race of the speakers but, at the same time, arguably correctly, discounts that fact as pertinent to the sociolinguistic inquiry. Nichols, a sociolinguist herself (though her more frequent role in the correspondence was that of advice seeker rather than advice giver), does not address Heath's choice not to reveal the race of the community members. She instead responds by suggesting, "Labov has probably given Bernstein his bad name in this country, probably largely because of the *use* to which B. has been put." She suggests that perhaps Bernstein's work has been misunderstood in this country and offers that "the Bernstein pitfall" might be the fault of educational psychologists who latched onto Bernstein's notion of restricted code to support theories of deprivation. She asks Heath how she determined the degree of closedness of the community but does not at any point in the letter probe the implications of obscuring the race of the community. The topic of the race of the communities is dropped in subsequent correspondence; in a later letter, Heath responds to the inquiry about how the closedness of the community was established:

March 15, 1975

You ask how I arrived at the 85% figure on closed community. I asked them to tell me about their exits from the community on certain days of the week at different times of the year. The figure ran closer to 90% and confirmed with the observations I made on the days I was in the community. I thought 85% more conservative, however, since I did not have as much data from certain times of the year as from others. With regards to proving informative function of language in school, I think samples from text books, reading workbooks, etc. could be useful here. In addition, when I get graduate students again, I can see

> if one of them will do a survey in her classroom of the percentage of types of language, and that would prove the point.

This last question—of how the informative function of school discourse might be proved—indicates a shift in the direction of Heath's project, and in its audience; instead of bringing the findings of sociolinguists to prove something about language to an audience of teachers, she brings the findings of teachers to prove something about language to an audience of sociolinguists. This letter was written a year after Heath's visit to the eye doctor. Even if sorties from Trackton into the mainstream community were a rare occasion, those exits were enough, as the visit to the eye doctor illustrates, to put the community in contact with racism. Racism is not something the members of Trackton can completely close out. It is in the water, as the saying goes.

Reimagining Community

That Heath put great consideration into defining the closed nature of the community—how closed, how dependent on internal culture—suggests the theoretical framework within which she was working. Heath's naturalistic approach to the communities she studied was quite different from Bernstein's method of controlled interviews and owed a great deal to ethnographer of communication and sociolinguist Dell Hymes; the acknowledgements to *Ways* attest that "Dell H. Hymes is behind this book more than any other single individual" (p. ix). Hymes's innovation to linguistics involved recasting Chomsky's notion of competence as a social phenomenon; while Chomsky described competence in terms of grammar, Hymes recast competence in terms of use. He viewed the "speech community" as the matrix of speech styles, defined as "a community sharing rules for the conduct and interpretation of speech" (1977, p. 54). For the purposes of study, then, a given speech community must be defined and bounded and its rules of interaction defined.

Subsequent to the publication of *Ways*, Hymes's notion of the defined and bounded speech community has been challenged. Extending the implications of historian Benedict Anderson's (1991) conception of the "imagined community" into the field of linguistics, Mary Louise Pratt (1987) argues that research drawing on the work of Hymes tends to create "linguistic utopias" by overdetermining the boundaries between speech communities. Pratt suggests that speech communities are constructed and maintained by lin-guists who approach difference by imagining "separate speech com-munities with their own boundaries, sovereignty, fraternity and authenticity" (p. 56). The communities of Roadville and Trackton in part 1 of *Ways,* though certainly located in the very real Pied-mont, are in other ways imagined as discrete utopias, suspended in an ethnographic and somewhat allegorical present. *Ways* relies on a formulation of monodialectical speech communities throughout part 1 of its analysis as it details language practices in the "rela-tively self-contained worlds" of Roadville and Trackton (Heath, 1983, p. 11). And yet in the prologue, Heath situates the region in historical time. Heath provides a sweeping history of the Piedmont region, one that highlights the social and economic forces that have kept the two communities separate for generations. Race is inevi-tably invoked as a category in this prologue as one of those factors keeping African Americans and Whites virtually separate for two hundred years. Heath notes that "new mills along the rivers' banks spawned mill villages for white workers" around the turn of the century, and while she acknowledges that the history of African Americans in the area was harder to reconstruct, she traces their movement from tenant farming to the late start in the mills (p. 21ff.); Heath writes of Roadville and Trackton specifically that through "both geographic location and historical patterns of choice of neighbors and circle of friends, each community tended to be closed, somewhat set apart, with an evolved identity and inner life of its own" (p. 6). Said differently, this history also reveals a con-tinuing pattern of segregation. Although the prologue to *Ways* serves the purpose Pratt identifies as crucial to sociolinguistic in-quiry, that of constructing homogeneous communities, the descrip-tion perhaps overemphasizes choice and does not account for the role of the Jim Crow laws and illegal acts of terrorism in encour-aging much of the communities' separateness.

The format of *Ways* further encourages the reader to imagine Roadville and Trackton as discrete bounded communities. The chapters in part 1 detail sense-making practices of the two towns separately, if not by chapter then by section. Heath refrains from drawing explicit comparisons between the practices of Roadville and Trackton, though implicit comparisons are drawn in that Heath details similar activities in both towns (e.g., how the baby is brought home, how children are taught the meaning of a stop sign). In chapter 2, separate maps of the two communities describe their proximity to the larger (also pseudonymous) towns but not to each other, so the reader has little sense of where Roadville and Trackton—really both intersections of a few streets with less than ten families on them each, according to the map—are in relation to each other. The focus in these early chapters is on the linguistic practices within each bounded community. The chapters in part 2 are more "perspectivistic," but the angles of perspective are prescribed; in part 2, interactions are described between Roadville and Trackton students on the one hand, and teachers on the other, but interactions between Roadville children on the one hand and Trackton children on the other are not described. The focus in these chapters is on mainstream teachers' attempts to bridge communicative gaps by explaining their own "ways with words" and by studying those of their students. A kind of equivalence is created between the two communities of Roadville and Trackton through the dual narratives of part 1. This equivalence is in part the result of Heath's strategy to avoid the pitfall of reinforcing deficit models of African American literacy practices; because the communities are not discussed in relation to one another, the reader is discouraged from comparing them—although a conscious attempt to do so makes obvious that the economic situation of working-class Roadville is not nearly as dire as the economic situation of working-class Trackton. Heath's letters indicate that she did not initially intend to study White working-class literacy practices at all. She began the study of Roadville when she considered publishing her work as a way to avoid the "pitfall."

Readers are taught in more explicit ways to avoid judging the communities under study. In the prologue to *Ways*, Heath describes her commitment to observing language practices "without preconceived judgments" (p. 3). She has subsequently expressed some regret over rejecting a colleague's advice and publishing "Ethnographer Doing," the second part of *Ways*; she refers to the section as "more celebration than description" (1993, p. 265). In advocating ethnographic practice as a classroom tool to bridge communicative gaps in home and school, part 2 ironically diverges from the ethnographic goal of impartiality as Heath defines it—that it is not the ethnographer's place "to suggest that subjects *should* be doing something other than what they do." Ethnography describes what is happening, not what is not happening[7] (1993, p. 263).

The nonjudgmental stance implied by the conventions of ethnography at the time Heath was writing, however, mitigates against an approach that would take as its focus racism and its possible impact on the community members of *Ways;* simply to identify "racism" in the communities in the years Heath was writing would be to cast a pejorative eye on the subjects of the study, rendering a judgment on their practices and violating the precepts of cultural relativity. Heath (1993) discourages such judgments of the subjects of her study:

> What outsiders call poverty, marital troubles, racism and crime appear in the communities of WWW, but without comment from me (see, for example, pp. 34, 39, 51ff.). From the contemporary situation of finding drugs, violence, and crime in every nook and cranny of the nation, we find it hard to believe that in the 1970s, any of these occurred as the rare exception and not the rule. Close-knit communities in which everyone knew everyone else's business and older members and women stayed home all day provided, along with an intense environment of religious life, the surest social control on child and spousal abuse, thefts, and the introduction of anything new and destructive into the community. (p. 262)

In reading this comment, I find myself forced into the role of the "outsider," positioned there not only by my focus on racial discrimination but also by the fact that I grew up in New Jersey. As an outsider to the communities of *Ways,* then, I have no authority according to the terms by which ethnographic practice dictates authority (i.e., extended direct contact with the subjects under study). But for the purposes of my inquiry, I would like to undo for a moment Heath's innovation to literacy research and extend the operative imagined community past the subcommunities Heath delineated to the level of the national community. Whereas Heath saw her subjects as individuals struggling with "the forces of capitalist economy and the state" (1993, p. 258), I'd like to see them as constituting the capitalist economy and the state. To illustrate this point and provide relevant historical background to the national community I imagine, I recall some of the observations made by the legal analysts profiled in the last chapter—that this country was founded on property rights and continues to develop ways to ensure those rights over human rights; that the Constitution was constructed in such a way as to ensure that Whites would be able to maintain control over African Americans by defining African Americans as property and as three-fifths of a person for representational purposes; that concessions (like school desegregation) are only given to African Americans when they benefit Whites while ensuring that African Americans remain economically and politically at least one down. Accepting these observations, one would conclude there isn't anybody in any nook and cranny of the nation who can claim to exist "outside" racism. The change here in the unit of analysis—from the subcommunity to the national community—places the communities of Roadville and Trackton and the townspeople in contact, allowing for an approach that examines what communicative rules might be shared by all the participants in a given interaction.

"Now That You Bring It Up": The Return of Race

I began this chapter discussing a Roadville man's attitude toward Blacks in his workplace. I'd like to continue by looking at the mainstreamers, the symbols of Everyamericanmiddleclassperson in *Ways,* and their attitudes toward Blacks in their schools. Significantly, when the book turns away from the ethnographic allegorical present toward the mainstream teachers' attempts in the 1970s to work with the students from Trackton and Roadville, the racial distinction between the two communities must resurface. The race of subjects is recorded, for example, in a table Heath created that documents teachers' impressions "from early desegregation" of their "Black" and "White" students. (See table 3.1.) When I teach *Ways,* my undergraduate and graduate students alike are quick to notice that the tone the teachers quoted in this table take toward the "Black" students they have encountered is markedly more negative than the tone taken toward the "White" students. Although ostensibly this table shows how the communicative practices of the children of both Roadville and Trackton caused their mainstream teachers consternation, the difference in tone seems so stark in some cases that I find it difficult to imagine that readers of *Ways* are not meant to notice it and factor it into their understanding of African American student school performance.

Though race is not mentioned in the table title, "Black" and "White" at the top of the columns indicate the race of the "working-class" students. The reader of *Ways* knows from the context of the discussion of the table that Heath has worked with the teachers making the comments in her classrooms and collaborated with them in her research; chapter 7 of *Ways* is devoted to describing

Table 3.1
Examples of Teachers' Evaluations of Working-Class Students Having Discipline and Academic Problems

Black	White
"verbally & physically aggressive"	"quiet, laconic"
"disrespectful"	"respectful"
"never says he's sorry"	"know how to let me know they're sorry even if they don't always say so"
. . .	. . .
"has no respect for private property; thinks anything in the class 'belongs' to him"	"often shy about sharing; wants 'one of her own'"
"young children will almost never tell me who did what; my friends who teach at the jr. and sr. high school levels tell me it's the same way there. They'll never identify who started a fight"	"getting them to talk, especially the boys, is hard, but if I can find a girl who saw what happened, and I talk to her alone, she'll tell me"
. . .	. . .
"they'll never tell a story straight—if there ever was a grain of truth in what they say, it's lost when they get through with it. If they only used that imagination in some constructive way . . ."	"needs help in moving beyond the bare essentials of restating reading stories or social studies materials"

Source: Reprinted with the permission of Cambridge University Press from S. B. Heath, 1983, pp. 268–69.

the reading, writing, and speaking practices of the mainstream townspeople—the greater socioeconomic group these teachers represent—so as to defamiliarize these practices for the middle-class and mainstream audience to which the book was written. In the endnotes to this chapter, Heath carefully defines her use of the categories "mainstream" and "middle class," explaining that "terms such as *mainstream* or *middle class* are frequently used in both popular and scholarly writings without careful definition" (p. 397). She notes that middle-class habits "are rarely specified in ethnographic detail, and numerous accounts of life in these homes portray these behaviors and values as universal and 'natural' rather than as the learned and shared habits of a particular social group" (p. 398). She then points to several studies that identify patterns of middle-class behavior.

This care with which the terms *middle class* and *mainstream* are defined is a contrast to the manner in which the terms *Black* and *White* are invoked. Reflecting the theoretical discourse on race at the time, categories denoting race are not singled out and cited for the way they are frequently used without careful definition; unlike class categories then, race categories appear natural rather than socially constructed. Because racial categories are invoked to delineate students but not the teachers making the comments, the teachers are maintained in a race-transcendent position. It is not possible from the table or from the surrounding discussion to pursue questions about how a teacher's race might have affected his or her approach to the students. It is only possible to consider how a student's race might have factored into the evaluation.

The categorization choices of the table reflect the purpose of Heath's research; she was trying initially to provide knowledge of cultural variation in language practices to teachers. Teachers were not the subjects of her study in the same way that students were. Although she provides pseudonyms (like Roadville and Trackton) for the working-class communities she studies and for the people and places of the book, she cites the journals of the teachers from which the comments in table 3.1 were excerpted as collected when these teachers were in her courses at Winthrop College and at the University of North Carolina at Charlotte, as well as at various workshops from the period 1969 to 1977 (p. 400). Her relationship to these teachers—her students—had of course some bearing on her representations of them. She was in representing them faced with the "fishbowl" dilemma, as she depended on them as informants. In fact, the data for this chapter, which focuses on the townspeople, was collected by "townspeople students" themselves—from her courses—and so represent at least partially the townspeople's "self-identification" of their own values and practices (p. 397).

As a reader of *Ways,* I am privileged; unencumbered by the constraints imposed by Heath's particular relationships to her informants, I am free to mine the data collected in the book for evidence of how the teachers' subjective attitudes might have affected the students of Trackton—indeed this investigation is necessary if an account of literacy practices that acknowledges the impact of endemic racism be told. While the design of table 3.1 echoes the rest of the book in identifying an equal number of "problems" in Roadville and Trackton students, other comments suggest that teachers found dealing with Trackton students particularly difficult. Heath writes of the teachers' first encounters with Trackton children: "Even the most patient teachers found it hard not to question the 'kind of homes these students come from' and whether or not they and their parents had the 'right attitude about school'" (p. 280). Teacher attitudes about students are also revealed in this comment made by a young adult from Roadville: "You know I think that's one of the reasons so many of our teachers hated the nigger kids so, they never would say they were sorry" (p. 143). Such comments suggest that African American students encountered negative subjective attitudes along with merely different ways of using speech and print when the schools were desegregated and White teachers were at the head of the class. This is not a gratuitous observation, although at first it might appear one. I would like to acknowledge again the impetus for the study—desegregation. *Ways* documents that Roadville children had been in the schools with mainstream teachers for some time before the study, in basic classes getting a slowed down version of what the mainstream children got. An investigation of methods begins when Trackton students enter (described as "foreigners" by one of the teachers [p. 270]). While *Ways* constructs Roadville and Trackton as equally estranged from school practices, the social logic of the institution of segregation operated to make Trackton children more different. Taking a critical race theory approach to the text, I might posit that the problem the teachers have with Trackton students is partially that they're different, but mostly that they're Black and different.

By including Roadville in her study, Heath was attempting to make working-class White children at least as different; she was trying to point out that African American students weren't the only ones failing to live up to mainstream standards in the schools. Yet the historical situation in which Heath was writing and the patent racism desegregation mandates were confronting suggest that it was not in her power to address racialized perceptions of difference. One of the major conclusions of *Ways* is that patterns of language use "are in accord with and mutually reinforce other cultural patterns"; Heath labels "group loyalties" among those other cultural patterns (p. 344). My investigation of the impact of racism on the subjects in Heath's study is an extension of thinking about how patterns of language use accord with group loyalties. From the standpoint of investigating group loyalties, it is worth observing that while people from Roadville refer to "niggers," they don't refer to "townspeople" (at least not in Heath's presence or at least not as recorded in *Ways*), suggesting an unwillingness to acknowledge class divisions. From the dynamics of desegregation in the area and patterns of demographic movement, we can imagine the groups of people Heath studied had imagined communities of their own—identifications based on race that crossed class lines.

Chapter 7 reports on the townspeople and reveals how within one monolithic class there are racial identifications and group loyalties with bearing on attitudes toward school sponsored literacy. The townspeople are described as falling into two groups—old-timers and newcomers. The White old-timers are those Whites who have long-standing family ties to the area through businesses or farms; the Black old-timers are described as descendants of free, propertied Blacks whose families have established themselves in farming or business. The newcomers are either Whites whose industries have relocated them in the South or Blacks who have returned to the South. But it seems at times that the townspeople identify with others based on race, rather than by where they came from. In discussing the civic concerns of the townspeople, Heath notes, "By the end of the 1970s, there are very few who express resentment of black representation on the city council or the school board; they simply weigh the relative merits of the ideas and manner of presentation of black as well as white members" (p. 239). Said differently, for most of the time that Heath was collecting data on the townspeople (from the late 1960s to the late 1970s), there were more than a very few townspeople expressing resentments over Black representation—perhaps a few, perhaps many. It's not possible to give an accurate portrait of the racial dynamics among Black and White mainstreamers from this vantage point, but the history of school desegregation in Charlotte, North Carolina—the city where many of the mainstreamers in *Ways* worked even as they lived in South Carolina—gives some indication of why the Black townspeople placed, as Heath put it, "a more recent and more cautious" value on school than the White townspeople (p. 239).

Unlike the state of South Carolina, which engaged in notorious open defiance of *Brown* in myriad ways,[8] Charlotte, North Carolina, enjoyed a national reputation as one of the first southern cities to voluntarily desegregate. This early desegregation, however, was not exclusively or even primarily motivated by altruistic concerns, nor was it even effective desegregation. Davison Douglas (1994, 1995) draws on an impressive number of primary documents and oral histories to demonstrate that Charlotte's White elite, fearing the economic toll of a bad reputation, urged voluntary integration of the schools in 1957, well in advance of local legal challenge. As a consequence of this decision, Charlotte did not experience the considerable economic setbacks suffered by southern cities that strongly resisted desegregation.[9] Charlotte's chamber of commerce and the Charlotte school board realized that they could control the pace of desegregation through voluntary integration, and they did so for years, letting only a few African American students into White schools. In 1957, Charlotte assigned four African American students to White schools; in 1958, the school board approved only two out of twenty-three transfer requests filed by African American students; in 1959, every transfer request was denied. As a result, "only one black student attended a white school in Charlotte during the 1959–1960 school year" (Douglas, 1994, p. 711). Severe racial imbalances existed throughout the early 1960s. Later, literacy tests were used as an obstacle to integration, as African American student applicants were required to take entrance examinations to some formerly White schools.

Racial desegregation plans in other areas of the Piedmont similarly indicate that as late as 1970, "freedom of choice desegregation" provided a small degree of integration in formerly all-White schools, and no degree of integration in formerly all African American ones (*United States v. Fairfield County School District,* 1970). A student paper from Heath's class at Winthrop suggests that real desegregation came no speedier to where the mainstreamers of *Ways* lived. The student notes that efforts to encourage applications that would change the homogeneous atmosphere of the Winthrop kindergarten failed: "[O]ut of the approximately ninety applications for the forty available places in the 1974–75 class, only one was from a black family. The remainder of the applicants were from white, predominantly middle-class families" ("Resource Unit" p. 5).

Seemingly, at the point at which the cultural capital of going to an all-White school outweighed financial concerns, White resistance to integration increased nationwide. Charlotte's commitment to even token integration in the schools ended when confronted with the issue of busing. While some in the African American community worried that their children would be harassed in predominantly White schools, the main opposition to busing came from the White community. In February 1970, U.S. District Court Judge James McMillan, in deciding *Swann v. Charlotte-Mecklenburg Board of Education,* ordered the most radical desegregation plan to date involving extensive busing, a decision the Supreme Court upheld in 1971. This decision opened up the possibility of federally mandated busing throughout the country, and virtually the whole country has participated in resisting it ever since. Finally, in 1999, at a time at which White elite had nothing to lose and Charlotte's reputation was no longer at stake, many northern and southern cities having already gone this route with impunity, seven White parents—none of them originally from Charlotte—brought suit against the Charlotte school board, and *Swann* was reversed.

Charlotte's history of desegregation only reflects what critical race theorists have argued occurred nationally, that many Whites—mainly those with money already—profited from integration, politically and economically. The prologue to *Ways* further demonstrates how northern Whites' economic interests played a role in desegregating the area industry of the Piedmont. Heath documents that when the civil rights movement forced the breaking of the color barrier in hiring, African Americans began to move from menial jobs at the mill to the production line, a move that was primarily a boon to mostly northern factory owners who, Heath notes, without unionization and with the new labor source, could now keep wages low (p. 27). Describing how these changes affected African Americans, Heath calls the move to the mills a step up: "They could now model their futures on the lives of young white families" (p. 28). But this situation no doubt did little to ease racial tensions in the area. Heath documents that as desegregation set in, "resentment over unionism, health hazards and blacks in the mills runs high among the young," and the young of Roadville began "looking to be on their way up and out of the mills" (p. 29). I would like to return to the comment made by the Roadville man who described the need to leave the mills to seek greater opportunities in the tech school in "Alberta." It would seem that for him, literacy became a useful commodity when it was perceived as the mechanism through which he could escape African Americans and the loss of status that working with African Americans signified to him and his family. As the discussions in the previous chapter revealed, since Whiteness itself has been assigned property value, the mere presence of African Americans on one's social level is enough to threaten White property interests. I would argue that while occupying the same jobs on the production lines, African Americans and Whites were in two effectively different class positions, one moving up and one moving down, the trajectories of that movement determined in terms of racial capital. I would also argue that the history of desegregation in the area suggests that White mainstreamers and the White working class had an imagined community of their own—an identification based on race that crossed class lines. Schools were seen as mechanisms through which those racial lines might be maintained, even as economic disparities became starker.

Racial group identifications have significance not only for how schools were perceived but also for how language use was perceived. While Heath refers to the townspeople as at times "middle class" and at times "mainstream," Annie Mae, one of Heath's main informants from Trackton, refers to "White folks" and contrasts their "ways with words" with those of Trackton: "He gotta learn to *know* 'bout dis world, can't nobody tell 'im. Now just how crazy is dat? White folks uh hear dey kids say sump'n, dey say it back to 'em, dey aks 'em 'gain 'n 'gain 'bout things, like they 'posed to be born knowin'" (p. 84). Heath at one point gets lumped in with Trackton's "other": "We don't talk to our chil'rn like you folks do. We don't ask 'em 'bout colors, names 'n things," Annie Mae observes (p. 109). Racial identifications surface in Heath's account of her own position as ethnographer, and her explanation of her own language development. Explaining her access to the communities in the opening pages of *Ways*, Heath describes herself as White and follows this description with a qualification of how the proximity of Black neighbors led her to have shared "unconscious habits of interaction" with the communities of *Ways*:

> I am white, but while I was growing up, my family's nearest neighbors were black families; the black church was across the road from my house, and the three black school teachers in our area lived just down the road. In our area, both white and black children lived too far from the nearest school to walk, so we took buses to our respective schools, but in the afternoons and summers, we joined each other for ballgames, bike-riding, and trips to the creek to look for "crawfish." In the summers, we all worked for local tobacco farmers, black and white. These shared experiences and unconscious habits of interaction eased my transition into both Trackton and Roadville. (p. 5)

Subsequently, Heath has offered that because of her upbringing, she knew Black English vernacular as well as the vernacular dialect spoken by uneducated White people. Yet there are other ways, besides dialect usage, in which Heath is a kind of insider, given the broader imagined community framework within which I am working. Her reflection on her childhood demonstrates the inconsistencies of the institution of segregation, that African American and White children who were together in every other way were separated at school. Thurgood Marshall pointed to this inconsistency in arguing *Brown* and argued (contentiously even among the NAACP's legal team) that it had a damaging psychological impact on African American students. Heath's account of her upbringing demonstrates how the social landscape of segregation shaped her identity, her language practices as well as those of her neighbors. Heath's letters and the papers of her students can therefore tell us more about communicative practices in a zone marked by a history of legalized segregation.

Heath has written that she wished she had added an appendix to *Ways* to include details of her personal background, self-reflection on the fieldwork, the "ups and downs" of her own life in the communities, and "critical incidents" (1993, p. 264). One incident reported in Heath's letters that would qualify as critical from a perspective that considers the context of desegregation vital involves Heath's attempts to find a nursery school for the young son of the family she was closest to in the African American community. She writes in August 1975 to Nichols of her efforts to ease several of the children into different scholastic environments, and of the opposition of the children's father:

August 31, 1975

I got the two five-year old twins from the community into Head Start, went with the Mother for interviews, etc., and will do so again one day this week. Then I thought I had had the 3 year old in Day Care, but that fell through ("because the family is not on welfare!")—(note that the fact that there are 7 in the family—and only a $7000 a year income counts for nothing!), so I spent the rest of the week trying to find some school for him. The father is opposed, but if I get the child in school, it will be accepted, I think. Finally I am in step three of a series of six steps toward getting him in a two-day a week morning program. This is the child on whom I have the most complete language record. He is extremely bright, healthy, and super-charged.

Two weeks later, Heath writes again to Nichols of what she calls a "strange experience" in which she and the father discuss the issue of the three-year-old's schooling directly. In this conversation, the father questions Heath about her research and her concern for his family. Heath views this conversation as a breakthrough, a rare moment of informative exchange between genders. But it seems from the father's response to Heath's informing him that his son will be the only Black child in an all-White school that gender isn't the only issue; the father takes the opportunity that this mention of race presents to broach the question of "this black-white thing." I quote from this letter at length because the details of Heath's report of the event are significant to my analysis:

September 13, 1975

I greeted him more responsively than usual, I'm sure, because I had particularly wanted to see him to discuss putting the 3 year old in a nursery school. He sat beside me, and for the first time, I felt we really communicated on what mainstreamers would call an information level. We did so while I told him about school, etc. He then said, I want to ask you something—I've heard my wife say you study me and other people, and I want to know how you do it and why. I tried to answer as directly as I could. He then said, I also want to know why you care so much about my wife and my kids. Again, I tried to answer directly, putting it on the level of learning, sharing, no need to be what I wasn't with them, etc., etc. He seemed satisfied, and then I went on describing the school, and telling him this child would be the only black child in an all white school. (I had tried the only black nursery, to no avail, because the family is not on welfare!) He hesitated, and then he said, "now that you bring it up, there is this black-white thing. I am what I am and you are what you are." I realized he was not talking about the black-white "thing," but rather the "amness" the <u>being</u> of two humans. I double-checked that notion by saying something about how easy it was for [another Trackton resident] and me to sit in the park with the kids and just talk, each of us not having to say "pleasant" things, or expected things, but just what we felt that day at that time. He responded by talking about his "not talking." He went on to explain that sometimes he could talk about things (give information), and sometimes he talked just to be "his way." But he said, even if I don't talk, and if I don't say this again, you and your family, the kids and all, are welcome at my house. He then went into performance talk and starting talking about a barbecue at his house. Rest of the conversation was all show, style, tone, etc., very different. [emphasis in the original]

Heath's decision to double-check what the father might have meant—when he said, "now that you bring it up, there is this black-white thing. I am what I am and you are what you are"—speaks to her uncertainty of the meaning of his phrase, but her double check doesn't involve asking the father a direct question as to the meaning, even though he had just asked her several direct questions in a row and even though they are, in her terms, engaged in information sharing. She tells a short anecdote about her interactions with another member of the community to double-check his meaning. Her final interpretation of the father's turn is unique in that it does not draw on an observed rule of the community (not one recorded in *Ways* at any rate), unlike her parsing of the father's talk into informative and performative, which draws extensively on her understanding of different communicative practices in Trackton and the mainstream community. Instead, to interpret his meaning, she relies on privileging certain lexical terms over other terms without any contextually based explanation for the choice. In determining that the father "was not talking about the black-white 'thing' but rather the 'am-ness' the *being* of two humans," Heath selects the verbs over the nouns and adjectives as the meaning makers of the phrase. Heath therefore perhaps hopefully reads his comment not as an act of division in which the father defines himself as part of one group and her as part of another but rather as an act of identification in which both she and he are united in "am-ness" as "two humans," and the history of segregation that stands between them is for a moment removed. But what if the father had been trying to indicate a racial distinction between himself and Heath? Why was such a meaning, if intended, less apparent or desirable given the framework Heath was working within, and the reading Heath settled on, in which an appeal to universals is invoked, more available?

To pursue these questions, I would like to turn to another report of an interaction that was not recorded in *Ways,* this one between a young African American student and one of the teachers in Heath's classes, reported by the teacher in a paper for Heath's course. As previously mentioned, papers from Heath's courses archived with her correspondence indicate that teachers she worked with were learning to describe everyday interactions in sociolinguistic terms. Interactions recorded in their notes include bits of language use from their surroundings, from TV, and from comic strips. These interactions were in turn identified as exemplifying some linguistic principles; for example, this is an example of elaborated code; this is example of ideational function; this is an example of the Black Rural Cultural practice of "X." One teacher, describing the "performance" behavior of one of her Black students, recorded the following interaction:

> During my first year as a teacher, there was one little Black girl who seemed determined to shock me or enrage me by certain references to Black people and White people. For example, she would say, "You don't never call on no Black children."
>
> One afternoon, I was sitting in a child's chair, watching the children as they played. Lisa sauntered up behind me and said, quite casually, "Going to a wedding Saturday."
>
> I replied "Oh really?"
>
> She said, "Yeah, Black man and a white girl gettin' married."
>
> My reply, "Oh, that's nice."
>
> After a moment of somewhat stunned silence, Lisa returned to her friends. She never again made a remark like that to me.
>
> This is an example of performance by a Black child. In the Black community, children are encouraged to give these verbal performances. It gives them prestige and status in the eyes of the community and the amount of "glory" received from these performances is often determined by how much of a reaction comes from the person to whom the remark is directed.

There are a couple of ways to read this interaction, though each one reveals the necessity of considering the atmosphere of strained racial relations in which it took place. In one reading, one could assume that the teacher is right in categorizing the child's utterances as a "performance" meant to get a reaction out of the teacher. But to explain how a comment like "Black man and a white girl gettin' married" might be designed to "shock" or "enrage" the teacher, that comment must be seen as transgressive in some way. Such a comment could not be socially transgressive outside of the context of a history of segregation understood by both Lisa and the teacher. Comments by students to teachers about their weekend plans are hardly abnormal. The comment "man and a girl gettin' married" might not have provoked the same reaction from the teacher, but this we can only speculate. Without a shared understanding of endemic racism between both interactants, the child's comment could not be construed as a performance.

In the second reading I propose, one could assume the teacher is wrong in her analysis of Lisa's utterance. Comments like "You don't never call on no Black children" and "Yeah, Black man and a white girl gettin' married" are fine examples of informative comments at face value. Again, speculating, we might imagine that rather than trying to shock and enrage, Lisa might be seen as trying to provide information and feedback ("You don't never call on no Black children") that the teacher might need in order to correct a racial imbalance in her pedagogy. It must be acknowledged that if Lisa's observation was informative, its message did not reach its source. By designating Lisa's utterance as performative, the teacher shunts her back into the rules of her imagined home community and denies any relevance to her observations of the classroom community Lisa, like the teacher, also inhabits.

As the teacher reports it, the interaction is followed by a period of stunned silence, followed by the lack of repetition of any similar communication. According to Hymes, "In general, instances of the breaking off of communication, or uneasiness in it, are good evidence of the presence of a rule or expectation about speaking" (1968, p. 123). If there is a rule in this interaction, it seems most obviously a prohibition against African American children making comments about Black people and White people getting married. The lack of further speech on the subject attests to the maintenance of a taboo—a situation Hymes acknowledges can limit otherwise grammatically possible expressions (1968, pp. 113–114). The interaction between the teacher and Lisa reveals the integral nature of racism to communicative rules while the interaction itself creates and sustains the racist nature of the culture. The interaction reasserts the teacher's power to enforce the taboo, to determine what is performative and what is informative, the power to deem utterances culturally unintelligible and essentially meaningless (i.e., to deem an utterance performative and not informative). Similarly, with regard to Heath's conversation with the father, the father's hesitation and introduction "now that you bring it up" to his comment "there is this black-white thing" suggests that he is following her lead and also indicates some taboo attached to the subject of race, particularly if an African American is the one to broach the subject.

These two sets of interactions illustrate the limits of the approach Heath took in *Ways* because they suggest that the problem isn't a lack of mutual understanding but rather too much understanding. Tom Fox's (1990) reading of *Ways* as an example of a "Clash of Cultural Styles" explanation for student failure is relevant here. In such an explanation, he notes, the teachers are always "well-meaning," and the interaction always goes awry because of some "misunderstanding," which will assumedly disappear once appreciation of different cultures on both sides of the interaction is developed. Such an assumption is a naïve one, according to Fox, and he suggests that the "misunderstandings" might have root in histories of power imbalances. Henley and Kramarae (1991), in analyzing "miscommunications" between men and women, also reject cultural mismatch explanations for miscommunication based on the creation of two different sociolinguistic subcultures; they suggest gendered hierarchies of power determine whose version of the communication situation will prevail, including "who will be required to imitate the other's style in order to fit into the society" (p. 20). In the context of cross-gender communication in sexual situations, they argue that greater social power gives men certain rights—"the right to pay less attention to, or discount, women's protests, the right to be less adept at interpreting their communications than women are of men's, the right to believe women are inscrutable" (p. 27).

The issue in the end is not merely a matter of whether etic or emic frameworks prevail; I don't see the teacher's analysis or Heath's as any less contextually oriented than Lisa's or the father's if the context is understood as one of shared rules of interaction derived from histories of interactions, both local and national. While Heath's research might be seen as an attempt to create a shared community between home and school where all the rules of language use are understood by all, the interaction between the student and teacher suggests that there is already a shared community, one in which some of the rules involve allowing people with certain skin color to dictate the terms of interaction. Under these circumstances, there can be no real shared understanding beyond understanding the rules, those rules ensuring that students of color will often be placed in a deeply paradoxical position, learning in an environment where logic is subservient to the maintenance of cultural taboos.

A rereading of *Ways* that is sensitive to these rules demonstrates the implications for sociocultural theories of language use and literacy of factoring racism into culture; critical race theory's conception of racism as the rule and not the exception discussed in the last chapter is valuable for understanding the communities of *Ways*. Trackton children are not simply engaging in strategies to survive in the community of Trackton and are not ignorant of linguistic practices outside their community. They are always/already socialized into discourses of racism and very aware that group identifications based on race significantly shape their everyday experience. Strategies for dealing with the basic inconsistencies and inherent contradictions of life in a racist society can be seen as part of the Trackton way of life. Heath notes that Trackton children are adept at adapting to the "shifting sands of reality":

> Annie Mae, the community cultural broker, who seems to know *and* be able to explain many of the mainstream cultural practices as well as those of Trackton, sees these shifting sands of reality as a good training ground for children. . . . Across sets of situations and actors, children learn the domains of applications of a particular word, phrase, or set of actions and the meanings conveyed across these are often neither literal nor predictable. (p. 84)

One Trackton mother suggests that learning is learning to cope with this unpredictability: "[H]e see one thing one place one time, he know how it go, see sump'n like it again, maybe it be the same, maybe it won't" (p. 105). Heath comments that Annie Mae's view of language indicates that "Trackton children are expected to recognize that the same form of language—or anything else—is not expected to carry the same meaning at all times" (p. 105). Heath's "or anything else" puts me in mind of rights. The learning to deal with inconsistency that children do in Trackton seems appropriate given Mari Matsuda's analysis of the position of people of color in the United States—a position, Matsuda argues based on the history of Japanese American internment in World War II, in which people of color have to believe that they have a right to participate equally in society and yet live with the experience that rights are whatever people in power say they are (1987, p. 339).

Heath wrote of *Ways* that she was attempting to tell the "true" story of school reforms, "to ensure ongoing openness that is truly open and not merely adhering to current ideological tenets" (1993, p. 267); indeed, desegregation—the school reform attempt of the century—is a subject from which Heath consistently maintains a certain distance, a stance she shares with many critical race theorists who now question many of the mechanics and even the motives of desegregation (e.g., Bell, 1980b). Nevertheless, current ideological tenets influence the writing and the reading of any ethnography. In the end, the most interesting question is not how a study that takes as its problem space desegregation could ask its readers not to think about race—the inability of social research to theorize race outside essentially racist constructions at that time is evident—but how those readers could comply for so many years. Readers have embraced *Ways* for its demonstration of how the practices of reading, writing, and speaking are richly embedded within group identities, values, and activities and have found in the text vital arguments against strategies for scholastic success based on the simplistic formula "If parents do X, then children will achieve Y." Less embraced of rejections of simplistic formulas are the implications Heath's research uncovers—that desegregation would not in and of itself cure educational disparities in the face of pervasive racism and a history of segregation. It should be remembered that while reporting on the late 1960s and early 1970s, Heath's work was published in 1983, after both the hope of integrationists and the rage of the Black Power movement had been submerged by a wave of government-supported backlash against the gains of the civil rights movement. (This backlash will be the focus of the next chapter.) Certainly, the revival of scholarly interest in theoretical articulations of race has made possible my rereading of *Ways* not as a study of literacy that documents the occasional aberrant act of racism but as a book about the pervasive influence of racism through social structures, identity formation, and communicative interaction. Without racism, there would have been no segregation, no need for desegregation, and no impetus for Heath's research. Practices of reading and writing that do not acknowledge much less explore the impact of racism on language and literacy are not viable alternatives to essentially racist theories in scholarly and public discourse, not the best means to side-step the "pitfalls" such theories create, not the best way to address the limits of desegregation that *Ways* portends.

As James Clifford observes, "[T]he meanings of an ethnographic account are uncontrollable. Neither an author's intention, nor disciplinary training, nor the rules of genre can limit the readings of a text that will emerge with new historical, scientific, or political projects" (1986, p. 120). The continuing institution of segregation demands a new look at *Ways,* and an unsparing look at the history that surrounded it.

4 ✦ GIVE ME YOUR LITERATE: LITERACY AND THE AMERICAN DREAM

During the 1970s, while Heath was documenting educational change in the wake of *Brown* at the elementary school level in the South, debates were going on nationally over issues of literacy and racial justice at the college level. Questions arose as to whether the frequently required first-year composition course was a tool to help students of color adjust to academia, or a gate-keeping mechanism to fail out those students. In 1974, the Conference on College Composition and Communication (CCCC) responded to concerns over the stigmatization of Black English in these courses by publishing the final draft of the resolution *Students' Right to Their Own Language*. Noting that language scholarship has long disproved the myth of a standard American dialect, the resolution begins: "We affirm the students' right to their own patterns and varieties of language—the dialects of their nurture or whatever dialects in which they find their own identity and style." And it ends with a pedagogical imperative: "We affirm strongly that teachers must have the experiences and training that will enable them to respect diversity and uphold the right of students to their own language"[1] (*Students' Right,* 1974, pp. 2–3). The resolution was accompanied by a background statement that explained the nature of dialects, the process by which some dialects acquire prestige, and the implications of enforcing prestige dialect usage. The *Students' Right* resolution in its theoretical orientations was informed strongly by research, but in its intent, it was an antidiscrimination measure, a use of rhetoric to indict language discrimination based on racial discrimination and move people to combat it; as such, it reflects a reaffirmation of the rights of all in the tradition of the Fourteenth Amendment to the Constitution. Geneva Smitherman, one of the authors of the *Students' Right* resolution, suggests that the statement was designed in part to resolve the organization's contradictory stance on what was then referred to as Black English for those people who had qualms about it; more practically, it was intended to help teachers frustrated by the challenges presented by the "new and different student clientele"[2] (1999, p. 359). The authors of the resolution clearly hoped to persuade teachers not to fail African American students out of college on the basis of their language usage. As one of the committee members and the then chair of CCCC, Elisabeth McPherson wrote in a letter to a CCCC member: "[T]here is no real evidence that correcting student papers for so-called errors has any effect other than eliminating from a chance at education those students whose language choices differ from our own"[3] (qtd. in Parks, 2000, p. 176).

The *Students' Right* statement did not emerge from a cultural void but was proceeded and followed by many efforts by many literacy scholars to marry the causes of literacy research and teaching with racial justice. When it emerged, a pressing civil rights issue in literacy and racial justice was confronting the near obsession with correcting Black English. Educators and researchers challenged the construction of Standard English and the assumption that writing or speaking in certain ways was necessary to literacy development. After hearing that Martin Luther King Jr. had just been shot, for example, Ernece B. Kelly of Chicago City College delivered an impromptu speech to the attendees of the 1968 CCCC annual meeting, in which she called for a reassessment of the CCCC pedagogical direction. Declaring her frustration with the persistent lack of Black representation in the field and the "violence" of the field's efforts to "upgrade" or "replace" Black dialect, Kelly implores her audience—which she identifies as "white educators"—"to understand the terrible depth of racism that rages through this land," to "really work to undo the damage you may have done in trying to reshape the Black student in your own image." She warns in the end that it might be already too late to act to undo past damage, as she finds herself, among many others, moving toward "a blackness which approaches violence" (Kelly, 1968, pp. 107–8). The speech was later published in the pages of the journal *College Composition and Communication (CCC)*, under the title "Murder of the American Dream."

Kelly's speech, and a subsequent volume of *CCC* she coedited on issues of language diversity recognition, played a role in generating energy for the later *Students' Right* resolution (Smitherman, 1999). Other African Americans questioning in strong terms the role of the required first-year English composition course would follow her. In 1971, in the pages of *CCC*, Marilyn Musgrave of Miami University in Ohio charged, "Freshman Composition courses seldom meet the needs of minority group students, and in fact often destroy these students" (p. 24). She questions the then newest incarnation of the literacy myth, that Standard English use ensures academic progress in college and subsequent professional advancement, and identifies this myth as a tool of racial exclusion.

> This country is filled with Blacks who speak SE while they carry suitcases, wait table, strip tobacco, and, if they're lucky, sort mail. The new insistence by whites on SE indicates to many Blacks its intended use as an exclusion clause, a weapon against the larger number of Blacks now trying to enter colleges which are lily-white under the ivy. (p. 27).

Around the country, though more in areas where faculty and students of color were pressing the issue, universities were facing challenges to White dominated faculty, curriculum, and literacy practices. The published reports of teachers give some indication of the ways faculty in many places were trying to change first-year composition from a gate-keeping course and tool of racial exclusion to a course explicitly connecting the development of literacy with racial justice goals. Marie Lederman reports in a 1969 issue of *CCC,* for example, the use of "hip" language in her composition classroom at City University of New York.[4] She introduces her report with comments on the struggle for Black equality and draws directly on the rhetoric of Malcolm X's human rights movement to identify the study of language with the struggle for human rights. Racism is treated as an almost indisputable fact of society in

Lederman's report, and the need to combat systemic racism emerges as the rationale for changes in language arts pedagogy. In the process of compiling a list of "hip" words students use, Lederman recounts how discussion of prejudice emerged in the class:

> For a time we left discussion of language and wandered into discussion of prejudice, the problems of ghetto life for blacks in America. . . . I sometimes listed on the board some of the controversial ideas implied by the students' use of certain words and suggested that students use some of these as a basis for later papers dealing with analysis and argumentation. (p. 212)

In the 1990s, college teachers remained concerned with discussing racism and prejudice in their writing classrooms, but their reports also capture something else worthy of note—resistance from students. As Geoffrey Sirc's (1994) "*The Autobiography of Malcolm X* as a Basic Writing Text" shows, Malcolm X was still inspiring approaches to teaching in the mid-1990s, yet through Sirc's report of the responses of his basic writing students at the University of Minnesota to the story of Malcolm X, one can detect that something has changed since the 1960s and early 1970s. One White student reacts:

> I am so tired of hearing about racism that I would love to scream at everyone whining about America to go home! I have never discriminated against anyone purely based on race. Those people that yell about "black pride" and us "white devils" should journey back to Africa. Then make a choice to stay there or return. The same is true for every ethnical group. (Sirc, 1994, p. 54)

This student protested the inclusion of *The Autobiography of Malcolm X* on the syllabus on the grounds that it contained things that were offensive. Sirc observes of his student, "A racist student like Rhonda then, speaks in a kind of code, in which the complaint about racism is the real problem, not the object of the complaint" (pp. 55–56).

Also in 1994, Helen Rothschild Ewald and David L. Wallace document White student resistance to affirmative action in a discussion in Wallace's first-year writing class at Iowa State University. TJ, an African American student writing about his own experiences with employment discrimination, announces that his paper's thesis is "stereotypes have made it difficult for unemployed African American males to find suitable employment"—just the kind of thesis Lederman had been encouraging from her students twenty-five years earlier. A White student counters TJ's thesis, however, arguing, "Afro-Americans are getting a . . . a better hand deal" (Ewald & Wallace, 1994, p. 344). A debate over whether affirmative action constitutes a form of reverse discrimination follows. Even though what constitutes reverse discrimination here is contested, reverse discrimination emerges in the discussion with the students as an uncontested term, a fact of society.

The tacit understanding of White hegemony documented by college composition teachers in the late 1960s and 1970s is questioned by some of the students in Sirc's class and in Wallace's class; assertions of rights denied in these classes are just as likely to emanate from White students. In the 1990s, the question of who is discriminated against is up for grabs, and the construct of reverse discrimination is invoked as a direct challenge to the changes the civil rights movement brought to the classroom. This move from discussion of "racial discrimination" in classrooms to discussion of "reverse discrimination" witnesses in part the influence of the *Bakke* decision. In pondering the *Bakke* case, Justice Stevens suggested that reverse discrimination "poses problems unique in our history" (J. P. Stevens, 1977, p. 1). In my review of over one hundred studies and teacher reports since 1965, I indeed did not find any mention of reverse discrimination before the *Bakke* decision. The concept of reverse discrimination, however, really masks the real issue, which is eliminating any remedies granted for past racial discrimination that could be perceived as harming Whites. This goal of preventing perceived harm to Whites governed the majority of the justices when they decided *Bakke* and put affirmative action programs on ideologically shaky ground. As legal scholar Michael Selmi (1999) observes, the legacy of *Bakke* is a divorce of questions of affirmative action and other remedies from discussion of past or even present discrimination against people of color. *Bakke* thus legitimized the replacing of discussions of remedy with discussions of reverse discrimination.

In Sirc's class, some of the students not only challenge the notion that African Americans were discriminated against; they challenge the very discussion of racism in the classroom. Such challenges were coming not only from isolated students in the 1990s. When the president of the University of Texas overrode the English department's attempt to implement a syllabus for first-year composition entitled "Writing about Difference," in which exploration of racism and sexism through study of civil rights law was to be an explicit focus, the incident made national news. Linda Brodkey, the director of the program, who had helped design the syllabus, received hate mail, and pundits denounced the discussion of issues pertinent to women and minorities in first-year composition. As Brodkey (1996) documents in reflecting on the controversy, critics of the syllabus had charged that writing and basic skills should be taught without discussion of social issues or oppression. President Cunningham of the University of Texas, for example, followed up his abridgement of academic freedom by denouncing multiculturalism to school donors as "a code word for some people, a signal of efforts—real or imagined—to use the curriculum to promote 'politically correct' ideologies or viewpoints. We must not, and we will not, permit such a development at the University" (1991, p. 2). President Cunningham's statement asserts that the project of racial justice is an unnatural intrusion on the project of literacy development.

President Cunningham and Geoffrey Sirc, though writing from ideologically opposed viewpoints, interestingly both identify discourse around issues of racial justice and literacy as coded. All this coding is the natural consequence of the taboo on discussing or acknowledging the country's history of racism, and the incompatibility of that history with the ideal of America as a democratic nation. Yet if Sirc is right and his student, Rhonda, is speaking a "kind of code" in which complaining about racism is the only form of racism, it is a code many people apparently embraced, one that found greatest expression beginning in the Reagan era. Scholars have shown that the Reagan administration's backlash against the civil rights enforcement agencies that had been built up over the previous few decades was accomplished in part by Reagan's skillful use of the rhetoric of racial equality and color blindness to exercise neglect toward discriminatory practices (Crenshaw, 1988; Lipsitz, 1998; Omi & Winant, 1994). My contribution here is to show how conceptions of literacy as White property were marshaled to serve that backlash as well.

In the first part of this chapter, I explore what I call "the Reaganomics of race and literacy," Reagan's philosophy about race, literacy, and economic sensibility, which both reflected the tone of backlash against the civil rights movement in the country and informed Reagan's policies toward civil rights enforcement. Reagan was invested in the notion of literacy as a set of universal "reading, writing, and arithmetic" skills and thought that public education for Whites had been ruined by "minority interests" and the goal of eliminating prejudice in students. Like Sirc's student Rhonda, Reagan analogized the experience of people of color to the experience of White ethnic immigrants to this country in a denial of the reality of racism, and the reality of immigration (Omi & Winant, 1994). With deceptively simple rhetorical appeal, this immigrant analogy became the greatest rhetorical weapon against both affirmative action and racially just literacy instruction. Literacy scholars who wish to study the impact of racial injustice on student language practices understandably, then, set themselves to the task of dismantling the immigrant analogy. Many point out that the experiences of African Americans, Latino/as, and Asian Americans have been distinct from other groups of immigrants, putting those people of color at a long-ranging disadvantage in literacy environments.

Such observations, while true, only partially address the fantasy of immigration at the heart of Reagan's philosophy. They are complemented by historical studies of immigration demonstrating that White ethnic immigrants to America were not necessarily born "White" but rather became so through the process of assimilation (Jacobsen, 1999). These studies remind us that immigrants acquired not only a new nationality but a racial identity as part of becoming American. Significantly, scholarly interest in intersections of race and immigration burgeoned after David Roediger's (1991) charge that labor historians had ignored race in studying the development of working-class identity. Since, as I will discuss, the laborer and the literate were historically cast as contradictory figures in immigration debate, it is unsurprising, if problematic, that attention to literacy in labor-based histories has been spare. In actuality, conceptions of literacy, particularly those forwarded by well-educated elites, played a crucial role in the process of creating White identity through immigration.

From roughly Reconstruction through World War II, immigration restriction debate was prominent and dominated by discourse about literacy. Literacy tests were continually offered by nativists as the most efficient means of preserving what was viewed as the racial integrity of the United States, and literacy restrictions were eventually enforced, though haphazardly, in immigration. Furthermore, a racial bar to citizenship was in effect from 1790 to 1952 whereby naturalization in this country was predicated on one's being able to prove one was "White" or, after 1870, of specifically African ancestry (López, 1996). Evidence of literacy was often marshaled in naturalization court cases to bolster an applicant's argument for being White. The alliance of ideologies of literacy with ideologies of race damned groups of immigrants in two ways: Either they were denied at the border, or if they entered, they were faced with a naturalization process denying citizenship and opportunities to acquire and capitalize on literacy to those configured as non-White. Thus the process of immigration, of moving across borders, is one that has both created "White" identity and reinforced the conception of literacy as a White trait. This history discussed in this chapter provides further context to the *Brown* decision, as it shows that the pervasive cultural belief in literacy as White property had to be challenged continually at the highest governmental levels at the time the *Brown* case was being argued.

Awareness of this history, however, was absent from Reagan's understanding of the relationship between race and literacy. Instead Reagan revived and acted upon a fantasy of immigration that not only bolstered the cultural belief in literacy as White property but also undermined those institutions that would redistribute literacy more evenly. The link between White identity and literacy that guided pivotal court cases and legislative hearings in the nineteenth and early-twentieth centuries was therefore sustained throughout the post–civil rights era under Reagan, and literacy instruction and scholarship both suffered as a result.

The Reaganomics of Race and Literacy

Given that presidents rarely write and speak their own words, Reagan's distaste for the civil rights movement and its effects on public education are perhaps most visible as his (as opposed to his speechwriter's or advisor's) in the radio addresses he wrote himself in the late 1970s, just before he became president. In these recently published addresses, which reached twenty million people each week as they were heard on 286 radio stations and printed in 226 newspapers, Reagan bemoans the decline in the quality of education and dates the beginning of the decline to the late 1950s, a few years after *Brown v. Board of Education* was decided. In 1976, the same year many of the Supreme Court justices hearing *Washington v. Davis* were suggesting that a high school public education was no longer sufficient to guarantee a standard of literacy necessary for civil service positions, Reagan declared, "[I]n the last 20 [years] the quality of [education] has declined by anyone's standard." He attributes the decline to the schools' new agenda to create "citizens free of prejudice"—Communists by implication: "We've all been aware of educationists claims that the old fashioned 'reading, writin & arithmetic' was no longer relevant. School was going to mould the 'now' generation into world citizens free of prejudice, hostility or even a competitive instinct"[5] (Skinner, Anderson, & Anderson, 2001, p. 344). This comment shows Reagan's tendency for nostalgia. Although Reagan, unlike the Supreme Court justices discussed in chapter 1, was too much of an anti-intellectual to invest much in any one particular literacy institution—or, for that matter, in education in general, as he was much more preoccupied with stopping the spread of Communism to the Arabian gulf—the few addresses he gave on education show his investment in the kind of literacy instruction he felt he was given as a child. He stressed repeatedly the importance of the "old fashioned system" and saw this system threatened by emphasis on "minority affairs" brought by the civil rights movement. In an address given in 1978, the year *Bakke* was decided, Reagan wrote: "[A] flood of progressive innovations—teaching consumer ed., environment, minority affairs and others heavily larded with cultural relativism have replaced 'reading, writing & arithmetic'" (Skinner et al., 2001, p. 345). In this address, he voiced the same insistence on divorcing the learning of basic skills from the content of "minority affairs" that critics of the University of Texas first-year writing syllabus would voice later.

Reagan's nostalgia for pre–civil rights era literacy instruction features prominently in a 1979 address he drafted about Nancy Reagan's visit to a Harlem parochial school.[6] This school, in which students pay a tuition fee and parents volunteer to do custodial work or serve as teachers' aids, is lauded as a big improvement over public schools. The improvement apparently consists of shifting the economic burden for education from the federal government to the individual. Reagan writes:

> One mother with an income of $6300 pays $1100 of that in tuition. She says she does without things, dosen't [*sic*] buy many clothes because education is the most important thing. By reading and other tests these schools top the N.Y. public schools in educational quality and the total cost per students averages less than $500. Per student cost in the public schools is OVER $2600." (Skinner et al., 2001, p. 358)

Reagan's vision of economically disenfranchised African Americans sacrificing most of their livelihood and much of their time to educate their children outside the public school system nearly duplicates the terms African Americans in many areas were forced to adhere to in order to educate their children, from Reconstruction up through the mid-twentieth century. In the 1920s, for example, when Reagan was attending elementary school, many public elementary and high schools were closed to African Americans who, as James Anderson (1988) documents, often conducted school in their churches, under conditions that had improved little since Reconstruction.

Reagan was not inevitably interested in salvaging public education. He saw public education as spiraling downward since *Brown,* as a cost and a burden. He relied greatly on standardized test scores for this assessment of public education's progress. In 1979 he wrote:

> Well over the last 14 years spending has vastly increased from around $400 per student to $1400. . . . In these SAME roughly 14 yrs. the scholastic aptitude tests—the college entrance *exams* called Sat's for short—have dropped every year for totals ranging from 50 points in verbal, to 30 in math. (Skinner et al., 2001, p. 346)

Reagan had other complaints against public schools beside the cost. He resented the ban on school prayer in public schools and favored private and parochial schools without that ban. These schools he wished to keep as White as possible. In 1978, he charged the IRS with threatening religious freedom by denying tax exempt status to private schools "that fail to meet an arbitrary quota of minority enrollment & hiring. Pvt. & church supported schools will have to institute minority recruitment, minority hiring programs & provide minority scholarships to increase minority enrollment" (Skinner et al., 2001, p. 355). Reagan again focuses on the economic and cultural cost of remedy, claiming here that affirmative action in educational settings threatens one of the first goals of the nation—religious freedom. Many of Reagan's speeches construct a binary opposition between "freedom" and inclusion of people of color or what he conceived to be their issues or their language.

Reagan had special words for the notion that students have a right to their own language. He complained in a 1979 address about the director of the Office of Bilingual Education's statement that, in Reagan's words, "being taught in one's native language perhaps should be considered a 'human right'" (Skinner et al., 2001, p. 346). Reagan alludes in this address to the Supreme Court decision in *Lau v. Nichols* (1974), which held that Chinese students were discriminated against in California schools and allowed for the possibility of special federally funded programs for Chinese-speaking students to learn in their own language.[7] Reagan invokes the image of the melting pot to argue against such bilingual education:

> Today our govt. spends $150 mil. a year teaching children of other cultures in their own language. The melting pot tradition in which we taught the foreign born how to fit into our society has been forsaken in favor of teaching them how to be different & remain apart from the mainstream of American living. (Skinner et al., 2001, p. 347)

"Our society" in this formulation is clearly imagined to be a perennially English-speaking one, and the opposition created between "our govt." and "children of other cultures" assumes a monocultural government. Reagan never mentions the discrimination that these programs were meant to redress; instead, like Justice William Rehnquist of the Supreme Court (who Reagan, once president, promoted to chief justice), he worries about where all this change is going in quantitative terms: "What is next—traffic signs etc. in 70 different languages?" (Skinner et al., 2001, p. 347).

From Reagan's radio address, a Reaganomics of race and literacy can be deduced. In Reagan's imagination, public schools, particularly those with programs that address the needs of non-White students, are merely a drain on the government and the White American taxpayer. Non-Whites are entitled to literacy, but only if it does not cost Whites anything either now or in the future. The Reaganomics of race and literacy therefore presumes literacy to be the property of Whites.

Certainly Reagan only reflected the sentiments of many Americans. Not many Americans, however, were in a position to effect the changes Reagan did when he became president. While in 1977 Reagan wrote of his opposition to the proposed international Genocide Convention on the grounds that "our own public officials & individual American citizens could be prosecuted & punished for causing mental harm (and who defines what that is) to members of a national, ethnic, racial or cultural group" (Skinner et al., 2001, p. 166), when he became president of the United States, he did whatever possible within his domain to forestall prosecution of public officials and citizens for racial discrimination. The Reagan era rollback of civil rights gains was facilitated by disabling those federal and judicial organizations that were set up to enforce non-discriminatory policies, partially through appointments and vetoes, and by allowing those organizations to ignore race and racial discrimination. Reagan attempted to fire members of the U.S. Commission on Civil Rights and vetoed the Civil Rights Restoration Act (Crenshaw et al., 1995). The Reagan-appointed assistant attorney general for civil rights, William Bradford Reynolds, upon gaining office immediately called for reductions in the enforcement budget of the Civil Rights Division of the U.S. Justice Department and opposed busing for school integration. Furthermore, Reynolds all but stopped the filing of housing discrimination suits, using the Paperwork Reduction Act to excuse Housing and Urban Development from gathering racial information on those participating in housing programs.[8] In 1981, the Federal Deposit Insurance Corporation (FDIC) ceased keeping records based on race when a court order enforcing the 1974 Equal Credit Opportunity Act prohibiting discrimination in real estate lending expired. In 1983, Reagan appointed Clarence Thomas, a foe of affirmative action, to direct the EEOC. Reviewing Reagan's record, Lipsitz (1998) suggests that the Reagan administration affirmed support for integration in the abstract while actively preventing many mechanisms designed to make integration possible from functioning effectively. Racial minorities still had civil rights, but they had fewer and fewer ways to see that those rights were enforced. Unsurprisingly, Reagan historically had no real commitment to civil rights; he opposed the Civil Rights Act of 1964 and called the Voting Rights Act of 1965 (which called for the end of literacy testing in voter registration) humiliating to southerners (D. Carter, 1996).

Looking at his approach to civil rights, it seems clear that Reagan didn't really believe race discrimination to have been a reality of American history at all. As Reagan's policies were tailored to his conception of the "melting pot tradition in which we taught the foreign born how to fit into our society," they strongly embody what Michael Omi and Harold Winant (1994) call an "ethnicity theory" approach to race. In ethnicity theory, integration is seen as an uncomplicated good and assimilation a necessary eventuality. Failure to assimilate is read as a conflict of cultural practices or norms. Although the conflict might be benign, those practices the newcomers bring with them from wherever they came from are inevitably to be adjusted rather than circumstances external to the group. This narrative of immigration is incompatible with discussion of systemic discrimination or persistent prejudice because it assumes equality of opportunity and a fundamentally benign majority society. Even if initial prejudicial opposition to a group is recognized, it is assumed to be aberrant and imagined surmountable as the group adapts to the norms of the majority.

This narrative of immigration had been around long before Reagan. Post–civil rights movement, however, it was specifically deployed to counter the challenges to the conception of a fundamentally benign society that the movement had brought. But the narrative of immigration in which racial discrimination plays no part and normative conceptions of literacy only play a benign or enabling role does not hold up under historical scrutiny. Looking at the actual history of immigration reveals not how literacy instruction taught the foreign born to "fit in" but rather how ideologies of literacy were marshaled for the project of keeping the foreign born out of what was imagined to be a "White" nation.

Literacy in the "Melting Pot"

As we know, anti-immigrationists operated powerfully on both coasts beginning in the mid-1800s. On the West Coast, immigrants from Asia and Mexico were the frequent targets of exclusion legislation, while on the East Coast, nativists were working to restrict immigration from eastern and southern Europe. Anti-Chinese sentiment in the 1870s began the period of closing America's borders. In 1875, the Page Law was passed disallowing entry of almost all Chinese women on the assumption that they were prostitutes. Following a recession in which cheap labor was no longer perceived of as scarce, the Chinese Exclusion Act was passed in 1882, disallowing Chinese laborers. Pan-Asian restrictions were passed in 1917 and later in 1924.[9] Segregation of Asians in the California school system was common long before *Plessy* for Chinese and later Japanese, Korean, and Indian students. But the anti-Asian sentiment sometimes carried with it tolls on literacy of a different and more difficult to document nature. During the height of nativism, White violence made the streets treacherous for the Chinese, and Chinese parents kept their children home from any school (Delgado & Stefancic, 2000, p. 1564). Anti-Asian sentiment having set the pattern, the children of later Mexican immigrants were segregated or tracked into vocational settings often on the basis of standardized test scores (p. 1572).

On the East Coast, Henry Cabot Lodge led the anti-immigration platform. An affluent Harvard-educated Bostonian, Lodge devoted much of his political life to the question of how to limit what he saw as undesirable immigration from southern and eastern Europe. So attracted to the notion of heredity that he married his cousin Anna Cabot Miller Davis, Lodge was sure that a literacy test would restrict those groups he found unfavorable without invoking a national origins quota. Lodge was not alone in his faith in literacy. By the time Lodge had reached the Senate in 1894, the Immigration Restriction League of Boston had formed, as other Harvard alums began to advocate the use of a literacy test to curb immigration. In 1896, Cabot introduced the literacy test to Congress explicitly as a means of racial restriction on immigration. The report presented tables showing that southern Europe had a higher rate of illiteracy and argued that

> the literacy test will affect almost entirely those races whose immigration to the United States has begun within recent time and which are most alien in language and origin to the people who founded the 13 colonies and which built the United States. (Senate Report 290, pp. 22, 23)

President Cleveland, however, vetoed a bill requiring a literacy test, but it did not die. Other bills advocating a literacy test were introduced in almost every subsequent session of Congress until 1917, when one was passed (M. E. Brown, 1999).

When a bill advocating a literacy test for immigration restriction came up under President Theodore Roosevelt's administration, an interesting coordination of interests led to its defeat. The empire of Japan was concerned about the segregation of Japanese children in schools in California. Under pressure from President Roosevelt over the foreign crisis this segregation was creating, the school board of San Francisco offered Roosevelt a deal: They would desegregate their schools if Roosevelt agreed to limit immigration of Japanese laborers (M. E. Brown, 1999; Delgado & Stefancic, 2000). In order to get this racial restriction on labor passed through Congress in 1907, Lodge let the literacy test be dropped. Proponents of the literacy test continued to advocate for its use in immigration restriction, however. Prescott F. Hall, one of these proponents, argued in 1908 that a literacy test "furnishes an indirect method of excluding those who are undesirable, not merely because of their illiteracy, but for other reasons. . . . The hereditary tendencies of the peoples illiterate abroad . . . cannot be overcome in a generation or two."[10] Finally, in 1917, over President Wilson's veto, an immigration act was passed barring immigrants over the age of sixteen who could not read or write in any language.

Still the debate over literacy restrictions did not end. In 1924, the United States Committee on Immigration and Naturalization conducted hearings in connection with the Immigration Act of 1924. These hearings included the lengthy testimony of Dr. Harry H. Laughlin of the Eugenics Record Office of the Carnegie Institution of Washington, who felt that unrestricted immigration had suited the purposes of the country at a time when it was starving for immigrant labor, but times had changed. Arguing that the development of the United States as a country was now threatened by the practice of allowing ignorant laborers of inferior strains to settle in its borders, Laughlin, an outspoken eugenicist, warned that

> America is a melting pot whether we like it or not. . . . We should be found admitting only sound metals, and those in such proportions as would alloy well with the earlier American elements already in the crucible, and should take great care to reject and eliminate all dross.

Laughlin believed that "natural intelligence . . . should weigh heavily in emigration and immigration standards" (Hearings, 68th Congress, 1924, p. 1277). He presented the committee with a table detailing twenty-five different quota formulas for immigration, including the number of people each formula would exclude from each country. Most of these plans are variations of restriction on the basis of nation of origin. One, however, plans to restrict on the basis of "hereditary quality" defined as "the biological principle which admits only immigrants of demonstrable individual and family stock qualities of higher value than the average already established in the United States." It is under this column that literacy tests appear as a "condition limiting opening and extent of immigration." The plan calls for "Mental and educational tests: Descriptive records. Special tests of literacy." Graphically displaying the link between literacy and racial taxonomy that was in the minds of immigration restrictionists, this column lists literacy tests right below "anthropometrical and racial tests and measurements" (Hearings, 68th Congress, 1924, p. 1290).

The tests Laughlin had in mind would be based on the Army Intelligence tests, the results of which Laughlin also submitted broken down by ethnic group (Hearings, 68th Congress, 1924, p.

1278). Laughlin's charts place people from England and Scotland at the top of the list of natural intelligence and "Southern American Negroes" on the bottom; (in this respect, these charts are very similar to the charts Herrnstein and Murray (1994), authors of *The Bell Curve,* would construct seventy years later). But despite the claim of universality, Laughlin's test of "natural intelligence" deserves a closer look because it is actually quite culturally specific. Along with his testimony, Laughlin submitted the results of the experimental study of "J. B.," a thirty-one-year-old Belgian woman who had undergone his physical and mental tests to determine her hereditary value. J. B. was asked in the intelligence test to, among other things, "choose prettier in each of three pairs of pictures," "count backwards," "repeat sentences," "see absurdity in 5 different pictures," and define charity, obedience, and justice. J. B. apparently failed to define obedience and justice. Although the pictures J. B. was asked to evaluate are not presented, arguably the meanings of "prettiness" and "justice" are subject to cultural variation. J. B. did not do very well on the tests, and the summary of the case finds "neither personally nor in blood would she add intelligence or initiative to the average of these qualities already established here." She in this regard apparently shares much with other Belgians who tested third from the bottom of the intelligence chart, right above the Polish and "Southern American Negroes" but below Italians. Yet she is somewhat rescued by a qualifier attached to the mental test about the test not having been given in ideal circumstances "on account of the language (J. B. speaks a Brussels' Flemish dialect)." It is further noted, "What J. B. lacks most is instruction. She reads and writes French very poorly. On the other hand she seems to have a practical sense of things and to be a good housekeeper" (Hearings, 68th Congress, 1924, p. 1347).

It is difficult to imagine the immigration situation in which this un-ideal circumstance of language interference would not frequently occur. Natural intelligence in Laughlin's test is more attainable if the applicant shares not only the cultural assumptions about beauty and justice but also the language of the test giver. But the qualifier about J. B.'s test circumstances is interesting for other reasons. As it happens, J. B. is from the northwestern part of Europe, which Laughlin and many other restrictionists favored; his testimony includes a map defining this region. Her poor performance on the test, then, must somehow be explained away, and some other shining quality of hers brought to light. The comment that J. B. would make a good housekeeper suggests that although J. B. is condemned by her intelligence score, she is rescued by the ideology of domesticity, her inability to correctly define obedience notwithstanding. The qualifier "she seems to have a practical sense about things" in its vagueness stands in bizarre contrast to her raw intelligence score at the bottom. In any case, Laughlin's research on intelligence tests did not prove convincing—and given the results and the goal to restrict non–Northwestern European immigration, one can easily see why. Instead, the Immigration Act of 1924 was passed with a blunt national quota system that would ensure an overwhelming majority of German and English immigrants. Although this act did not institute the kinds of tests that Laughlin suggested, it did retain the requirement of demonstrating the ability to read and write and so preserved the notion of literacy as a White trait.

All the while racial limits were being debated in immigration, in and through and around the subject of literacy, racial restrictions on naturalization remained firmly in place, as the Naturalization Act of 1790 limited citizenship to "free White" people. Ian Haney López (1996) demonstrates through an analysis of the fifty-two court cases recorded between 1878 and 1944, in which applicants for U.S. citizenship attempted to prove that they were White, that the courts of the nation played a role in forming the "White race" as it is presently understood in the American context. In documenting how widespread nativism and fears of miscegenation informed the process, López notes no mixed-race person was ever naturalized as White in a recorded court case, even a drop of non-White blood being considered enough to render one non-White under the "one drop of blood" rule (1996, p. 27). López determines that all the prerequisite cases recorded were decided based on the following rationales: legal precedent, common knowledge, scientific evidence, and congressional intent. In pronouncing the decision of each case, morphological features such as skin color, jaw size, cranial capacity, and hair texture were discussed through and against such considerations as character, language aptitude, and profession.

A proto-form of literacy expertise was also brought to the task of making racial distinctions in these cases. When some of the physical characteristics were beginning to seem a little murky and the reliability of color as a signifier of race had been challenged, the taxonomy of ethnologist A. W. Keane (1908) explaining differences in "mental" characteristics was invoked in *In re Najour* (1909) as incontrovertible scientific evidence. Keane found the "Negro or Black Division" to be

> sensual, unintellectual, lacking the sense of personal dignity or self-respect, hence, readily bending to the yoke of slavery . . . mind arrested at puberty owing to the early closing of the cranial sutures, hence in the adult the animal side is more developed than the mental; hence also no science or letters. (p. 16)

Keane found the "Mongolic or Yellow Division" to be "nearly all reckless gamblers, science slightly, arts and letters moderately developed" (p. 18). With blatant favoritism, Keane described the "Caucasian or White Division" as "highly imaginative and intellectual, hence science, arts, poetry, and letters fully developed, to some extent from very early times; most civilizations . . . have had their roots in Caucasic soil" (p. 25).

The judge deciding *In re Najour* used Keane's taxonomy as scientific evidence proving Syrians are White. The use of Keane in this case demonstrates how developed literacy was equated with White identity in an effort to stabilize the concept of a "White" race when it was under threat and to preserve the concept of America as a "White" nation. But evidence of literacy, like other forms of evidence, could be used capriciously. When Keane's taxonomy was rejected and "common knowledge" rather than scientific evidence offered in the decision in *Ex parte Shahid* (1913), literacy was still used to assess the application to naturalize. In this case, the judge found reasons to disqualify Syrians as White based on "personal disqualifications" including the evidence of illiteracy in English. The applicant, the judge wrote, "writes his name in Arabic, cannot read or write in English and speaks and understands English very imperfectly" (López, 1996, p. 213). Although the judge in this case dismissed as ambiguous the "general question of admissibility," he did provide a long discussion of why "free White person" should be taken to mean of European background.

The shift in rationales from *In re Najour* to *Ex parte Shahid* proved to be part of a trend. When the tide of anthropology turned toward questioning the coherence of morphological and mental attributes as signifiers of race, scientific evidence factored into the rationales less and less; judges could appeal to common knowledge or legal precedent to override potentially subversive scientific evidence. López's analysis demonstrates that "evidence" including evidence of literacy or illiteracy could be marshaled to support the arbitrary views of any judge. Through such forms of reasoning, each nationality or ethnicity not previously raced was assigned a racial identity upon application, a process that solidified the value of being "White" whether the applicant won or lost. Reviewing the result of *United States v. Cartozian* (1925), for example (a case in which the anthropologist Franz Boas—in a probably pragmatic moment—testified as scientific expert for the defendant), López notes not only that Armenians were pronounced legally White but that "this pronouncement allowed them a prosperous and privileged position in American society. This prosperity then confirmed the common knowledge of their Whiteness, which in turn served to justify the judicial treatment of Armenians as White persons" (1996, p. 131). Through the process of immigration, immigrants become "White," the country becomes "White," literacy becomes "White," and "White" as a racial identity is further reified.

In 1952, the racial bar to naturalization was lifted when the McCarran-Walter bill passed, over President Truman's veto, to become the Immigration Act of 1952. In returning the bill, Truman commended the lifting of the racial bar to citizenship but found unacceptable the system of national origin quotas to immigration that the bill imposed, calling it "a constant handicap in the conduct of our foreign relations" (*Whom*, 1953, p. 277). He invoked the debt Americans owed to allies from World War II and pointed out the inanity of restricting immigration from those countries where Communism had prevented significant emigration. This system of quotas, Truman argued, reinstated the very injustices that were operating in the past. Certainly vetoing the bill was part of Truman's efforts to preserve America's reputation as a desirable democracy in a Cold War era. Considering that the U.S. Commissioner of the Immigration and Naturalization Service, Earl G. Harrison, had resigned in 1944, complaining that besides America, the only country having a racial bar to naturalization was Nazi Germany, Truman was well aware of the stakes of removing all racial bars to immigration and naturalization (López, 1996, p. 44).

Although not discussed at length by President Truman in his veto message, the McCarran-Walter bill also retained literacy requirements for immigration and naturalization. After the House and the Senate overturned his veto, Truman established the President's

Commission on Immigration and Naturalization to address issues he felt arose with the influx of refugees from Europe. Lengthy hearings ensued as senators, House members, and representatives from various interest groups that had by the 1950s formed organizations in the United States voiced their favor or, more frequently, their disfavor of the new legislation. The issue of literacy testing of immigrants was a frequent focus of these hearings.[11]

The American Jewish Congress, for example, testified to the dismal history of the relationship between literacy testing and the motive of racial exclusion in immigration legislation. Echoing the American Jewish Congress's concerns, Alice O'Connor, secretary for the Massachusetts Displaced Persons Commission, quoted Henry Cabot Lodge's claim before Congress in 1896 that literacy tests will bear upon "Italians, Russians, Poles, Hungarians, Greeks, and Asiatics, and lightly, or not at all, upon English-speaking immigrants or Germans, Scandinavians, or French." O'Connor labeled Lodge's arguments "nativism or Nordic superiority in its most outspoken phase" and advocated "a long, considered campaign of education to balance at least 23 years of the bland acceptance of a theory so closely akin to that of the Nazi doctrine of Hitler" (Hearings, 82nd Congress, 1952, p. 315). A representative from the Order Sons of Italy also objected to the requirement that an immigrant demonstrate the ability to read and write a language or dialect. Reversing the logic that had cast illiterates as undesirable, the representative, Palmer Di Giulio, characterized literates as toil phobic "cream puffs":

> Many illiterate but honest people have come to the United States and contributed to the progress of this great Nation their useful toil. The fallacy of this policy lies in the fact that learned people do not like to work with a pick and a shovel or at jobs which require willingness and a strong back. Had we depended upon cream puffs to build railroads we would still be traveling by oxcart. (Hearings, 82nd Congress, 1952, p. 658)

The irony of this construction is that the Chinese men who had been instrumental in building the railroad, though denied citizenship, were popularly configured as something like the "cream puffs" of American society. Immigration restrictions barring the entry of Chinese women and antimiscegenation laws threatening White American women with loss of citizenship if they married noncitizens, left Chinese men without the choice to form legally recognized families, all circumstances leading to the feminization of the Chinese male in the American imagination[12] (Eng, 2001; Lowe, 1996).

Objections to the new immigration act were objections not always to a literacy restriction per se but to the kind of literacy the act presumed useful. Edward Heims, chairman of a committee on immigration for the Commonwealth Club of California, objected that the government sought to measure the wrong kind of literacy. Heims offered that his committee had drawn up a report on measures of selection based on objective tests. During the hearing, he produced a letter he had solicited from the president of the Educational Testing Service (ETS) in Princeton, Henry Chauncey, stating ETS's interest in helping develop such tests. Chauncey wrote: "I was naturally especially interested in your recommendation that tests be used in the selective-immigration program that is recommended. There is no question in my mind that tests effective for this purpose can be devised" (Hearings, 82nd Congress, 1952, p. 1031). Apparently having in mind some kind of intelligence test similar to those presented during the 1924 immigration hearings by Laughlin, Heims explained that these tests would not measure particular skills so much as "the real innate constitutional abilities to develop into desirable personalities." Making explicit the connection between literacy and Whiteness, he bemoaned the past immigration of Chinese and Africans, "which gives anyway now occasion to frictions and makes so much of our problems, has been caused because one wanted to fill temporary needs" (Hearings, 82nd Congress, 1952, p. 1032).

Others turned their attention to challenging the literacy requirements restricting naturalization. Eugene Freeheim of the Welfare Federation of Cleveland objected to the naturalization requirement that a prospective citizen be able to read and write in English, offering that many newspapers including the *New York Times, Washington Post,* and *Harvard Crimson* had also published editorials condemning this requirement. Elizabeth Wilson, executive secretary of the International Institute of Gary, Indiana, also argued that literacy tests for naturalization enacted were too high. She objected that it was a "waste of the time of the teacher" to teach people a few words in English if they were illiterate in their own language (Hearings, 82nd Congress, 1952, p. 720).

In 1953, the President's Commission on Immigration and Naturalization published their report, pointedly entitled *Whom We Shall*

Welcome. The report criticized national origins quotas and explicitly addressed the assumption that a literacy test would keep out those imagined undesirable by supporters of the tests.[13] Countering claims originating in the work of Henry Cabot Lodge and the Immigration Restriction League that illiteracy was higher in new rather than old immigrants, the report notes:

> All reliable evidence shows that illiteracy is more closely related to opportunity than to any other single factor. The literacy of persons admitted under the Displaced Persons Act showed a surprising degree of similarity to that of the American people as a whole. The theory of inherent racial tendencies to illiteracy is completely disproved by the 100 years experience of the American public school system which shows that there are no substantial differences in the capacity of different groups to be educated and Americanized. (*Whom*, 1953, p. 95)

The report also contains less stirring language grounding the call for increased immigration in the need for more manpower to meet labor shortages and bolster national security. Nevertheless, these statements about literacy from the commission are noteworthy for the faith they place in American public schools to educate and "Americanize" in a period of Cold War anxiety. This faith would be reaffirmed by the Supreme Court in the decision of *Brown v. Board of Education,* one year later.

A Literate America

As I noted in chapter 1, and again in discussing Reagan's radio addresses, this faith in public education was not to endure. Lester Faigley (1992) reads in the decisive victories of Ronald Reagan in the presidential elections an indication of public abandonment of the idea of social equality and education for all. This public zeitgeist had a trickle down effect on the building of knowledge about literacy. Faigley has aptly characterized the 1980s as a decade in which published writing research, for example, took a decided turn away from radical or political scholarship. In part, he suggests that the near discipline-wide embrace of "the writing process" left writing scholars little, conceptually or rhetorically speaking, with which to confront escalating attacks on affirmative action and open admissions. But the political climate in the 1980s, Faigley argues, also tended to discourage scholars from exhibiting the zeal toward social issues characterizing scholarship in the early 1970s, unfavorable tenure decisions serving as one form of disincentive (p. 66). Central to the deployment of the political climate of the 1980s, I have offered, was the retroactive imagining of immigration as a time when people of all races from around the world were welcomed into the United States and given literacy as the key to the American dream. Such imaginings became the ideological root of attacks on multicultural education, dialect recognition, and bilingual education. In short, such imaginings fed the backlash against post–civil rights era attempts to combine literacy instruction with the goal of racial justice.

Making a connection between the conservative academic climate of the Reagan era and literacy scholarship, Geneva Smitherman (1999) points out that linguistic-cognitive deficit theories of African Americans reemerged during the 1980s.[14] Possibly such returns to essentially racist explanations for disparities in achievement between African Americans and Whites were indirectly facilitated by the inattention to racial discrimination in the 1980s that Faigley describes. Counter-explanations offered for disparities in achievement did not often draw on evidence of discrimination, but rather they would pick up the immigrant analogy so available in the public discourse. Such explanations attributed problems in academic achievement to clashes of cultural styles between the academy and incoming students, even, as Horner and Lu (1999) have observed, conceptualizing the newcomer to the academic environment as a "foreigner."

Horner and Lu's critique of the immigrant analogy echoes others. Arnetha Ball (1992), for example, challenges the analogizing of African Americans to other ethnic groups, arguing that "the experiences of many African Americans distinguish them from other ethnic groups, both culturally and linguistically" (p. 507). Ball points out that African Americans from the time of slave trade up through and after desegregation have faced language policies designed to prevent their acquisition of education and literacy on par with other ethnic groups. Carol Severino (1992) attacks the "melting pot" image charging, "The melting pot doesn't describe the experience of African-Americans, Native Americans, Hispanics, and Asians who, confronted with discrimination and prejudice, find "melting" difficult if not impossible" (p. 5).

Musgrave's much older (1971) critique of the immigrant analogy is the most telling, as it acknowledges not only that people of color have been treated differently but also that judgments about literacy are used to "race others." Unmasking the illusory role of literacy in securing the American dream, Musgrave argues the assumption that "SE [Standard English] is the only hurdle left for Blacks, then welcome into the great society is a flat lie" (p. 27). Further exposing the practice of racializing devalued dialects, she offers, "(For 'black' read Appalachian, Spanish-American, etc.)." Musgrave's parenthetical aside reveals how any deviation from a cultural norm is aggregated and raced "Black," a function Omi and Winant (1994) note as characteristic of ethnicity theory. Here, the norm is imagined to be Standard English, and any deviation from that norm is racialized and seen as evidence of illiteracy. Musgrave concludes that the conflicts between students and teachers are attributable to the greater climate of endemic racial discrimination. Cutting right to the chase, Musgrave entreats her audience, "If you have difficulty understanding a student, try to bring the reason to the surface. You might be reacting to his skin color" (p. 29). In Musgrave's analysis, the norm that must be confronted in American culture is not most importantly a standardized form of English but the fact of racism.

The field of literacy research in the 1990s has emerged from what Zeni and Thomas (1990) have termed "an obsession with the differentness of Black oral style" (p. 25); nevertheless notions of students as having a culture incompatible with school culture remain, and the predominant explanation for disparities in achievement is still seen to be a failure of assimilation. The voices of students, embedded in the literacy research reports of the past few decades, however, call into question the idea of education as uncomplicated assimilation undistorted by race. A student in Freedman and Calfee's (1984) study, for example, cites prejudice during a student-teacher conference about past experiences and current feelings about formal written language; of her failure to succeed in school she remarks, "As a whole I found that there is a lot of discrimination that's going on in the classroom" (p. 476). Sternglass (1974) documents an African American student's complaint about having to write in "standard white English." In an essay, a student in Zak's (1990) study writes, "I faced a lot of discrimination at the high school I attended," and cites as an example of discrimination receiving a note about "foul-mouthed, over-sexed, garishly-dressed Puerto-Ricans" (pp. 44–45). Dean (1989) records the words of one of his students who was writing an essay about the difference between university and home: "I was so upset about leaving home and coming to Davis. . . . My anger grew when I realized I was a minority at Davis. My whole town is Mexican and I never thought of prejudice until I came to Davis" (p. 32).

In thinking about the silences in the *Bakke* decision around the topic of racism, Dean's study is particularly illuminating because it documents the experience of being in the minority and encountering prejudice at the University of California at Davis. Significantly, this student was not introduced to the idea of racism in her first-year composition class; she encountered the fact of racism in the climate of the school. As many legal analysts have noted, the most flawed element of the record presented in *Bakke* was the lack of documentation of discrimination in California schools. As a result of this lack of documentation, race consciousness seems to be a post–civil rights phenomenon, an imposition into otherwise pure environments, even though the history of race conscious immigration restriction and race-based school assignment and segregation in California is lengthy. Dean also documents forms of racial discrimination that demonstrate how literacy continues to be conceived of as White property; he notes the "increasing incidents of hostility toward Asians (as reflected in bathroom graffiti 'Lower the curve: kill a chink')" (p. 34). This slur suggests that literacy is considered the possession of Whites whether racialized students are performing well on tests or not. Such details provide vital evidence against what are imagined to be merit based arguments that after a fixed period of remedy for past discrimination, discrimination will no longer be a problem, literacy itself serving as the ticket into "the great society," as Musgrave termed it back in 1971. The history I have outlined in this chapter on the contrary suggests that education could rightly encompass an investigation of how the American literate culture has been racialized in the American imagination as a primarily White one. An education truly suited to the project of creating informed citizens would involve understanding the history of this country as it is, not as we would have liked it to be; it would assess the impact of that history in the present and would imagine a more just society not based on nostalgic fantasies of past fairness but based firmly in accountability and acknowledgment. This may not be education as we know it today, yet a literate America requires nothing less.

5 ✦ LITERACY AND RACIAL JUSTICE IN PRACTICE: HIGH SCHOOL X

Ronald Reagan's protestations about the mixing of literacy and "minority issues," however motivated by fantasies of the American past, nevertheless indicated that education had in some ways changed since he was a boy. The late 1960s and early 1970s saw an explosion of alternatives in education—schools inspired by the civil rights movement, Vietnam War protests, and general parental and student dissatisfaction with the traditional public school system.[1] Many of these new schools represented attempts to make issues of racial justice a focus of instruction. Few schools, however, have gone as far in terms of striving to create "citizens free of prejudice" (as Reagan dubbed them) as the one I profile in this chapter, High School X. The study of this school will suggest possibilities for developing democratic education that has as a core principle acknowledging past and present social inequities and conflicts. Yet the difficulties and limitations involved in a school's efforts to address a legacy of discrimination while still being affected by it will be described here as well.

High School X is a public alternative secondary school that was established in 1971 and named after Malcolm X. High School X is of course not the school's real name. After I briefed the students of the classes I observed on the conventions of anonymity in research reports, they suggested that I call the school "High School X." They were aware, as I was, that the school's name was more than just a word that could be interchanged with any nonconnotative pseudonym like "River Valley High"; learning about Malcolm X is a requirement of every student at the school, so important is the figure of Malcolm X to the school's sense of itself. Yet while I can't talk about the school without mentioning its connection to Malcolm X, I have not compromised the school's anonymity for two reasons, both of which are pertinent to the following discussion. First, there are numerous schools named after Malcolm X throughout the country; this proliferation is another testament to the influence of the civil rights era on literacy institutions (however superficial that influence may be in some cases). Second, Malcolm X had several names, suggesting his various identifications with certain organizations and beliefs throughout his life.[2] For this reason, among others, Malcolm X has become one of the more flexible symbols of racial justice. His flexibility would emerge, as I will show, in the literacy practices of High School X's students as they tried to represent his life. The fault lines in post–civil rights movement era racial justice—tensions between integrationism and separatism as paths toward racial justice, and tensions between and among groups claiming the need for recognition and remedy—would emerge along with it.

High School X (HSX) has struggled throughout its history with these tensions. One of the very first pieces of printed matter describing HSX that I saw—and certainly one of the first that students see—is the cover of the HSX course timetable, the design of which suggests an opposition between HSX and traditional public schools. The traditional public school is represented by a rectangle containing fourteen identical plain "smiley" faces and one patterned "frowny" face; HSX is represented by a rectangle containing fifteen differently patterned smiley faces. Underneath is the question, "Can you appreciate the difference?" In this representation, the salient difference that makes a difference is that between institutions—HSX versus the traditional school—all other distinctions being conquered in that larger one, unranked, unnamed, and unmarked except that those other differences are implied to have something to do with visual representations and faces. Racial difference thus makes a coded appearance in this image. The image, though, also suggests a generic and ahistoric conception of difference and alterity, one that does not give an indication of the school's efforts to acknowledge historical conflicts. It does, however, suggest the post–civil rights era climate of racial justice as Gloria Ladson-Billings and William Tate (1995) describe it in the course of exploring the shortcomings of "the multicultural paradigm." Ladson-Billings and Tate suggest that the awareness of diversity has not led to productive discussion of growing tensions

> between and among various groups that gather under the umbrella of multiculturalism. . . . We assert that the ever-expanding multicultural paradigm follows the traditions of liberalism—allowing a proliferation of difference. Unfortunately, the tensions between and among these differences is rarely interrogated, presuming a "unity of difference"—that is, that all difference is both analogous and equivalent. (p. 62)

HSX was more ready to confront racism than most schools; an antidiscrimination course was required and further made redundant by the larger curriculum that focused on issues of racism frequently. And yet, through its history and into the present, the school would struggle between encouraging a proliferation of difference and exploring tensions between groups. HSX thus serves as one site to examine the ambiguities inherent in imagining literacy instruction in the service of racial justice today.

I entered HSX's history in 1996 first as a tutor, then as a researcher, assistant teacher, and general community member. Most of the data I present in this chapter were collected during that year I spent at the school (see table 5.1 for sources of data). In May 2000, however, I returned to HSX after a three-year absence and a move to a different part of the Midwest because I wanted to interview some of the key staff members involved in the school's development. When I went to meet the teacher I had worked with most, Lyla Holmes,[3] I was a little early, having arrived a few minutes before the end of the hour. Because HSX students don't have bells reminding them when to change classes, and don't have hall monitors or security guards keeping the halls absolutely devoid of student life between classes, I was only vaguely sure of being early. I stalled for time by going to the rest room and was virtually surrounded by student literacy practices; while washing my hands, I was looking at a sign reminding other students of how nice it is to have a clean rest room and of their responsibility for keeping it that way. A reflective piece of paper posted next to the hand dryer told me that I

Table 5.1

Data Sources and Research Activities

Date	Site or Source	Activities
November 1995–May 1996	Academic Study Skills class taught by Lyla	Became familiar with school, teachers, and students by tutoring in ASSC. Negotiated parameters of research with school staff.
September–October 1996	HSX I taught by Casey and Judith	Acting as participant-observer, took field notes daily of class activities and dialogue. Collected copies of assignments, photocopied written work submitted by students, photographed final projects, audiotaped one small group's final presentation. Interviewed teachers periodically.
	HSX II taught by Aiden and Lyla	Acting as participant-observer, took field notes daily of class activities and dialogue. Collected copies of assignments, photocopied written work submitted by students. Interviewed teachers periodically.
September 1996	Staff meeting	Acting as participant-observer, took field notes of activities and dialogue.
September 1996	School improvement planning meeting	Acting as participant-observer, took field notes of activities and dialogue.
November 1996–January 1997	New Visions taught by Casey	Acting as participant-observer, took field notes of class activities and dialogue. Audiotaped panel discussion of alternatives in education.
January–March 1997	Academic Study Skills class taught by Lyla	Conducted follow-up interviews and observations. Tutored in ASSC.
May 2000	Lyla, David	Follow-up interviews.

Note: ASSC = Academic Study Skills class.

was looking at the most common victim of rape, with a statistic that most rape victims are under age nineteen. (I was not the intended audience for this.) As I turned to go out the door, I noticed another poster announcing a course's engagement with a nonprofit organization, urging other students' participation. It reminded me of the first time I came to HSX, also near lunch hour, when students from the "Amnesty International" course were assembled in the cafeteria wearing placards urging fellow students to buy locally produced pizza for lunch instead of dictator-supporting corporate-chain pizza.

Even before I first stepped into HSX, I had suspected that this kind of evidence of critical and socially conscious literacy would abound, and that is why I went there in the first place. Its long-standing reputation in the district had preceded it. In fact, as well as in representation, HSX differs in many ways from traditional public schools. All courses are pass-fail. The school doesn't track by ability level or grade.[4] Student-teacher ratios tend to be smaller, about 10 to 1. In the classrooms, chairs are arranged in circles instead of rows. In the school lounge, students congregate between and sometimes during classes to relax, do work, or listen to music on one of many couches. Students are permitted to eat in the classes, go to the rest room without asking permission (though this privilege is sometimes taken away when it is perceived to have been abused), wear what they want, doodle while their instructors are talking. Music, either staff or student selected, is often played while students are working. Staff and students are on an entirely first-name basis. As traditional public schools become ever more marked by rules regulating student movement and dress, HSX is perhaps even more "alternative" now than it was when it first began.

HSX was founded first as a charter experimental program seeking to meet the needs of parents and students who were looking for alternatives in education. From an experimental program serving only juniors and seniors, it developed in a few years into an alternative public school, the fifth public secondary school of the district. Now students who elect to go to HSX tend to be students who, for whatever reason, feel uncomfortable in one of the city's other four traditional high schools. The reasons for discomfort tend to be varied. Some students may not have been achieving academically; others may be achieving academically but may express boredom with their school's curriculum or frustration with a curriculum exhibiting a lack of multiculturalism or lack of choice. Other students have suffered harassment at their home school and have come to HSX for its nonharassment policy. A significant percentage of the student body at any one time is pregnant or has children. Some students are out gays and lesbians. The school has at times had a reputation as a dumping ground for kids who are failing, but this reputation is not entirely accurate and represents an interesting construction: Those who are not comfortable or performing up to expectations in the traditional public school environment are those who failed it, rather than seeing the students as the ones the traditional school has failed. Part of the purpose of HSX seems to be to convince the students that this is a construction that doesn't serve them well.

After greeting Lyla, I sat on a couch next to her small desk to start setting up for the interview. Most of the students in Lyla's room sit on the couches arranged in a circle surrounded by desks and chairs. On my first day at HSX years before, I was sitting in one of those chairs as I was introduced along with several other tutors from the nearby university (all White-appearing[5] including myself) to the students in Lyla's Academic Study Skills class. Lyla, a self-identifying African American teacher, asked the students to welcome the tutors (we were called "JaGoras"—the Swahili word for guide) "from our community." An African American–appearing student looked up at us and said, "They ain't from *my* community."

Despite this inauspicious beginning, this particular student was a joy to work with, and a frequent commentator on the nature of community; reading Chinua Achebe's *Things Fall Apart* for his "Africa" class, he commented, "Man, these people eat a lot of goddamn yams!" But his drawing a distinction between the community he understood himself to be in and the community he saw the tutors as being in interested me, because HSX was invested in unifying itself as one community of those present—teachers, students, tutors, and staff.[6] Lyla corrected him. That was the spring of 1996. In the fall of 1996, I was back in HSX with the intent of studying constructions of community and student investments in the school through its only two required courses, High School X Experience I (HSX I) and High School X Experience II[7] (HSX II) (recently renamed Mirrors of Discrimination), and, the subsequent quarter, through New Visions, the course on school reform, which also functions as the student government for the school.[8] Concerned as they are with explicit teaching of alternatives in education, conflict resolution, and histories of racial discrimination, these courses are rare curricular tools in a secondary school. They presented an opportunity to see how attempts to promote racial and social justice were realized through pedagogical literacy projects in one site of school-sponsored literacy development. These courses, at least in part, redefined literacy as including the pursuit of racial justice.

A Course in Racial Justice

HSX's entire curriculum reflects its community building efforts through study of historically disenfranchised groups and critique of American domestic and foreign policy. Courses like "Native American History," "The Juvenile Justice System" (a look at why it's not working [popular with the HSX students who have experienced it]), and "Chicks, Babes, Broads . . . NOT! (An exploration of women's issues in American Society)" reflect student and staff interests. The "Chicks" class, for example, was proposed by a student and co-taught by that student and one of the staff. Having students guide the curriculum is one way the school tries to encourage students to take ownership of their learning. These courses and others are taught periodically, however, unlike HSX I and II and New Visions (the courses I observed), which are taught continually and are devoted explicitly to maintaining the school as a community. All incoming students take HSX I, which is designed to introduce them to the school. All students take HSX II before they can graduate. New Visions had been recently created as part of the staff's efforts to bring back student involvement in the school's direction, which had all but disappeared in the school's middle years, roughly the 1980s, according to David Gregory, one of the founders of the school and a math teacher.[9] The subject matter of the course is educational policy and whatever needs attention at HSX, whether litter or harassment problems or school trips. Students can take New Visions repeatedly, but they must be in the school for at least one quarter before they take it. These three courses are all mechanisms to support the school's anti-harassment policy, a centerpiece of the school's purpose, ensconced in HSX's mission statement, which defines HSX's attempt "to create a harassment-free learning environment where all people, regardless of previous academic performance, family background, socioeconomic status, beliefs, abilities, appearance, race, gender, or sexual orientation are respected." While I knew these courses were important to how HSX defined itself, I knew little of their history before observing them or after, until my interviews in 2000 with Lyla and David Gregory. Through talking with these two pivotal figures in the school's history, I came to see the courses as social artifacts not only of the school's development but also of unresolved civil rights and post–civil rights era tensions over how to put racial justice into practice.

I asked Lyla about HSX II, the antidiscrimination course she was instrumental in creating. The course description at the time I observed the class read:

> This required antidiscrimination class goes hand in hand with our non-harassment policy and is a central part of the [HSX] philosophy. In this class we will address the complicated and emotional issues of racism, sexism and homophobia in our society. The course is divided into five units: first we will look at our own backgrounds and beliefs in the hope of recognizing and celebrating our many differences. Then we will study the history and culture of four groups in our society. . . . For each group studied we will bring in guest speakers from the community.[10]

As the course description suggests, racial justice isn't the only item on the agenda; sexism and homophobia are treated as well. Such was not always the case. HSX II developed from a course entitled "Malcolm Shabazz X. The Man and His Times," which Lyla had taught a few years after she joined the school. This course, which focuses specifically on the civil rights struggle and racism, was one in which Lyla was personally invested. Lyla was born in Mississippi in 1949 during an era in which, as she put it, there were only a few professions open to African Americans—teaching, social work, and preaching, and preaching was out because she was female. She felt that teaching was the obvious choice because she enjoyed public speaking and because her family of landowning farmers had always stressed the importance of education and self-determination.

> We didn't stay home to work for Mr. Charlie, which is what I call the local White folks in the area, at the exclusion of our education. We were also landowners, and if you were Black and you owned land, you could chart your own course as to what you wanted to do in terms of your work, in terms of the education of your children and so forth. And that's what we did.

As Lyla indicates, property ownership was linked to owning one's education, yet her efforts to own that education were challenged by half-hearted attempts at desegregation in her school district. Up until the last year and a half of high school, Lyla was educated in all African American schools within a segregated school system. In January of 1966—a full eleven years after "with all deliberate speed"—she and her cousins became some of the first to integrate the local formerly all-White high school. Everything in this integrated school, however, was segregated except sitting in classrooms, and even in classrooms, there were attempts to get the students to sit in certain sections. The African American students, therefore, took segregated busing to an integrated school with segregated rest rooms and segregated seating in the cafeteria. Lyla remembers the cafeteria's seating arrangements as particularly public and humiliating. She wrote to the U.S. Justice Department about the situation and representatives were sent to the school to investigate:

> We had this big meeting, and they had them get rid of all these segregated things within the school. We even had a separate Black study hall. I remember very well the principal said: "Why now, [Lyla], I guess you're happy now because you can't have your fun in that room, throwing stuff out the window and enjoying yourself up in that special study hall." I said, "Sir, I think I can handle that."

Integrating the cafeteria, however, proved to require teamwork on the part of the African American students as they fought to counter dining hall White flight:

> I directed the students to sit at separate tables. There were like eight of us and there were only like nine tables in the cafeteria. So we'd sit at a table and they would fly like white birds, running from us. But they didn't have nowhere to sit because we had all the tables covered. Then they stopped running.

Lyla joined HSX in 1982 after she had been, as she put it, "surplussed" at one of the city's main traditional high schools where her teaching career had begun in 1972. At the traditional high school, she had been the only African American woman in a department of White men. According to Lyla, the then principal of HSX had heard that Lyla had a reputation among the other principals of the district as "a loud-mouthed Black woman" and recruited her. Although worried about the school's reputation at that point in time as a dumping ground, Lyla was lured by the open curriculum, which would allow her to teach whatever social studies classes she or the students wanted. Lyla said that the students in her "Malcolm Shabazz X: The Man and His Times" class felt that the material of that particular course was significant for HSX's anti-harassment mission. She recalled that the students said that even though HSX had a policy of anti-harassment, there was still discrimination and harassment at the school, for example, name-calling in the hallways or the occasional swastika scribbled on the wall. The students felt the class should be mandatory and took that suggestion to the staff. A mandatory class of any kind was a big step considering that HSX had a tradition of few rules and a flexible curriculum, yet the staff agreed that an antidiscrimination class should be required, and Lyla, David Gregory, and an English teacher no longer working with the school began to design the course. Making the course a requirement, however, led to philosophical differences between Lyla and the English teacher about what constituted an antidiscrimination course. As Lyla describes her position during the controversy:

> It was along the lines of: This is not just another feel-good class where we've come to study literature, okay? This is a class where we will seriously look at the issue of race and racism and homophobia and how each of us has been impacted by it and what we have seriously done about it, or failed to do about it—that social class, having a focus such as that, where you looked at self, where you analyze self, and you did that through many group activities in the class—triads and dyads and guest speakers coming in to share their stories and trying to walk a mile in their shoes and so forth—until we do, and at such time that we do those types of things in the class, we cannot call it an antidiscrimination class.

The philosophical differences eventually were resolved in Lyla's favor, and the course became a requirement of the social nature Lyla suggested, emphasizing nonfiction texts over literary texts. This course, developed during Ronald Reagan's presidency, directly confronted the myth of America's immigration history that Reagan had promoted. The first piece of written material handed to the students of HSX II the quarter I observed it read: "In this class we reject the notion that our society is a 'Melting Pot.'" The class work began with investigation of each student's own sense of identity and experiences with discrimination. Students were invited to draw their conceptions of their identity in pie-chart form, considering "gender, racial heritage, sibling status, son/daughter, religious beliefs, dating status, economic status, political beliefs, athletic interests, mother/father and others of importance to you." The sample chart on the handout divides the pie into Jewish, son, sixteen, male. Aiden (self-identified European American), who co-taught the course with Lyla, explained that identity was complex and shifting. He demonstrated his pie chart on the board and offered that a section devoted to being a father had been added in the last year, and as a result, the section devoted to work had shrunk, as his time priorities had shifted. A few days later students were asked to make "ancestral" charts in some creative form. They were given readings on different ethnicities to complement the charts. Although the pie charts portray identity as a complex of social interests, the class moves from this point on into a discussion of specifically ethnic culture and conflict (except for a short section on gay rights at the end, which many students wrote in their evaluations felt less complete).

After the unit on exploring self, HSX II students began exploring history with an emphasis on racial oppression. The building of America was discussed primarily and not secondarily as a history of subordination of people of color, from Columbus's subjugation of the indigenous people he encountered, to the Trail of Tears, up to the present use of Native American mascots by sports teams. Students uncovered the myths propagated by the media about people of color's acts of resistance to this subordination; for example, students learned that Rosa Parks, far from being an elderly lady acting on impulse when refusing to sit at the back of the bus, as has been popularly portrayed in history textbooks, was a member of the NAACP and part of an organized and long-standing resistance movement in the area. They read a poem by Richard Olivas entitled "I'm Sitting in My History Class," which asks, "If George Washington's my father / Why wasn't he Chicano?" They watched a video about the Southern Poverty Law Center. They read and discussed Peggy McIntosh's (1990) essay "White Privilege: Unpacking the Invisible Knapsack," which lists the privileges Whites can take for granted and defines racism not as a matter of "individual acts of meanness" but rather as a system giving Whites dominance (p. 31).

After this section, a more celebratory look at European Americans began with a discussion of the Freedom Riders of the civil rights movement, who worked to integrate interstate bus terminals in the South. Lyla gave some background on the Freedom Riders and talked of her experience in Freedom School when she was sixteen. The students were shown a clip from the film *Mississippi Burning* and then read "My Son Didn't Die in Vain," written by the mother of Andrew Goodman, one of the three civil rights workers killed in Mississippi. Afterwards they were asked to write responses on a work sheet to open-ended questions about the reading, to define their values and discuss any occasion where they were forced to defend those values. They were also asked to assess the impact of the civil rights movement by the question, "In your opinion have developments in Civil Rights since 1964 fulfilled or disappointed Ms. Goodman's hope that good would come from Andrew's death? Explain."[11]

The next day of the European American unit, two of the teachers discussed the traditional celebration of poet Robert Burns's night in Scotland. One of the students (White-appearing) challenged this lesson asking, "Why are we learning about this?" Despite what the course description suggested about the emotional and complicated issues involved in the curriculum, this was actually the only open dissension I witnessed during the class; possibly the objection to the Burns lesson arose because it strayed from the usual practice the class had established of exploring cultural clashes and political movements in the United States. Throughout the quarter that I watched the class, I observed that many of the students seemed interested, but also carried an air of knowing much of this already. One student, in answer to the question on the evaluation form at the end of class of whether his views had been changed, wrote that he'd been at the school too long for this class to have had any particular impact. Another student (self-identifying in the class as one-quarter African American, one-quarter White, one-quarter Latino, and one-quarter Native American) wrote, "Well to tell you honestly I knew about 90% of all the material that was went over in class already." Another student suggested the course could be improved by bringing "the study of Native America closer to home" and listed tribes around the region closer to home than the far-off Cherokee the class had studied. These tribes in fact had whole courses devoted to them at HSX. It seemed that the larger curriculum of the school, multicultural throughout, had made this course redundant by the time many of the students took it.

I noticed, however, that although many of the students in this class seemed already absorbed into the High School X community, others were not to remain long. In the first week that I observed HSX II, I sat next to a student (White-appearing) who was picking at a design he had carved into his arm the night before. Each line of this design was about a quarter of an inch thick, and I could smell his flesh from where I was sitting. When asked by the teacher what his experience with discrimination was, he offered that people mistook him for a skinhead. When asked how he dealt with that, he said he beats them up. He dropped out inside of a week. At the end of that hour, another student (self-identifying as Jewish) was asked by a fellow student what she would do now that her parents have been arrested "again"; she listed the friends she could stay with. She dropped out within two weeks. Although I spotted both of these students in town periodically, I didn't see them at HSX again that semester. Even though most of the original students who began the course with me were still there at the end, attendance fluctuated quite a bit. Because the course was not required during the first nine weeks that a student was at the school, one could be in the HSX community for a period of time and not have taken the class, it seemed. This was not so with High School X Experience I.

The Making of a School

Every student entering HSX takes HSX I in his or her first quarter. HSX I also came about in the 1980s and is, even more than HSX II, explicitly designed to create community at the school, in part around the figure of Malcolm X. The course description reads: "This course introduces new students to the theory and realities of HSX as an alternative school. Units of study include: Community building, policies and procedures, conflict management, a study of education, and the life and times of Malcolm X." To understand the purpose behind HSX I, and why learning about Malcolm X plays such a role in orienting people in the school, it is again helpful to know something of the school's history. Like HSX II, HSX I was designed to improve implementation of the school's anti-harassment policy, and like HSX II, it is a social artifact of influences of the civil rights movement, though its relationship to those influences is more mediated. David Gregory suggested that the school, in designing both courses as requirements, was "just trying to make [the anti-harassment policy] work on a regular basis and trying to figure out ways to best make it work." David recalled that the policy itself was something the students pushed for early in the school's existence. That the students took the initiative in this case was not unusual. Students helped determine a great deal of the school's functioning—hiring staff, advising on admissions, determining curriculum—and were even instrumental in generating enthusiasm for the school's existence.

David recalled that although the original impetus for the school came from elements of the community, including students looking for alternatives in education, the actual paperwork involved in starting the school was put together by a professor in the nearby university who wanted to use part of a university grant to run an experimental high school program. In 1970, the professor approached a less than enthusiastic school board for approval. David suggested that the board approved the program only because they thought it wouldn't succeed; they had been under pressure from students and parents to provide alternatives in education that they didn't want to provide and were therefore looking for an alternative school to fail:

> [The professor] went to the school board and said, "Look, you have agitation from parents and students to create an alternative high school. I have funding from the Ford Foundation. They'll fund this program in total for two years, or if you want to do it partly, to fund it over a period of time, they'll work with you that way with the same amount of money. But you need to administer the program." The school board agreed, and I believe at the time the feeling was, here's an easy way to do this. We don't have to put out any money, and it'll fail, and then we can say we tried. But it won't have cost us anything. This happened in the fall of 1970. I think they accepted it all in October, or maybe early November. But that just gave you very little time because the start-up was supposed to be at the beginning of the second semester.

With two months to prepare, the most racially diverse staff in the district was assembled and volunteers were recruited like David (White-appearing), then a graduate student in educational policy who worked at the university's Drug Information Center. A lottery was held to determine which of the almost three hundred students who applied would take up the seventy slots the school had available. The staff made a concerted effort even at this early point to strive for an integrated and racially balanced student body. As David recalls:

> [W]e attempted a half and half racial balance. But in fact I don't think we had enough applicants from minority communities to get to half. So we ended up taking all the minority students who applied. I think there were maybe about 20 to 25 at the time, and then the rest of the students were chosen strictly by lottery.

Many of the students who did not make the cut kept showing up to classes anyway, rather than go to their traditional school. Slowly the school was allowed to expand its student base.

David acknowledges that getting and maintaining racial balance of the student body was difficult: "We couldn't get the Black community to actively support us. . . . We never had quite the numbers that we wanted." The staff asked the first group of African American students at the school what was missing from the traditional schools and what they wanted at HSX. What they wanted was a room of their own, in terms of a Black Studies Center, but also in terms of curriculum. They wanted a focus on Black history. David recalls that this posed a "difficulty" initially but that the school was able to accommodate the requests:

> They said, "There's nothing that applies to us in those schools. There are no programs that deal with Black history; we feel like we're not there, that we don't exist. We don't have spaces to ourselves." It was a difficulty, because we had this general community room, but they wanted a place that they could call a Black Studies Center, so one of the social studies rooms actually became a place where they just regularly hung out together. And they wanted courses that applied to them directly. So we created a curriculum, created as many Black studies opportunities as we could.

A December 1972 booklet discussing High School X's program of study describes the Black Interdisciplinary Program. The booklet argues that the program is necessary because Black students in questionnaires and interviews had expressed feelings that their needs were not being met at any of the city's schools. These needs could not be satisfied in other ways because "the absence of specific courses related to Afro-Americans or Africans tends to perpetuate institutional racism. The failure of a school to address itself meaningfully to BLACKNESS is the point which evokes criticism."[12] Vestiges of the psychological rhetoric informing the *Brown* decision and the civil rights movement as a whole seem to be present in the description of the purpose of the program—to develop "psychologically healthy human beings"—yet in a Malcolm X-ian reversal of the logic of *Brown*, psychological health is seen to be the outcome of separate rather than integrated education. The booklet reads:

> [B]efore we can develop to this state of civilization, we must redefine the Black man in a psychologically healthy framework so that other

human beings—white, yellow, or red—are able to relate to a healthy, self-defined being. In other words, before we can relate to others about us, we must learn to relate to ourselves.

By this time, the students had chosen to name the school after Malcolm X, having considered and rejected a few other options, including naming the school after a member of the Black Panthers who had just been shot by police, or—a more abstract homage to alterity—naming the school after a character in a comic, Olio, who has a round head and lives in a land of points. Although the school as a whole was to be named after Malcolm X, the separate institutional space for Black students was not to last more than a couple of years, replaced eventually by the anti-harassment policy. As David described the end of the Black studies program:

> The aim and intention of the school as a whole is to integrate everybody and to meet those needs in terms of Black studies, but not to have people separated off into different rooms. We worked hard at—within a year or two the students came up with the idea of an anti-harassment policy, and that helped us to start bringing people together in a more significant way.

As David's comments suggest, the anti-harassment policy was an integration-oriented measure, part of a struggle to provide an environment that met the needs of everyone, superseding the need for separatism in a school whose aim was integration. Nonetheless, maintaining racial balance in the school population remained difficult as the number of students of color dwindled for many years, even though HSX retained a more racially diverse (though majority White) staff than any other school in the district and was the first school "not named after a White man or a point on the compass," David observed. While not sure exactly why HSX could not entice greater participation from the African American community, David suggested that the legacy of segregated education in the nation made an alternative school less appealing to those who were trying to assert their presence in the mainstream: "[T]hey felt that it was important that they be accepted in the regular high schools." Yet for some of the students of color who came to HSX the year I was there, the problem seemed to be that the school wasn't alternative enough. Despite the anti-harassment policy, the name of the school, and the multicultural curriculum, there still seemed to be a desire on the part of the African American students in the HSX I class that I observed to have their own institutional space. There were some issues of alterity, in other words, that the anti-harassment policy did not completely resolve.

The fall of 1996 at High School X was, as principal Mike Dean (White-appearing) described it in retrospect to New Visions, "a very hot quarter. There was a lot of conflict." He was referring mostly to a couple of visible expulsions that took place that quarter—one for weapons carrying and another for racist remarks. Less dramatic but nonetheless telling conflicts were evident in HSX I, however. Conflicts were in many ways overt—as one student commented anonymously to the teacher on the final evaluation form, "This class was hard because there were a lot of disruptive students, but you did a good job despite the problems." But conflict was also manifested in the literacy practices of the students. The spoken and written work of the class gave students opportunities to identify with their new school and with the school's namesake, Malcolm X. The literacy practices of the students in the class demonstrate how these opportunities were received, embraced, or rejected. Given the school's close identification with a figure whose position vis-à-vis what constituted the best path to racial justice was shifting, the literacy practices of the students also reveal much about the cultural milieu of the post-civil rights era. In 1996, the commodification of Malcolm X was at an all-time high with the recent release of Spike Lee's film *Malcolm X*. Baseball caps with X's on them were everywhere, and anyone could claim Malcolm X as a role model. The fluidity of Malcolm X's meaning sparked conflict in HSX I as Malcolm became for many students, but not all, removed from historical context and put in the context of the school. Discussion of this conflict and students' representations of Malcolm X serve as a starting point to address the nature of history and multiculturalism in the post–civil rights era.

This study also reveals the effects of delayed racial justice on the practice of literacy research. As a participant-observer, I was in no way exempt from the conflict, and I learned much about the limitations the racially identifiable body places on research. Although Casey and Judith (identifying as European American) were the two main teachers of the HSX I class, I counted in many ways as another teacher. I had been a JaGora with the school the spring before, so I continued to fulfill many of the roles I had been fulfilling previously. My engagement was welcomed and encouraged by

the staff; it is part of the school's ethos (and one of its main sur-
vival strategies) to make use of whatever resources are in its midst.
Accordingly, during my time observing at High School X, I did the
following: completed assignments; helped teachers in classes; tutored students; recruited tutors; helped train tutors; traded teaching ideas with staff; sat in on staff training; joined staff, students,
parents, and social work interns on one of the school improvement
planning committees; helped the school with its publicity efforts;
drove a neighboring student to school. I was so thoroughly confused
with actual staff that students generally asked me for instructions
or for permission to leave the classroom. I am not sure in retrospect
how much this actually helped me to observe literacy practices at
the school, as frequently I was unable to write down what was happening because I was so much a part of what was happening. On
the other hand, in working closely with individual students in classrooms, or serving as a tutor in the Academic Study Skills class, I
got to know more about students and their literacy practices than
I would have otherwise. I worked with one sixteen-year-old White-
appearing woman with a young son, for example, and noted that
although she rushed through her biology homework, she read all
the library resources on teen parenting between classes. She was one
of many students who challenge the presumption that literacy practices observable within classrooms are adequate evidence of the
extent of a person's uses of literacy.

I believed initially, as Daniel Jorgensen (1989) has argued, that
being a participant-observer allows one to be less obtrusive. As I
discovered, however, some students found me more obtrusive than
others, whether I was participating or observing. To the degree to
which I was allowed to wander freely in the "school" community,
there was also a degree to which I was not always allowed free access to the group of African American students in HSX I. I spent more
time with them, particularly in Lyla's Academic Study Skills class
(which immediately followed HSX I); in the study skills class, for
example, I worked closely with Calvin, a self-identified African
American student, helping him read *The Color Purple*. But an indication that there would be disparities in data I could collect sur-
faced before any of the students knew me personally. In the first
few days of my observations, when students had had almost no
interaction with me yet past seeing me—a young (relative to their
teachers), White female—in their classroom, I discovered that three

out of the five African American students who had agreed to be in the study and to let me write down information on them and their work had declined to sign the portion of the permission form allowing me to audiotape them, while none of the White students in the study had so declined.

I have read several ethnographies of literacy practices that have acknowledged the constraints that gender places on collection of data.[13] I would say, echoing those observations, that I experienced slightly more ease of interaction with female staff and students. Yet probably not enough is said about how racial difference both constrains and enables data collection and analysis. I was conducting this study two years after *The Bell Curve* was published and followed by very public discussion of intelligence and literacy achievement along racial lines. Deficit models to explain African American students' achievement in school were freshly in the air, not that they had ever been definitely put to rest in the minds of many Americans. I felt their presence in my permission forms.

High School X I

The quarter that I observed HSX I, there were twenty-four students in the class, nineteen appearing or identifying as European American and five appearing or identifying as African American.[14] This was an unusually large class for High School X, a school with only 150 students overall.[15] On the first day of HSX I, Casey greeted the students and told them how glad the staff was that the students chose to come. She emphasized that it was a choice they made. The students' first task (and first verbal input) was to introduce themselves, say something about themselves, and say why they came. Almost all students responded to the "why they came" portion of the question by declaring their hatred for their old school. The building of solidarity and student investment in the school, crucial in an alternative school where turnover is high, thus began early and continued throughout the first week. On the second day of class, students watched a news-station-produced documentary about High School X that I had seen years before on TV. Its coverage of the school was structured around a typically TV news-style dichotomous question: HSX—dumping ground or creative learning environment? In the documentary, student testimonies attest to discontent with traditional school settings, interestingly the same discontents the HSX I students in the class I observed had just expressed. One student in the documentary confessed that she had spent all her time in her old traditional school getting high, but at HSX she was aided by a "Stay Straight" support group and was on the road to graduation. In HSX I, the new students were asked to respond in writing to the documentary by answering the following questions: What do you expect from HSX? What do you expect from yourself at HSX? Casey explained that one of the other classes was planning to do an updated documentary of the school, and added an additional question: What would you like to see in such a documentary? Student answers gave me an opportunity to observe who would profess immediate comfort with the new surroundings. A few students demonstrated their familiarity with the school's ethos and identified with the school in their writing. Don, a self-identified White student (on the first day of class, when asked to say something that would identify him particularly, he said, "I'm White") and one of the two seniors in the class, was one of the first to conflate his identity with HSX. He made this suggestion for the new documentary: "Maybe a few profiles, a compare and contrast to other schools, and then a large battle scene in which every student of [HSX] is put into an epic struggle against [his old public school's] students. I know we'd win." Don's old high school, located in the most affluent section of the city, was considered to be the most academically accelerated school in the state. Don appeared to be academically accelerated in his own right. On the reading survey students filled out in the early days of class, he listed *Gödel, Escher, Bach* as the last book he enjoyed reading. He was soft-spoken and dressed like many other HSX students—in a hooded sweatshirt, cap, and loose-fitting pants.

Janice, a White-appearing and self-identified lesbian student, was another early identifier with the school. In the first diagnostic writing assignment in HSX I, she chose to write about violence in her old school:

> I was already in E.D. [educational disability] classes and that's something that I kind of expected. . . . Plus I know someone that got stabbed thair a couple years ago. And I don't wanna have to worry about that happen to me someday. . . . I didn't want to be a drop out and be a nobody. So I set up a interview for HSX. And at that interview thay told me that I had a 99.9 chance of getting into HSX. So that's were I told myself were I had to go, and that's were I am today. I like a lote better than [my old school].

Janice wasn't always as compliant and academically motivated a student as Don. I was sitting next to her when she declined to take one of the many handouts passed out by the teachers in those early weeks. As Casey attempted to give Janice the piece of paper, Janice said, "Get that the fuck away from me!" The next day she spontaneously apologized. She'd been trying to quit smoking, she explained. She hadn't been penalized for the outburst. I found that the teachers at HSX try to give students space if they seem emotionally unable to work on any particular day. "I used to take them home," Casey said of students whose home circumstances were overwhelmingly difficult.[16] Janice, who generally wore a leather jacket and jeans, had identified herself on the first day of class as "sensitive, loving, strong inside, short, silly." Despite having different academic histories, both Janice and Don identified with the school early, and both could be seen to strengthen that identification as the quarter progressed.

This could not be said of Lenny, one of the minority of African American students, perhaps the student who was recognized by the staff and many of his classmates as being the most bright of all the new students. "Extremely bright" was the first thing Lyla said about him when I asked her years later what had happened to him. Lenny stuck out among all students at HSX because I never saw him wear a pair of jeans. He always wore neat, almost pressed, warm-up gear. Soft-spoken, with a look on his face Lyla later described as "haunting," Lenny didn't say much about HSX—complimentary or not—in the first couple of weeks and kept writing to a minimum.[17] At the end of the first unit, however, when Casey introduced the class to the major project of the course—learning and teaching the life of Malcolm X—Lenny distinguished himself as the Malcolm expert by giving a fifteen-minute speech about Malcolm X's life, virtually by memory; he was holding note cards, but he rarely looked at them. The speech contained mostly the facts of Malcolm X's life, though Lenny did editorialize at one point, noting that it was interesting that the FBI didn't have a file on Malcolm X when he was a criminal but started one when he joined the Nation of Islam. Referring to Malcolm's eventual turn away from the Nation, Lenny said: "I look up to him, and I respect him, but a lot of stuff he did at the end I just don't understand." Lenny had not in this speech made references to the new school and how he expected to feel comfortable there. By the time Lenny gave this speech, two weeks into the quarter, all the African American students but one were sitting on the direct opposite end of the room from the teachers, where they remained for the duration of the quarter, and relations between them and the staff would shortly begin to degrade.

With that speech, Lenny had completed some but not all of the Malcolm X project, the major project of the course. Two days after his speech, on September 13, Casey explained the rationale for studying Malcolm X, giving some history of the school: "The students named the school after him for reasons they felt strongly about and we kept those names all these years. We want you to know something about his life." The students needed to know four things about Malcolm X: his basic biographical data and the important details of his life and times, the stages of his life, his beliefs, and why the school was named for him. The students were asked to choose to do one of the following with the information they had collected: make connections between Malcolm's life and their own, explain why Malcolm was so threatening in his own time to both Blacks and Whites, or explain why Malcolm matters today. Casey told the class that they had options as to how to demonstrate this knowledge: "We talk a lot about different learning styles and we decided we should practice what we preach." To illustrate the range of ways students had previously approached this project, Casey showed a collage of fabric swatches a student from a previous HSX I class had put together demonstrating the stages of Malcolm's life. She passed around a board game and a tape of music other students had made. Although the project allowed students many options as to how they might demonstrate their knowledge, everyone in the end had to teach the sixth graders who share the building with HSX about Malcolm X.[18] For extra credit, students could read *The Autobiography of Malcolm X* by Alex Haley and answer a series of work sheet questions on each chapter. Casey tells the class that they used to have everyone read the book, "but not everyone can read it. It's at an 11th grade reading level." Lenny, a tenth grader, has no problem taking this option and for the next few weeks tried to help Calvin get the extra credit as well.

Later in the week, the class began their review of the school's anti-harassment policy, attendance policy, and alcohol and drug policy, all of which contain information regarding the terms under which students are allowed to remain at HSX. Much time was devoted to the anti-harassment policy, which protects students from harassment not only on the basis of race, gender, class, religion, and sexual orientation but also on the basis of clothing and political beliefs. Students were trained in conflict resolution and given scenarios that put them in the position of judging infringements of the anti-harassment policy. Ironically, on September 18, most of the way through the unit on conflict resolution headed by Judith, the school social worker, conflict in HSX I between staff and students began. During the opening segment of this class period, Judith and Casey stopped class repeatedly to address the constant discussion going on across the room where Ginger (White appearing) and Shirley, Calvin, Lenny, and Georgia (identifying African American) were sitting. Some of these students left in the middle of class. Casey went into the hall to address them as they returned. Judith said that they might have to go to assigned seating if the disruptions continued, apparently hoping to break up the block of students causing the disruptions.

The next day Casey resumed discussing the options for the Malcolm X project. Students were told they could write a paper or write and perform a play based on his life. "For those of you into mythology, you can write a hero's tale because I think his life lends itself to mythology," she offered. She suggested that general information about Malcolm X could be gotten from several books in the library and from the recent movie directed by Spike Lee. Recognizing Lenny's expertise, she added, "You can use Lenny as a resource." Casey then introduced a unit on education, which would culminate in having students design their ideal school. She gave a short lecture on educational history, pointing out that all the African American students in the class could have been put to death if she taught them to read one hundred years ago in certain areas.[19] She asked Georgia to make sure she didn't talk for more than fifteen minutes. After class she told me that that was a trick she had learned—to choose the most disruptive student in class to tell you when to shut up so that that student stays focused. Both teachers had acknowledged Georgia as a disturbance at this point.

After the lecture, Casey told the students to get into small groups and begin planning how they would teach the sixth graders about Malcolm X. I observed a group of White-appearing students, Justine, Adam, and Dawna:

> *Adam:* Just teach them how to meditate.
> *Justine:* Do yoga.
> *Adam:* They have to contort themselves into Xs.

Justine: Is this just about Malcolm X or anything?

Adam: Talk about the stuff he did. Ask them how it relates to their life. . . .

Justine: How about a Frisbee with a face on it?

Adam: Every time you have to catch a Frisbee, you have to say something about his life.

Dawna: And yourself.

Justine: Shit. So what are we doing?

Adam: The Frisbee thing.

Dawna: I still like the meditation thing.

[The class at this point is moving toward share-outs and this group struggles quietly to figure out what to say.]

Dawna: Talk about the problems Malcolm X faced and ask them if they face the same problems now.

Adam: Somehow she managed to turn all the bullshit we were talking about into something real.

As I mentioned earlier, Malcolm X had become in the mid-1990s one of the more flexible and commodified symbols of racial justice in the culture. The conversation here is noteworthy because it enacted that flexibility and commodification as students discussed not what Malcolm X ever said but what shape he can be made to take, including the placement of his image on sellable products. At this point, they really were working with form, having little idea of the content of Malcolm X's life or times. The "something real" that they settled on, talking about the problems Malcolm X faced, would have to be filled in later when they knew what those problems were.

In a September 30 discussion of a Carl Sagan essay denouncing school's relevance, the conflicts between staff and students in HSX I continued and became more overt. Judith wanted the students to read the essay aloud. Lenny asked, "Can we read in small groups or by ourselves?" Adam echoed, "Can't we just read it to ourselves?" Judith said, "You know, because of people's different learning styles, it helps some people to read out loud." Ginger, Shirley, Calvin, and Georgia all left briefly. During the discussion of the relevance of school, Lenny commented, "In school they don't teach you real life. Like they don't want to talk about Black English." The teachers agreed with him. Later he got up to leave the room and was followed by others. Judith told them as they were leaving, "I'm going to start marking you absent or tardy. This is ridiculous. You choose. Would you like to be marked absent or tardy?" Everyone said "tardy." The exasperation of both students and staff was palpable.

On October 1, students began planning their ideal high school. I observed Lenny, Shirley, and Calvin, who sat on couches in the lounge with the radio on as they worked. As had become the norm, Lenny took the lead, guided by the assignment work sheet.

Lenny: Is it big or little? What time you go to school?
Shirley: 12 until 2.
Calvin: Man, no one's going to learn nothing.
Lenny: Yeah, but from 1–6 you work and get paid. . . . Okay 12 until 2 is too short.
Shirley: Okay. 11–2.
Calvin: I know that whole song.
Lenny: So do I. Stuff will be available all the time. You'd have to be under the age of 45.
Shirley: No.
Lenny: Huh?
Shirley: Thirty.
Lenny: Alright. Calvin, is 30 alright? The minute you turn 31 you're fired. Could anyone go to the school?
Shirley: Yeah.
Calvin: Hell no, you gotta go through an interview, too.
Shirley: Calvin, shut up.
Calvin: Lenny, let me take a look at that thing.
Lenny: 12–2 is too short, realistically.
Calvin: Some kids gotta eat lunch.
Lenny: 13 don't need to be coming up in no school with no 18 year olds. They'll start smoking. . . .
Lenny: [reading from the assignment sheet]. What would the physical environment be like. There'd be couches, no desks.
Calvin: You can smoke herb outside but not in the school.
Shirley: Why not?
Calvin: Cause if you smoking inside, everyone be wanting some. I don't know, Len, we're going to need security guards.
Lenny: We want computers.
Calvin: Every person got a computer.
Lenny: Heating, air-conditioning.
Calvin: We got a study room.

As Lenny, Calvin, and Shirley were deep within invention, generating ideas for the ideal school in terms of what they would like, Lenny, working to construct a more traditional kind of school than Calvin and Shirley had in mind, worried that students would start smoking or wouldn't get enough of an education. There are shades of High School X's influence peeking through this discussion. When Calvin suggested that students go through an interview (as they had, to get into HSX), Shirley dismissed the suggestion. The next day, Shirley, Calvin, Lenny, and Georgia were seemingly less focused on the assignment while working in small groups. When Casey went over to ask them what was wrong, she heard from Calvin and Georgia that HSX was not their ideal school:

Calvin: This school is boring.
Casey: More than other schools?
Calvin: We need more people here.
Georgia: More Black people.

Casey's response, characteristic of the school's ethos, was to encourage the students to take responsibility for the environment. She said, "You gotta go out and tell all your friends." Later in the hour, I was filling in for Casey, who was working with other groups in the lounge. She left me with the task of keeping an eye on the group's progress. I asked them how they were doing. "Would you leave us alone please?" Shirley asked. As I was turning away, I heard Georgia say, "Dyke."

As I mentioned earlier, confrontations between student and staff were not unheard of at HSX. I had seen Jackie blow up at Casey. I had seen Calvin get so angry he would stare into the distance, frozen, ignoring anything Lyla would say to him, refusing to do any work. Lyla would respond to this situation, which came up more than once, by saying that it was time to leave Calvin alone and would do just that. So there was no need necessarily to respond to this, except that when Casey returned and asked for a report on how the students in the classroom were doing and I mentioned this incident, she felt I ought to address it. The problem was that in the context of HSX, calling someone a "dyke" was a slur, an action covered by the anti-harassment policy and, therefore, worthy of comment. I discussed it with Georgia privately in Judith's office. What if Jackie had overheard her, I asked. She, Georgia, could have been thrown out of the school. She giggled, said she and Shirley were just joking with each other, and apologized. That was not the only aftermath of the incident, however, as I had an internal response as well. I took them on their word that they wanted to be left alone and made a mental note to give them more space. Nevertheless, I wondered from then on, why "dyke"? Why not "bitch"? Why not something like Jackie's "get that the fuck away from me" and leave it at that? Why a comment that would specifically challenge the anti-harassment policy that had been drilled into them during the first few weeks of class? I began to wonder if the particular choice of comment hadn't been a sideways critique of the definition of alterity that the school embraced and the anti-harassment policy embodied, under which almost any group, including Whites, could claim protection.

Georgia's comment barely registered in terms of anti-harassment issues the school faced that day. As if to back up my interpretation of what could happen to you if you flaunted the rules of the school, that afternoon was uncharacteristically full of expulsions and near expulsions—one student with a swastika tattoo was expelled for making racist comments on a school trip; another student was expelled for carrying a knife (ostensibly for self-protection); two female students were admonished for getting into a physical fight on the front lawn over comments about a haircut. In addition, the staff was concerned with a report that a group of students were making homophobic comments on that afternoon. An impromptu all-school meeting was organized later in the day to discuss these incidents. Students reported to me that the meeting ended chaotically and emotionally, as many blamed the problems on "new students." The following quarter, the New Visions class tried to come up with a new name for new students because the very term *new student* had become such a loaded one. Not surprisingly, they were not very successful. This tension between old and new students remained an acknowledged concern for the duration of my research.

On October 3, David Gregory came to address the new students and assure them that they were welcome, that he considered them "a good group." In the process of explaining the possible motivations for the hostility against new students, he drew an analogy between the experience of new students coming to HSX and the experience of the founders of the school:

Even the second semester we were in existence, people have been saying we're going downhill. You can bet on it, people do it every single quarter. . . . It is true that when students first come here, you're coming from some place you didn't like very much, so you think it's great here. We were on a high when we first started the school. We had to struggle against a tremendous amount of hostility from the school system and the community.

David Gregory called on the now familiar distinction between HSX and traditional schools to bring the students closer together. Later he compared the older students' actions to the behavior of his son who was about to embark for college. You've got to put down a place to make yourself ready to leave it, was his explanation for the old students' comments.

After David left, small group work on the "Design Your Own School" project continued quietly. Some worked on replicating HSX.

> *Janice:* Should we make the policies just like HSX? I think so. They're good policies. I'm just going to copy this down [picks up attendance policy].

Others unofficially parodied the school's principal policy of nonharassment, emphasized at the previous afternoon's meeting. Ginger, Georgia, and Tasha (African American-appearing) joked with each other while comparing darkness of shades of makeup compacts about whether their comparisons were racist. "She's harassing me," Georgia said, laughing.

Meanwhile Calvin worked on his Malcolm X project, asking Lenny questions that Lenny answered from memory while he seemed on the verge of napping.

> *Calvin:* What day he born, Len?
> *Lenny:* May 19, 1925.
> *Calvin:* What day he die?
> *Lenny:* February 21, 1965.

Students presented their "Design Your Own School" projects on October 7. These projects demonstrated, as earlier written work in the class had demonstrated, varying degrees of investment in HSX and opposition to traditional schooling. Justine, Janice, and Karen, all European American-appearing, designed the "Rosa Parks High School," which in policies and purpose was almost exactly the same as HSX—"a harassment free environment" where "[t]eachers and students alike are diverse and accepting." Like HSX, "[c]lasses are designed so each student learns in his or her best mode." The teacher-student ratio, the length of class periods, the enrollment process, and the basic policies all mimicked those of HSX. The biggest difference was that the only required course at Rosa Parks High was computer technology. The "Island School," designed by Lenny, Georgia, Calvin, and Shirley, also showed some similarities to HSX. They had settled on an attendance time of from ten to three. "We chose this number because it is similar to [HSX] and we feel that [HSX] is a comfortable environment." Like HSX, the Island School had 150 students, but the similarities ended there. Unlike HSX, the Island School was funded by hosting NBA games. The cafeteria offered vegetarian and nonpork options; this seemingly incidental feature of the meal plan was a sign of Lenny's investments, which would become more apparent as the quarter progressed.

October 2, the day of the all-school meeting, seemed to mark the lancing of the overt boil of tension in HSX I. After that meeting and David's subsequent visit, things were quieter. The students were left to their own devices much of the time to work in small groups; unlike previous units in the class, Casey did not at any point lecture on the subject of Malcolm X directly, and there was no class discussion on Malcolm exterior to the process of making the project. In the final week before they were to teach the sixth graders, work on the project stepped up, and students became visibly nervous. By October 14, students were asked to talk about some of their ideas. Lenny and Calvin presented the timeline Calvin had made in collaboration with Lenny. Lenny also presented his collage, "Things to do with Malcolm X"; they said they planned to show the sixth graders the timeline, the collage, "plus clips out of the newspapers to add some umph," though the exact nature of that "umph" was not discussed. Jackie looked the timeline over and asked Lenny, "How the hell do you know all them dates?" Lenny said, "I don't know them all by memory, but most of them." Jackie responded, "Because I was very impressed by that." Dawna presented her collage, and Lenny corrected a detail here and there. Justine played part of a musical tape she had put together ending with the Crosby, Stills, and Nash song "For What It's Worth." Most of the other students showed collages, and discussion was generally complimentary of students' efforts.[20] Harriet (White-appearing) drew pictures of Malcolm at different points of his life: "Then he goes to jail, Black power, and I drew them a lot darker." Casey looked it over and said, "The red also reminds me of how angry he was at that point."

Judith commented, "I like the way you played with colors and the faces because it's such an interesting place in his life."

Don and Cara (a White-appearing junior) presented material that looked very different because much of it was done on computer. Don had created a graphic representation of Malcolm X's life, including a paper doll of Malcolm X and cutout clothing to demonstrate the different stages of Malcolm's life in dress (see figure 5.1). The instructions were inset: "Hey Kids! Here's a fun Malcolm X play set featuring: A) The prison years! B) His Islam years! C) His early farm years! D) His hustler years! Just cut and paste, to dress up Malcolm the way YOU want to." Hats, books, and a gun were all provided as cutout accessories.

Figure 5.1. Don's graphic design

Another computer-generated graphic created by Don foregrounded the following quote from Malcolm X:

They called me a teacher, a fomenter of violence. I would say point blank: "that is a lie." I am not for wanton violence. I'm for justice. I feel that if white people were attacked by Negroes, if the forces of law proved unable, or inadequate, or reluctant to protect these whites from those Negroes, then those white people should protect and defend themselves from those Negroes, using arms if necessary. And I feel that when the law fails to protect Negroes from whites' attack, then those Negroes should use arms if necessary to defend themselves.

Lenny wanted that quote placed in historical context: "Do you know the date and year he said that?" Dan responded, "Not at all." Casey asked Don why he connected with the quote personally. Don responded by suggesting his empathy with Malcolm X and with oppression: "A lot of people are afraid of Malcolm because they think he's anti–White. But he really was for the oppressed against the oppressor, and I feel I've been oppressed, so I can connect with that." A third computer generated graphic of Don's showed a black-and-white pattern that became more and more complex in the center. Don explained, "Early Malcolm all you see are the contrasts, but later in life you see that a) all sides are the same and b) the sides can't exist without each other."

On October 18, small groups of HSX students were paired with small groups of sixth graders for the presentation of the final projects. I chose to audiotape and observe Don and Cara as they addressed one African American-appearing girl. In explaining the school's relationship to Malcolm X, they ended up promoting the school in terms of its difference from "regular school."

> *Don:* Let's see, Oh, I know. We gotta do why the school is named for him.
> *Cara:* Cause like, our school, the school that we go to, it's like, you know, everybody's different but we still get along, we still learn to accept each other and respect each other.
> *Don:* Just look around at all the kids from my class. I mean, I don't think there's a single person in this class who looks at all like me. Or anyone who listens to the music I listen to or does what I do. That's the same for every single one of us at [HSX], we all do our own thing. But at the same time, I'm not going to say, I do this and this and it's better than what you do. It's all just different. It's all different and it's all equal. [HSX's] main principle is respect.
> *Cara:* Would you like to go to a school like [HSX], or do you think you'd just like to go to regular school.

[student shrugs]

> *Don:* Well this is definitely not—[HSX] isn't for everybody.
> *Cara:* Yeah.
> *Dan:* A lot of people in this school wouldn't have made it through high school if it wasn't for [HSX]. I'm not sure if I would have.

> Right now I know I'm on the right track, going to college. It's all set. This school has saved me basically.

A few minutes before the end of the hour, the sixth-grade teacher stopped everyone and asked the students what they learned about Malcolm X. Don and Cara's student was the only one who raised her hand—which surprised Don and Cara because she'd been sitting quietly the whole time—and said, "I learned that he was like Martin Luther King."

Having taken the hint from the ideal school project observation experience, I didn't even ask to observe Lenny and Calvin, though given Lenny's ambivalent feelings about Malcolm X, I was curious. Lenny allowed me, however, to keep a photocopy of his "Things to Do with Malcolm X" collage; I realized, upon viewing it closely, that it was a very different statement from Don's collage (see figure 5.2). The biggest words on the collage were "The Hon. Elijah Muhammad." The collage had two photographs on it: one of Elijah Muhammad, the leader of the Nation of Islam during Malcolm X's affiliation with the organization, and one of Minister Louis Farrakhan, the most prominent figure of the Nation in 1996. A few short typescript phrases were pasted here and there: "justice," "justice applied equally to all," "freedom," "complete freedom," and "we cannot get along with them in peace." I later identified one prominent bulk of text as the last statement of "What the Muslims Believe" from "the Muslim Program," as articulated in Elijah Muhammad's teachings:

> 12. WE BELIEVE that Allah (God) appeared in the Person of Master W. Fard Muhammad, July, 1930; the long-awaited "Messiah" of the Christians and the "Mahdi" of the Muslims. We believe further and lastly that Allah is God and besides HIM there is no God and He will bring about a universal government of peace wherein we all can live in peace together.

The snippets of typescript phrases in the collage—"we cannot get along with them in peace," "justice applied equally to all," and "complete freedom"—also come from the "What the Muslims Believe" section of "The Muslim Program." The phrase "we cannot get along with them in peace," for example, comes from a larger phrase calling for separation in the face of four hundred years of oppression at the hands of White America. The whole phrase from the Muslim Program reads:

Figure 5.2. Lenny's collage

Since we cannot get along with them in peace and equality, after giving them 400 years of our sweat and blood and receiving in return some of the worst treatment human beings have ever experienced, we believe our contributions to this land and the suffering forced upon us by white America, justifies our demand for complete separation in a state or territory of our own. (Muhammad, 1973, p. 264)

The only mention of Malcolm X on the collage is the handwritten "Things to do with Malcolm X." I asked Lenny why there were no pictures of Malcolm X on his collage. He replied, giving a response that he has given since his first appearance at HSX, but in stronger terms: "Because I don't really like Malcolm X."

Malcolm

And what I'd be most interested in regarding any venture involving Malcolm X is what do students, especially adult education students (of whom Malcolm was one) think is the crucial lesson to be learned from his life? Do they accept the weak, tepid line that the central import of his life is that he overcame obstacles and had a tremendous capacity for reinventing himself? I know I don't accept it. You can run to your nearest politician and find a master of hurdling and rein-vention. Malcolm stood straight up and aimed a fiery verbal assault directly against white supremacy and economic exploitation. That is what thrilled me on the verge of adolescence. . . . While I am witness to the commodification of X, I'm looking for some X-ification, if you will, some basic decency and far less greed in our structures of com-modity. I'm seeking some X-ification, some gentle equalities and stu-dent empowerment, in our establishments of education. (Gilyard, 1996, p. 81)

Of course, the resurgence of interest in Malcolm guarantees nothing about the progressive character or radical direction of black politics in the future. Part of Malcolm's appeal is the openness of his narra-tive. This allows him to appear in myriad guises: as an orthodox member of the Nation of Islam, as a prototype for Minister Farrakhan or as a fledgling revolutionary socialist. We must try to make sense of the apparently limitless post-modern plasticity of Malcolm. . . . Like Malcolm's own story of transformation and redemptive change, the capacity to remake and mould his memory into a variety of contra-dictory but equally valid shapes underlines the impossibility of see-ing racial identity in mechanistically essentialist terms. . . . His living memory and the power of his image have created an important op-portunity to find new sets of racial tactics in circumstances where black nationalism and the economistic leftism against which it was so often defined have nothing left to offer. (Gilroy, 1994, p.13)

I began to see the extent to which a whole generation of us have grown up pretenders to the Malcolm legacy; I see it in the faces of my friends; I hear it in the inflections of our voices. I see it in myself; iconette in the making, dedicatedly pursuing the path of liberatory potential. Who knows if Malcolm would have approved. But that's the beauty of it all; the achingly postmodern transformativity of the singular imagination, floating somewhere in the misty blue angst of annibus domini 1980–2001. (Williams, 1995, p. 124)

These quotes from scholars published shortly before or during the time I was observing at High School X indicate that what Malcolm X's life was to mean in the post–civil rights era was a prob-lem not only to HSX but to America and beyond, as well. The "ap-parently limitless post-modern plasticity of Malcolm," as Paul Gilroy puts it, the "achingly postmodern transformativity," as Patricia Wil-liams puts it, the "weak, tepid line," as Keith Gilyard puts it, all in-dicate Malcolm X's life is easily appropriated to support a myriad of efforts, informed and not, to confront, or even sustain, racial injustice. For a compelling case in point, note that Williams's comment is occasioned by Clarence Thomas's public embrace of Malcolm X as a role model. As both Gilroy's and Gilyard's comments suggest, there are promises in teaching about Malcolm X's life, but certainly no guarantees that any such teaching will result in confrontation, equality, or student empowerment. Gilyard's comment also indicates that the open character of the Malcolm narrative (as opposed to, let's say, the Elijah Muhammad narrative as it is popularly documented) is exactly what has made it so adaptable to the classroom. First-year composition teacher and researcher Geoffrey Sirc, for example, having identified the Malcolm X story as that of a person who successfully makes a leap from one culture to another culture via privileged discourse, suggests this story is a fitting one for the basic writing student, raising questions about how students "join the institutional academic setting" (1994, p. 54). Yet the student responses Sirc reports from a class in which *The Autobiography of Malcolm X* was read reveal again the indeterminacy of the Malcolm X narrative. Some students viewed his life as a lesson to never quit hustling. Others think he's just plain racist.

Sirc notes that his students' opinions, while strong, were not necessarily all informed; as he points out, the Malcolm narrative is so available in the culture that some students discussed Malcolm without even reading his autobiography (which many consider to be the most authoritative source).[21] Most of the students in High School X did not read the book, either, other sources for the Malcolm narrative being readily available. Spike Lee's film, at the time recently released, embraced Malcolm's plasticity in its final moments as children from the United States and South Africa jumped up and declared "I am Malcolm!" and various celebrities were filmed wearing the Malcolm X hat the movie made popular.

All signs suggest either Lenny was a member of the Nation of Islam, or at least identified with the Nation strongly; hence there was a limit to how much he could like Malcolm X, much less shout "I am Malcolm" as a representative of a majority White school named after him. Elijah Muhammad condemned Malcolm X as a hypocrite and tool of the White man, specifically scorning the naming of schools after him. He wrote in *The Fall of America*:

> Malcolm fell out from us a hypocrite. He went and joined white people and worshiped them and he got what he preached for. Now

the white man names colleges after Malcolm only to get you to join in the philosophy which he left behind; that white people are good. (Muhammad, 1973, p. 95)

Given the fraught history between the Nation and Malcolm, it would be difficult if you favored one to favor the other except in the most historically abstract way. Far from historically abstract, Calvin and Lenny's Malcolm X timeline has a point in 1963 labeled "Becomes a hypocrite." Nevertheless, Lenny chose to go to High School X. His own relationship to Malcolm X therefore suggests a certain flexibility. It seemed the longer he was at the school, the more anti-Malcolm he became, the mission to teach sixth graders about Malcolm's life the seeming final straw.

The Monday after the visit to the middle school, Judith asked HSX I students to reflect on their experience teaching the sixth graders either by writing, drawing, or sculpting "more your feelings about you than your feelings about them." Play-doh was passed around. Don passed on the Play-doh and wrote the following about his experience teaching the sixth-grade girl:

> As we talked, I realized we had no way of knowing whether or not she was listening, whether or not she understood, or whether or not she cared. It was unnerving. But when we were finished, and the teacher asked for the kids to tell him what they learned, she raised her hand and made a comparison between Martin Luther King Jr. and Malcolm X. It was extremely satisfying. Maybe I would like to be a teacher.

At his turn, Lenny rendered a more global comment on the teaching exercise: "Waste of our time and theirs to do that."

The figure of Malcolm X obviously did not resonate with Don and Lenny in the same way, and yet, tellingly, they both approached the task to teach his life with similar rhetorical sensibilities. Both attended to the rhetoric of conversion in some form: Don in talking with the sixth grader professed acceptance of High School X as his savior through which universal harmony will be achieved, as well as pursuit of higher learning; Lenny ascribed the power to create universal harmony to Allah in the personage of Master W. Fard Muhammad—a position Malcolm X would eventually reject. Remarking on the rhetoric of conversion, Peter Dorsey (1992) observes that "in the process of testifying to a conversion experience, the autobiographer binds the self to a community of believers" (p. 78).

Lenny's collage, an anti-conversion statement, therefore suggested some ambivalence not only toward Malcolm X but also toward the community of HSX as well.

Both Don and Lenny's projects were also anti-harassment statements of a sort. Don's affirmed universal tolerance and the process of learning to live together in peace as the solution to harassment; Lenny's collage suggested that separatism, giving African Americans a space of their own, was necessary for peace, which could not be achieved through living together. Don suggested that the "sides"— Black and White—couldn't exist without each other. Lenny suggested that they couldn't exist with each other. But one of the greatest differences between Don's graphic and Lenny's collage had to do with historical context. Don's graphic did not place Malcolm X's words in history. His cutout game was the ultimate embodiment of Malcolm's postmodern plasticity. Lenny placed Malcolm X, albeit in a marginalized way, within a continuum of leaders of the Nation of Islam; his collage documented an even longer history, suggesting that one of the "things" that had to do with Malcolm X was four hundred years of oppression under White rule.

Considering the significance of history in the development of HSX's curriculum, I wondered what would have happened if the "life" of Malcolm X hadn't been separated from his "times," all those years ago, or if HSX I hadn't been separated from HSX II, the teaching of the anti-harassment policy from the course on discrimination in American history. Would it have made a difference to either Don or Lenny in their approach to Malcolm X? In HSX II, the students learned of many of the United States crimes against people of color, crimes that, as Jackson and Solís (1995) observe, abrogate any attempt to create a real multicultural literacy: "A pedagogy that asserts the celebration of difference must, by implication, affirm the struggles of oppressed and colonized peoples to self-determine, lest multiculturalism be reduced to yet the latest strategy of the colonizer to "deal" with its subordinates" (p. 6). Whether one agrees with the platform of Elijah Muhammad as a whole or not, one has to agree that he in some way stood for African American self-determination; he constantly reminded one of the struggle of an oppressed people. Lenny's collage, by invoking the figures of Elijah Muhammad and Minister Farrakhan, could be read as an effort to keep certain struggles alive in the historically amnesiac and commodified cultural present.

Although affirmed in HSX II, the anti-discrimination class, these struggles and histories were not directly affirmed through the Malcolm X project in HSX I, where the stakes of assimilating students into the school were perceived to be high. In HSX I, all readings of Malcolm X were allowed to coexist and were equally celebrated. There was no discussion of possible inconsistencies between readings or of the ramifications of individual students' identifications with certain representations. Lenny's collage stirred up no dust. The unit on learning the school policies was given long in advance of the Malcolm X project so that the interesting question of what Malcolm would have thought about the anti-harassment policy, and at what stage of his life, was not raised. In some ways, HSX was insulated from its namesake, Malcolm X, which is perhaps as it had to be. Integration oriented as the anti-harassment policy and High School X as a whole was, the namesake of the school was not. In a 1964 interview given after he had left the Nation, Malcolm X remarked of the integration remedy proposed by the *Brown* decision:

> So in my opinion, what the integrationists are saying when they say that whites and blacks must go to school together, is that whites are so much superior that just their presence in a black classroom balances it out. I can't go along with that. (Malcolm X, 1992/1970, p. 17)

HSX, an integrated school in the late 1990s, when Black separatist movements were not as prominent as they had been in the early 1970s, did not have that kind of "X-ification" on its agenda. The school offered explicit teaching of the environment of anti-harassment in place of separatism, even though that choice eventually led to mixed messages about racism and culture. The anti-harassment policy suggested that discrimination was a matter of aberrant acts to which anyone might be subject. The list of attributes for which people may not be harassed resembles "equal opportunity employment" statements at the bottom of job applications; it suggests the all-inclusive multiculturalism that has characterized the post–civil rights era approach to remedy and anti-discrimination, but this all-inclusive approach paradoxically does not sit well with all, not even with the school itself.

The quarter after I observed HSX I and II, I sat in on the New Visions class, the class responsible for maintaining the environment of the school and for enforcing the anti-harassment policy. With the help of Casey as teacher, the students put together anti-harassment workshops in the school, worked on the garbage problem, arranged school trips, and advised the principal and staff. As a member of the class put it to me with some authority, "If someone has a problem, they come to New Visions." But New Visions also represented the school to outsiders. Members of the class sat in on school district meetings, took notes, and reported back. During the quarter I observed the class, the students put together a panel on the need for alternatives in education and invited local newscasters and administrators from area schools to attend. During that panel, one of the students explained that the student body was one-third minority students, and that the HSX definition of *minority* included not only students of color but gay and lesbian students as well. The minority affairs officer from Don's old high school, an African American-appearing female, corrected the student, saying that *minority* refers only to people of color. Watching the tape of the proceedings later in New Visions, some students were livid at this suggestion, quickly pointing out all the crimes against gays and lesbians. In fact, HSX remains alone in the district in its broader definition of *minority,* but the school doesn't always act on that broader definition; the school has a second demographic category, "AHANA," to track the progress, retention, and recruitment of "African Americans, Hispanics, Asian Americans, and Native Americans." The School Improvement Planning notes from 1995/1996 evidence that retention of specifically African American students was a point of concern. The notes on recommendations from the staff for helping AHANA students pass classes read: "Increase partnerships with parents, language issues, power issues, attendance, black standard English (communication issues), high expectation with limits on behavior, bring in a speaker to address African American issues."

Certainly all schools need to address and condemn acts of hate speech and harassment, and the anti-harassment policy was critical to maintaining the school's largely peaceful climate without metal detectors, clothing rules, and hall passes. But in many ways, HSX offered competing definitions of multiculturalism through HSX I and II, one historical and one not. Although it let the unity of difference along the lines identified by Ladson-Billings and Tate (1995) stand in the most public images of the school, the staff remained concerned behind the scenes with having the school reflect the demographics of a surrounding community that included a large African American population.

Tensions between and among different groups were enacted in other ways, below the level of official curriculum and policy, and here I am thinking of Lenny's approach to the various teachers. I would like to return to HSX I, to another incident besides the Malcolm X speech, in which Lenny volunteered to be in a position to address the entire class. During the conflict resolution unit, Judith created four stations on the floor, marking the stages of the conflict cycle, and asked for volunteers to share a conflict with the class and walk through the cycle. Janice and Lenny both volunteered. The teachers demonstrated the exercise first. Casey began on the Beliefs and Attitudes station, explaining that as she was raised in an alcoholic home, she had a belief that conflict was to be avoided at all costs. Eventually, she married a difficult man. The consequence was her eventual divorce. After Casey, Judith began by explaining the beliefs and attitudes she learned from the alcoholic home she was raised in and related a recent conflict she had had with her husband about travel plans. Janice explained the conflict she had with her sister when her sister stole cigarettes from her. Lenny's conflict also revolved around being the victim of theft, as he recounted how his parents invaded his room looking for things to steal and then threw him down the stairs when he protested. He explained to a class now devoting its full attention to the exercise: "I don't mind when it gets physical, because at least people release their anger. I don't think it's fair when I get tag-teamed. I don't go home much no more. I don't have no trust in them." Judith asks, "So how if that's the mode of conflict resolution you learned, how is that going to work here where the consequences of fighting are so high?" Lenny responded, standing on the Consequences station, "[T]his situation makes me want to be in school even more."

Lenny did have some conflict resolution skills beyond fighting; he made ample use of his literacy practices to render critique, and he made ample use of the resources of the school. He volunteered to take the Academic Studies Skills class, even though, academically speaking anyway, he didn't need it. Yet he got other things there. Whereas with Casey and Judith he flaunted the rules of the class, and eventually marginalized the namesake of the school in the space of the page over which he had control, with Lyla, in the Academic Studies School class, he was mostly compliant and respectful. One day I witnessed Lenny acting up in HSX I enough to warrant a scolding from the teachers; in the very next period, in Lyla's Academic Study Skills class, he sat quietly while Lyla took attendance. Tears started rolling down his face as he told Lyla that he wasn't feeling that great that day, and then revealed a crushing family incident that had occurred the night before. For Lenny, as for many if not most of the students at HSX, things were almost impossible at home, and at least in part, being at school seemed to provide relief. For Lenny that part seemed to be Lyla's classroom. When I interviewed Lyla years later, I recalled this day and asked about their relationship:

> He had a thing about Black people sticking together. He would often say that. He would often say, "I respect you as a Black woman." I think that was part of the difference that you saw, that he was really trying to adhere and trying to do what he felt would make him a productive student in this setting with this Black teacher.[22]

Lenny's writing sample, the earliest piece of writing he did at HSX, suggested directly that Black people should respect each other and that Black men should respect Black women. He explained this in the context of arguing that rappers should not be censored. Given the assignment to write about something he felt strongly about, he wrote:

> I feel strongly about the lyrics in rap music. I feel that bad words should be allowed in music. I don't think anyone deserves to have their music censored. I also think that rappers should use their blessing for good though and send out positive messages. I think it would be better to fill peoples mind with positive stuff instead of negative. I especially think rappers need to quit talking about women by using the "B" word. Also black people need to stop reffering to each other as niggers.

For Lenny, all differences did not appear to be analogous and ahistorical, and the identities of the oppressor and oppressed did not appear to be completely interchangeable. Had Lenny attended the school in the early 1970s, he would have been within a cultural milieu that even if only briefly invited a majority Black institutional space in the form of a Black Studies Program. Arguably, in many ways, Lyla's class had become that space. By the 1990s, however, the idea of introducing such a space explicitly in an integrated setting was rhetorically off-register except as a support structure for literacy skills. Making a majority Black space outside of the rubric of literacy deficit became a function of individual students' literacy practices rather than a function of the school.

Lessons from an Alternative School

Lessons to be learned from this study of an alternative school cannot easily be boiled down to statistics of who graduated and who didn't, who received good grades and who didn't. The low enrollment at HSX renders most statistics unreliable. Students don't get grades, and because they sometimes choose to attend the school only temporarily, turnover is very high; at the end of the year, the school typically has a turnover rate in population near 50 percent, which is not a situation most schools face. Lyla and David Gregory both pointed out that while the school graduates about thirty to forty students a year, many students tend to go for a short period of time to HSX or on an as-needed basis. As David Gregory put it:

> You usually end up with having to take in what could be the equivalent of two large class—somewhere between 40 and 50 students in the first two quarters of the semester. That's quite a strain, having almost a third, sometimes more than a third of the school, being new students.

Trying to maintain its organic and student-involved nature with turnover of that size is one of the HSX staff's constant concerns. This situation presents challenges other schools don't have to face.

Because of the nature of the school, then, a qualitative study is likely to say more about literacy practices at HSX than a quantitative study or a comparison study with another school. Yet I can say that my experience also presents a cautionary tale of qualitative research. Researchers are often quick to point out that their own subjectivities affect how they analyze and make sense of data. I think more needs to be said about the data that one never does get to collect. Certainly as a participant-observer, I could not bring my racialized, gendered, university-identified body into this situation and expect to have access to all literacy practices equally. Many of the students in this university town have observation fatigue— doubtless that goes double for the African American students. I am sure that with many of these students, I saw what they wanted me to see. But they clearly wanted me to see something, as they chose their level of participation throughout. What I did see is that issues of racism's impact on literacy practices are more complex than single variable discussions of dialect difference, culturally based learning styles, or curriculum generally allow, and that the content of literacy practices—what those practices are actually saying—deserves much attention. Lenny's collage does not strike me as obtuse. Lenny shared with Lyla the practice of insisting that issues he felt important to African Americans be heard in written work and oral speeches, and he continually put himself in situations where he could be heard by the classroom as a whole. When it came to speaking against racial injustice, Lenny's conception of audience was generous. If he struggles after leaving HSX, it will not be through absence of literacy skill on his part, but rather it will be the fault of the larger national environment that with deliberate obliviousness, finds such expressions disutile, inappropriate, or culturally unintelligible.

Lyla continues to speak up as well, both inside and outside HSX. She has become an active participant in a Parents of African American Students advocacy group in the public school her sons attended (Don's old school). Almost thirty years after she integrated her high school, she found herself fighting racism in her son's school, using similar tactics of carefully orchestrated team work:

> I would go to the school board meetings and hold up these pictures of this all-White Homecoming Court, and talk about segregation within so-called integrated institutions. I mean, once I wrote a thirty-page speech because they would give you five minutes a piece to speak at school board meetings. So I divided it up among the people in my group, and so we went one after one. Gave the whole speech to them. So we would target racism in sports, you know, such as when our children would go to [a nearby school] and play, they would get called niggers and coons and goons down there.

Lyla told me the parents group was also instrumental in getting an African American history course accepted into the curriculum for required history credit. At other district high schools, such a class only counted as an elective. The parents group also engaged in a form of teacher evaluation that many of the school staff found unnerving; even if they were evaluated positively by the group, those who received awards for working well with African American students became targets of the other teachers' hostility.

> [W]e tried to use it as a way of encouraging people who did well with our children to keep doing that. So we actually set up a survey and would have our students evaluate, not a specific teacher but name the teachers who worked well with them and then give reasons why these

teachers worked well with them. Then the teachers who came out to be most successful with our students, we would give them plaques or certificates. That would really unnerve the rest of the staff, until in the end some of our teachers were afraid to accept the accolades from us because the other staff would come down on them so heavily.

That teachers who accepted accolades from the African American parents group were ostracized is evidence that there remain powerful culturally sanctioned incentives to promote African American student failure, evidence that in the project of making schools serve the entire population of the United States, much work remains to be done.

CONCLUSION: THE POLITICS OF LEARNING AFTER *BROWN*

In 1959, four years after *Brown v. Board of Education II* was decided, the U.S. Supreme Court upheld the use of literacy tests for voter eligibility in *Lassiter v. Northampton Election Bd*. Louise Lassiter, an African American woman, had charged that the North Carolina literacy test through which she was denied the opportunity to register to vote, and beyond that denied participation in activities such as serving on juries that are comprised of people on registered voter lists, violated her constitutional rights. The Court, however, determined that the requirement to "'be able to read and write any section of the Constitution of North Carolina in the English language,' did not on its face violate the Fifteenth Amendment" (*Lassiter,* 1959, p. 45). Justice Douglas delivered this opinion of the Court, and with it, a short disquisition on the nature of literacy:

> Literacy and illiteracy are neutral on race, creed, color, and sex, as reports around the world show. Literacy and intelligence are obviously not synonymous. Illiterate people may be intelligent voters. Yet in our society where newspapers, periodicals, books, and other printed matter canvass and debate campaign issues, a State might conclude that only those who are literate should exercise the franchise. . . . We do not sit in judgment of the wisdom of that policy. We cannot say,

however, that it is not an allowable one measured by constitutional standards. (*Lassiter,* 1959, p. 54)

Justice Douglas's opinion then concludes that although tests with arbitrary standards could be and have been designed for the purpose of racial discrimination, the requirement of the literacy standard in North Carolina for voter registration

> seems to us to be one fair way of determining whether a person is literate, not a calculated scheme to lay springes for the citizen. Certainly we cannot condemn it on its face as a device unrelated to the desire of North Carolina to raise the standards for people of all races who cast the ballot. (p. 54)

The language of this decision reflects a great but illogical investment in the primacy of literacy—illogical because it could well be argued that by 1959, with the rise of radio and television, printed matter was quickly becoming a redundant source of information on political matters, other sources being available to the populace. The Court's decision also assumes that people will not have access to the information conveyed by printed matter, yet people who are unable to read often get printed matter read to them by literates. The rationale here for upholding North Carolina's statute, couched the way it is and strictly interpreted, might also function as a rationale for restricting the sightless from voting.

So much can be observed from examining the decision "on its face" as it were. However, if considered in the context of past and future decisions, a more focused picture develops of the ideology of literacy's impact on the course of racial justice. The decision in *Lassiter* seems in some ways to be a step backward from the Supreme Court's opinion in *Brown*. The Court, having decided in *Brown* that segregated school systems in states like North Carolina have impeded students' ability to learn, in *Lassiter* finds literacy to be entirely race neutral. Past discrimination already determined by the Court to exist and to compromise the literacy of the state's citizens is not taken into account as the Court weighs Louise Lassiter's disenfranchisement against the state's desire to raise literacy standards. The move from *Brown* to *Lassiter* also seems to indicate a shift in the Court's conception of the state as an agent of literacy. Whereas in *Brown* preventing illiteracy seemed to be the state's responsibility, in *Lassiter,* it has become the responsibility of the individual, though the state can seemingly aid individual literacy development by manufacturing punitive consequences for illiteracy that impede democratic participation.[1] Overall, the decision in *Lassiter* shows the inclination the Court would take in subsequent decisions, a reluctance to condemn a statute that would raise literacy standards. This decision, however, abstracts North Carolina's literacy requirement from any historical context; the Court neglects to consider, for example, that up until 1957 North Carolina had on the books a grandfather clause exempting from the literacy test men registered to vote before 1867 and their progeny. In other words, by law most Whites would be unaffected by this statute. The only reason the literacy requirement existed was to disenfranchise African American voters. The Court, through its decision, effectively recognized White ownership over literacy, while African Americans had to prove theirs. Despite the discontinuities between the *Brown* decision and the *Lassiter* decision, there remains, then, this continuity: In failing to recognize the original reason for North Carolina's literacy requirement, the justices deciding *Lassiter* were governed by the same lapse in logic evident in the *Brown* decision, which failed to recognize that segregation existed solely to denigrate African Americans and protect White interests.

The Court in *Lassiter* not only failed to grant Louise Lassiter justice as an individual but also added to the ideological freight of racial injustice literacy would carry with it. Literacy, Harvey Graff (1995) suggests, is "the product of its own history" (p. xxix). We can only "know" literacy in terms of what it has meant to people over time and through specific contexts, so laminated is it with past understandings. Graff reminds us that "literacy" as a concept or a phenomenon cannot stand outside history. In the previous chapters, I have given some indication of the extent to which, in American history, literacy has been treated as White property, whereas the paths for groups of color to lay ownership to literacy have been more obstructed. Here I would like to explore some of the implications of that history for current literacy policy and scholarship.

Whose Accountability?

Despite the Court's attempt in *Lassiter* to declare literacy "neutral" on race, I would argue that such a statement is vacuous. The vacuous nature of that statement, however, has not apparently displaced its utility; literacy continues to be invoked as a race-neutral entity, even a race-defying one in current debates over standardized testing and school vouchers. For example, commentators have argued that the way to end the cycle of segregation and racism is to end the test score gap between African Americans and Whites.[2] Great social movement is thus imagined to develop from performance on literacy tests. The histories I have uncovered in the preceding pages suggest, however, that should the time come when Whites are no longer perceived to be outperforming racialized others on literacy tests, there is just as much reason to believe that segregation and racism will increase as it will decrease. I think here of the Anglo parent in the 1920s who, when asked why segregated schools for the Japanese were needed, remarked that the Japanese won too many academic awards (Delgado & Stefancic, 2000, p. 1568). The hostility of that parent seems similar to that inflicted upon teachers in Lyla's son's school who received awards for working well with African American students. Undergirding such hostility is the unexamined sentiment that literacy is first and foremost White property and that no attempt should therefore be made to redistribute the best goods. Should conclusions be drawn from history, it might be found that the day a gap between Whites and racialized groups on literacy tests ceases to become apparent will be the day state and federal legislatures end their love affair with high-stakes standardized testing and look for a new and more efficient means to identify literacy as White property.

Still, more and more literacy tests with higher and higher stakes are proposed with the justification that they will improve the opportunities of people of color (generally children of color) who are disadvantaged in underfunded schools. The rhetoric supporting high-stakes yearly literacy testing of elementary students nationwide even implies that this testing is a challenge to bigotry, providing the kind of equality that money alone has failed to bring.[3] It is further implied by the trend of giving only nominal increases to school budgets while instituting national tests that will have to be largely managed by private firms that these tests are intended to provide the transformation that public funds given directly to public schools cannot. The current policy, then, involves the giving of literacy standards instead of the giving of actual property in the form of funds for better schools and higher teacher salaries. The charge that increased literacy testing will ensure an end to "the soft bigotry of low expectations,"[4] however, is meaningless if there is no corresponding effort to confront the hard bigotry already firmly in place in the larger culture; literacy tests have most often functioned in an inequitable way in the American context of endemic racism and will likely, under current circumstances, continue to do so. Therefore the emphasis on testing coming from all levels of government as it is presently conceived is likely to be another burden on people of color, rather than a remedy. This testing can only reveal what we already know—that too many of the nation's schools are struggling.

Unfortunately, the debates over school testing and other policy issues seem to have displaced what could be a more fruitful debate over the essence of what literacy in this country should be. Less and less frequently do people talk about the actual content of instruction; discussion of what students read and what they learn about in school has faded into the background as policy makers seek to streamline education, guaranteeing certain readily measurable outcomes through testing.[5] But though the literacy these tests promote might be a measurable one, is it also a desirable one? In some cases, these tests seem to encourage what could arguably be called illiteracy rather than literacy. For example, the New York Regents exam, taken by all public high school students in New York State before they can be granted their diplomas, was recently found to have sanitized excerpts in the reading comprehension portion of the test of any mention of ethnicity or race. Excerpts from the works of Isaac Bashevis Singer deleted any mention of Judaism in the original text. Racial references were removed from a section of Annie Dillard's "An American Childhood," in which the author describes her experience as one of the few White people to visit a library in the African American part of town (Kleinfield, 2002, p. 3). Dillard's portrayal of American racial segregation is thus obscured through the editing process. This censorship not only perverts the meaning of each individual literary work but also sends an even more damaging message—that words have no meaning, no social worth outside of the exam context. Officials of the Education Department have defended the practice of altering the passages on the grounds that they did not want anyone to feel "ill at ease while taking the test" (Kleinfield, 2002, p. 3). Sadly, the student who might have been already acquainted with the literature seems unimaginable to the Education Department; that student might well be more discomforted by the alterations, pulled between his or her own experience with the literature and the false shadow of the text's meaning encountered while taking the exam. The New York Regents exam, then, is a bizarre kind of exit exam, seemingly designed to test not what students might have been taught but what students do not know. It further plays a role in ensuring that one thing students will not know about is the bigotry that has characterized American history. Standardized tests like the New York Regents exam are continually being proffered as measures to ensure school accountability; surely there is some need for such tests and the legislators who call for them to be accountable as well, to promote literacy worth having.

A Role for Literacy Scholars

What happened in New York State is not an isolated incident. In the post–civil rights era, the goal of ensuring sensitivity toward diversity in literacy education has frequently been hijacked, whether intentionally or not, in the service of obscuring histories of conflict. Literacy policy itself has been misguided by the inability to confront these histories and has badly misjudged their influence on the present. Scholars of literacy might work at this point toward pushing discussion of literacy in the public realm to a more informed and historically aware level. Over the last few decades, however, literacy scholars have themselves moved away from the kind of study that might challenge misconceptions informing current literacy policy directly. Scholars have tried to fight the drive toward standardized literacy by arguing for sensitivity toward a multiplicity of "local literacies."[6] Following Heath's (1983) *Ways with Words,* many studies have been conducted demonstrating that areas previously thought of as "illiterate" were, in fact, awash in literacy practices. However valuable the challenge to impoverished conceptions of literacy this work presents, too often "culture" in these studies is narrowly defined as local, nonnational, generally marginalized communities bounded by communicative norms. Leery of attributing meaningful literacy only to "great men," researchers have often chosen as their subjects people who are not historic figures.

Within this approach, literacy scholars have focused primarily on the mismatch between local literacy practices and school or national policy. Yet as Ralph Cintron (1997) suggests, literacy scholars could err in confining their critique to measuring the distance between a marginalized group's literacy practices and a powerful norm. Cintron observes that literacy as a scholarly focus as he understood it did not allow him to study larger socioeconomic power relationships or the embedded nature of textuality. His Midwestern Latina/o community field site, characterized as it was by immigration, made community and culture both seem more porous and unstable than literacy studies he had read had portrayed them to be. He began to focus less on cultural difference and more on the rhetoric of critique.

The civil rights era, I would argue, in challenging the rigid, artificial lines around communities, also saw the use of rhetoric to reveal the ways in which communities were more porous than they had been popularly acknowledged to be. Thurgood Marshall's argument in *Brown* serves as an exemplar of such challenges, as it deliberately pointed out the porousness of the White and African American communities in the South. He responded to the opposing counsel's argument:

> I got the feeling on hearing the discussion yesterday that when you put a white child in a school with a whole lot of colored children, the child would fall apart or something. Everybody knows that is not true. Those same kids in Virginia and South Carolina—and I have seen them do it—they play in the streets together, they play on their farms together, they go down the road together, they separate to go to school, they come out of school and play ball together. They have to be separated only in school. There is some magic to it. You can have them voting together, you can have them not restricted because of law in the houses they live in. You can have them going to the same state university and the same college, but if they go to elementary and high school, the world will fall apart. (Friedman, 1969, p. 239)

Marshall was a master rhetorician, and his argument about what "everybody knows" in the South was possibly more compelling to many of the justices than the ostensible reasons they gave for condemning segregation. Indeed, toward the end of the civil rights movement, one could say that the stockpile of what "everybody knows" had increased. The civil rights movement created many signs that have entered this nation's common language; catchwords, phrases, and historic figures have become the raw materials of the literate appropriations profiled in the previous chapters. This raw material has been variously adapted to suit individual purposes. Lenny, for example, was criticizing slavery, continuing racial injustice, and certainly the required Malcolm X project, in invoking Malcolm X the way that he did. As Gilyard (1996) points out, such a critique is not always a foregone conclusion when Malcolm X is studied in classrooms. As Heath (1983) observed, Trackton houses do have portraits of Dr. Martin Luther King Jr. and Coretta Scott King in them, whereas Roadville houses do not. This does not mean that anyone in Heath's study was ignorant of Dr. King. Rock Hill, South Carolina, the actual town Heath lived in while she conducted her research, was a stop for the Freedom Riders in the early 1960s. Likely, "everybody" in Rock Hill knew of Martin Luther King and was aware of the strong critique of racism in America he symbolized, just as "everybody" in America knew it.

One could overstate, then, the significance of cultural differences in a given conflict. Critique is part of any society, going on all the time, as anthropologist Marshall Sahlins (2000) reminds us; it is part of our shared culture and history. Sahlins notes:

> In the clash of cultural understandings and interests, both change and resistance to change are themselves historic issues. People are criticizing each other. . . . Still, all these processes are occurring in the same general way within any society, independently of radical differences in culture, so long as actors with partially distinct concepts and projects relate their actions to each other—and to a world that may prove refractory to the understandings of any and all concerned. (p. 68)

In Sahlins's model of culture, the cultural differences between Roadville and Trackton, Don and Lenny, and critical race theorists and mainstream legal theorists may not be as significant as their shared history. What may be of greatest value to those interested in striving toward equity is the critique of that history that is offered in a given conflict, and the potential of that critique to change circumstances for everyone.

Understanding the dynamics of literacy today entails, therefore, more focus on the national and global economic and political structures that affect literacy across locales, and on the events of our shared history. Literacy scholars might continue to trace the connections between sites of power and the seeming periphery, keeping history in mind as they study the present. The subjects of the first chapter—Supreme Court justices—are unusual ones for a literacy study, for example, but they are significant ones. Supreme Court justices, well-known figures at the top of the literacy pile, may not seem to be the proper subject of "cultural" analysis, as their writing is hardly obscure, and they are hardly struggling for "success." Yet "culture" includes those people who become historic figures sometimes by chance but often because they are put in positions of great agency by the larger culture. As Sahlins (2000) observes, the actions of such people are amplified. What the nine men of the Supreme Court thought about literacy at one point in time in the 1950s, I have argued, turned out to be pivotal for how people across locales thought about and invested in literacy. The Supreme Court, presidents, state legislators, heads of national committees, and CEOs of large corporations should therefore be the subjects of literacy study, where their actions bear greatly upon the literacy of others.

What are we to make, then, of the fact that these people who are in privileged positions in the nation often come from a handful of literacy institutions in the country? As I mentioned in the first chapter, three of the justices sitting on the Supreme Court deciding *Bakke* had received degrees from Harvard University. They did not all vote the same way in *Bakke*, however, nor did they all endorse the use of Harvard's admissions policy in the decision. It would be erroneous to suppose one could determine another's actions and preferences just based on the literacy training they received, as people are not simply reflections of their literacy institutions. And yet people's historic and affective associations with and investments in literacy institutions can play a surprisingly large role at crucial moments, as they did in the *Bakke* case. The literacy institutions people pass through are yet another aspect of their experience, leaving them not only with a degree but also with cultural capital, a way into social connections, and a sense of identity relational in part to the value of those institutions. For these reasons, many people make great emotional and material investments in literacy institutions, investments that generally operate below the radar of public attention to literacy.

Jennifer Holme's (2002) study of high-income home buyers who claim to choose their houses primarily based on the school district it is in bears witness to these investments. The parents Holme interviewed were all, as she noted, able to choose where to live and, therefore, really able to choose their schools. Despite the size of the material investment that the people in her study were contemplating for the benefit of their children's schooling, however, Holme found those she interviewed "obtained little firsthand information about the schools they chose or rejected before deciding to move 'for the schools,' relying instead on their social networks for school information" (p. 189). The parents she followed sought almost exclusively other high-status parents for their advice. Test scores were consulted secondarily, if at all, and the curriculum and instructional programs of the school were rarely considered in the decision, the content of instruction seemingly of little importance. One thing parents did weigh heavily, however, was White racial homogeneity, which many took to be an indication of high educational achievement.

Holme's study thus demonstrates how the economy of literacy as White property governs school choice. Based on her findings, Holme concludes that school choice programs will do little to help students of color, as "the most coveted schools are, from the most privileged parents' perspectives, those schools without low-income students or students of color" (p. 203). In his concurring opinion to the recent U.S. Supreme Court case *Zelman v. Simmons-Harris* (2002), Justice Clarence Thomas argued that the broad use of federally funded vouchers will help arm minorities with the education to defend themselves from the racial discrimination society has failed to end. Holme's study, however, suggests that given that broader context of discrimination, including residential segregation that leaves parents without another nearby school to go to, caps on enrollment at the schools that might be nearby, not to mention private schools with tuitions priced way beyond what the vouchers will provide, many parents of color will have nothing near the range of choice White high-income parents enjoy. Holme's study helps explain how a near exclusive franchise on choice of literacy institutions is brokered through a combination of accumulated capital, social connections, and White racial identity—even among those people who, Holme observed, possessed an abstract belief in the educational value of diversity. One of the lessons for literacy researchers that can be extrapolated from this case study is that calls for tolerance of culturally different literacy practices pose no fundamental threat to the current system of literacy distribution.

Literacy and the Reparations Movement

The U.S. Supreme Court's decision in *Zelman* supporting the broad use of federally funded school vouchers is one of the latest testaments to the degree to which literacy and racial justice continue to be conceptually linked in the American imagination. Vouchers are endorsed in Justice Thomas's opinion as the means to the long-awaited fulfillment of the promise of *Brown*. The failure of *Brown* to improve educational opportunities for African Americans, or to promote meaningful desegregation in the schools, is openly acknowledged. Not coincidentally, the worth of a public education is further denigrated by the decision in *Zelman*.

Literacy and racial justice continue to be linked in the public discourse, as well, though to far better effect through the reparations movement. A combination of assessing the material realities that have accumulated as a result of histories of discrimination and recognition of the disutility of civil rights approaches to further address those material realities has brought discussion of reparations to the forefront of current racial justice debates. Rhetorical and litigation strategies have both shifted as a result from an emphasis on pursuing rights to an emphasis on seeking reparations from private corporations. This shift itself signifies a growing recognition that most of the power in American government today rests in private, monied hands. Nevertheless, even given this shift, one thing has remained consistent in that literacy remains the focus of debates over racial justice.

The reparations movement has many facets and has weaved into its skein many interpretations about what reparations might constitute, and whom they should benefit. Most reparations advocates, however, give at least some attention to literacy. The literacy that is most often called for by the reparations movement is a socially conscious and historically aware one that renders a faithful portrait of America or, as the *Harvard Law Review* offers, "an unabridged version of American history" ("Bridging," 2002, p. 1708). Manning Marable (2001) most strongly conflates racial justice with literacy in his version of reparations, calling reparations an "education campaign." He explains:

> Demanding reparations is not just about compensation for the legacy of slavery and Jim Crow, however. Equally important, it is an education campaign that acknowledges the pattern of white privilege and Black inequality that is at the core of American history and that continues to this day. (Marable, 2001)

Although it is unclear exactly how successful litigation of the corporations that have benefited from slavery will eventually prove to be, one success of the reparations movement is already apparent: Debates over reparations not only hold promise for reviving struggles over racial justice but also stand to reinvigorate discussion about what one literacy priority in this country should be. The reparations movement has laid out a coherent literacy initiative in the form of a public effort to fill in the lacunas and right the distortions of American history. Of what consequence is such a restoration project to the work of building literacy in America? As the persistent protests by African Americans documented in this book show, any literacy project working toward racial justice is challenged to succeed in a climate in which national legislative bodies and large private corporations have failed to acknowledge the past and work feverishly to deny the impact of history on the present. Unless literacy projects work just as feverishly to point out the gap between what has been accomplished to promote equity and what remains to be done, they might continue to invite parody and apathy from the populations they most wish to engage.

Having for the greater part of this book reviewed the ways in which literacy has been tangled up in racial justice, it is now important that I untangle the two, as we conflate literacy and racial justice at our peril. There are aspects of the reparations movement that have little to do with literacy, as they are primarily concerned with seeking economic justice. Economic justice is not the inevitable natural outcome of education, as literacy scholars have amply shown. No measure of education is going to bring, for example, African Americans to a level playing field with White wealth. Economist Dalton Conley's (1999) study of the gap between White and African American wealth perhaps most succinctly reveals why. Although African American wealth has doubled since 1865, it has simply gone from 0.5 percent in 1865 of total wealth in the United States to 1 percent in 1990 (Conley, 1999, p. 25). Since, as Conley observes, it takes money to make money, the gap between White and African American net assets has grown, rather than shrunk, even in the face of civil rights victories. Conley's explanation of present conditions shows why literacy alone cannot fill in that gap:

> The locus of racial inequality no longer lies primarily in the labor market but rather in class and property relations that, in turn, affect other outcomes. While young African Americans may have the *opportunity* to obtain the same education, income, and wealth as whites, in actuality they are on a slippery slope, for the discrimination their parents faced in the housing and credit markets sets the stage for perpetual economic disadvantage. (1999, p. 152)

Conley notes that wealth gaps, where wealth is taken to include inherited assets such as property, stocks, and the like, persist even when salary gaps even out. Equal opportunity, then, only insures unequal outcomes. All the education in the world will not in and of itself make up for the failure to compensate African Americans for their contributions to the building of this country as well as to the fortunes of private corporations. More creative public policy in other realms besides education will be needed to offset the effects of past discrimination on the material lives of African Americans, Native Americans, and other disenfranchised groups. However, bearing the sweeping economic disparities in mind, one worthwhile step would be to end the strict scrutiny now seemingly reserved only for affirmative action programs, and to apply that scrutiny to any literacy initiative that serves as a gate to the democratic process or public funding.

Reparations, Erik Yamamoto (1999) reminds us, is not just about an apology; it is about a way to operationalize that apology, to change the structures of power in the United States so that the contributions of all citizens are recognized and valued. Each chapter of this book has isolated moments of critique in which those engaged in the enterprise of literacy are urged to seek that structural change. Taken collectively these moments suggest that the escalating literacy requirements that the country is moving toward do not in and of themselves constitute racial justice. Instead, these moments demonstrate the best values that literacy instruction can aspire to foster. At its best, literacy is a process of lifelong learning, a source of potential social engagement and critique, fuel for self-affirmation, and a means to restore justice to the law. At its worst, and too often in the present national dialogue on the subject, it is an excuse to delay long overdue reparations.

✦ NOTES

Introduction: The Tangled History of Literacy and Racial Justice

1. See Cornelius (1991) for an account of literacy restrictions faced by enslaved African Americans before the Civil War. Anderson (1988) documents the rise of industrial education for freed Blacks in the South. Royster (2000) writes of the restrictions placed on African American women's opportunities to acquire literacy.

2. In literacy studies, it has been well established that school privileging of certain cultural literacy practices functions as a form of racism (Delpit, 1988; Willis, 1995). Christopher Brown (1999) records the challenges now facing historically Black colleges and universities. Foster (1997) shows the cost of desegregation to African American teachers and administrators who lost their positions. Walker (1993) offers that integration changed the dynamics of African American parental involvement with school, often not for the better. Ladson-Billings and Tate (1995) remark on continuing segregation and call for a reexamination of *Brown v. Board of Education.*

3. See Bell (1980b) for a collection of essays by legal scholars reassessing *Brown.*

4. As Cornelius (1991) documents, however, reading and writing among those enslaved went on nonetheless.

5. Brandt (2001) argues that the economic structure of late capitalism demands more and more literacy from its workers, as literacy has become the raw material from which profits can be made.

6. Barton (1994a) dates the explosion of interest in literacy to the 1980s, though this date perhaps unnecessarily discredits the work the researchers in the 1980s were reacting to, particularly that of Jack Goody and Ian Watt, who were publishing on issues of literacy in the 1960s (Goody & Watt, 1988/1968). Kintgen, Kroll, and Rose (1988) suggest that interest in literacy

began with the publication of *Why Johnny Can't Read* in 1955. Graff (1979) dates interest in literacy in history departments to the late 1960s.

7. Nystrand (in press) argues that the development of thought about language in the late 1960s was affected by the social politics of the day, as the federal government collaborated with universities to an unprecedented extent. Harris and Willis (1997) suggest that Lyndon Johnson's administration's emphasis on education was motivated by the civil rights movement. They further suggest, as does Dressman (1999), that the nationwide reading research initiative, the 1967 "First-Grade Studies," was primarily motivated by desegregation and not by Sputnik, as has popularly been assumed. Labov's (1972) work on Black English vernacular was funded by the Office of Education, also as a response to perceived reading failure. Smitherman's (1977) *Talkin' and Testifyin'* reflected the ethos of the civil rights era: Smitherman identifies the Black Power movement as an inspiration to her work on Black English vernacular. Heath's (1983) work on cultural language patterns began as a way to answer teachers' concerns about the new population of students they faced when their schools in the Carolina Piedmont were desegregated.

8. One of the legacies of this cultural view of literacy is that scholars have begun to speak of "literacy practices" or "literacy events" as much as literacy (Heath, 1983; Scribner & Cole, 1988). Drawing on this work, I use the term *literacy practices* to describe the particular forms of literacy that are at play in a given context, as well as attitudes toward different uses of literacy, whether those attitudes are expressed in oral or written form.

9. For a cogent analysis of the flawed reasoning and statistical analysis on which Jensen based his claims, see Tucker (1994).

10. Gilyard (1996) has noted that *The Bell Curve* draws heavily on Jensen's research, citing twenty-four articles Jensen authored or coauthored in its bibliography (p. 114).

11. Delgado (1995a) and Crenshaw et al. (1995) are two anthologies of pivotal law review articles in critical race theory. The introductions to both volumes review how critical race theory developed as both a political and an intellectual movement.

12. High School X is a pseudonym.

1. The Economy of Literacy: How the Supreme Court Stalled the Civil Rights Movement

1. See Lamos (2000).

2. Brackets reflect the Supreme Court justices' amendments to the language of the district court judge in *Brown* (1951).

3. See Lòpez (1996).

4. Recordings of the oral argument were accessed online (Goldman, 2002).

5. Although transcripts of Supreme Court oral arguments do not reveal which justice is speaking, Justice Stevens is clearly identified in the context of the discussion as having asked this question.

6. The decision in the *Griggs* case established that employers must show that a standard for employment is necessary if it results in a racially disparate impact, hence the *Griggs* test (see *Griggs v. Duke Power Co.,* 1971).

7. According to Douglas (1995), the flight of White students from public schools in the South where desegregation actually was enforced was massive: "The average southern school system under a court-imposed desegregation order lost 38 percent of its white population between 1970–1984" (p. 246).

8. Applicants to the Recruit School must pass Test 21 in order to be admitted. Students at the Recruit School take the Recruit School training test during their training.

9. *Amicus* briefs are submitted by nonparties who have an interest in the outcome of the case.

10. When the University of California at Davis Medical School opened its doors in 1968, with no special admissions policy, it admitted no Blacks or Chicanos (*Petition of NAACP,* 1978, supra note 6, p. 21).

11. While laughter is documented in this written transcript, see also the audio of the oral argument in Goldman (1999). For identification of the speakers, see Dreyfuss and Lawrence (1979, p. 184).

12. The kinship between Cox and members of the Court was also evident in interactions not recorded in the official transcript of the oral argument. According to Gormley (1997), Justices Stewart and Brennan sent notes signed "Potter" and "Bill" to Cox's wife, in the audience. Justice Brennan's note read, "Phyllis—Byron and I are just delighted to see you there—it's like old times & should happen much, much more often" (p. 405).

2. *Bakke*'s Legacy: The New Rhetoric of Racial Justice

1. See Minda (1995) for a discussion of critical legal studies.

2. For the interview with Bell and other critical race theorists, see Wiener (1989, p. 246).

3. On the importance of narrative in critical race theorists' projects to expose the myths of the culture, see Delgado and Stefancic (1993).

4. Derrick Bell offered this explanation in response to the question that I, as a member of the audience, asked him during an address he gave at the University of Wisconsin in 1995: "Why do you often use the genre of science fiction narrative instead of the genre of legal argumentation?" (Bell, 1995a).

5. Richard Delgado (1995b) uses a similar technique in *The Rodrigo Chronicles* in which the first person narrator is the more traditional law

professor and Geneva's half-brother Rodrigo is the mouthpiece for Delgado's more radical assertions. Bell's use of Geneva, however, has been criticized by Patricia Williams: "She is the fiction who speaks from across the threshold to the powerful unfiction of the legal order; he argues with her, but he owns her, this destroyer of the rational order" (1991, p. 199).

6. I conducted a half-hour interview with Patricia Williams in her office at Columbia University on April 20, 1996.

7. "Muleheadedness" refers to *Of Mules and Men,* a collection of folktales about African Americans in the South by Zora Neal Hurston.

8. Jinks (1997) argues that critical race theorists should be more reflexive about the privileges of insidership they do have.

9. See "Battling against attrition" (Spring 2001) for a discussion of African American attrition rates, and the causes.

10. As Royster (2000) documents, James Forten, an African American businessman, wrote a letter to Congressman George Thatcher in 1799 pointing out the inconsistency of labeling African Americans as the property of Whites in an otherwise free society (p. 122).

3. Desegregation Comes to the Piedmont: Locating *Ways with Words*

1. See Heath (1993) for her discussion of the critical reception of *Ways.*

2. The archive included neither draft versions of *Ways* nor correspondence between Heath and the Cambridge University Press editors who published the book.

3. As I discussed previously, critical race theorist Charles Lawrence (1980) argues that since the courts and legislative bodies have consistently failed to devise a remedy in accordance with the moral mandate of *Brown,* the government has in effect found a passive way of condoning segregation by law.

4. At the same time as Heath was conducting informal research in these communities, her scholarly focus was mainly historical rather than ethnographic. Following her prize-winning account of language policy in Mexico, *Telling Tales,* she began researching language policy in early America.

5. See Saville-Troike (1982, p. 131) for a discussion of emic and etic frameworks.

6. See Bernstein (1975), *Class, Codes and Control,* vol. 3 (a volume which Heath cites in her bibliography to *Ways*), for Bernstein's discussion of educational time and space.

7. Heath has acknowledged the difficulties in adhering to this principal. She has written in response to criticisms identifying shades of allegory in her descriptions of the communities of *Ways* that these criticisms revealed to her the influence of her literary background on her rendering of the data: "I . . . wrote their lives into an encompassing story of repeating cycles of

fate, human will, and classical struggles of power between individuals and the forces of a capitalist economy and the state" (1993, p. 258).

8. See Patterson (2001) and Tushnet (1994) for documentation of resistance to desegregation.

9. For one description of the economic toll of segregation on the South, see Brumley (1957).

4. Give Me Your Literate: Literacy and the American Dream

1. The text of the *Students' Right* resolution reads:

We affirm the students' right to their own patterns and varieties of language—the dialects of their nurture or whatever dialects in which they find their own identity and style. Language scholars long ago denied that the myth of a standard American dialect has any validity. The claim that any one dialect is unacceptable amounts to an attempt of one social group to exert its dominance over another. Such a claim leads to false advice for speakers and writers, and immoral advice for humans. A nation proud of its diverse heritage and its cultural and racial variety will preserve its heritage of dialects. We affirm strongly that teachers must have the experiences and training that will enable them to respect diversity and uphold the right of students to their own language.

2. The *Students' Right* committee members were Adam Casmier, Nina Flores, Jenefer Giannasi, Myrna Harrison, Richard Lloyd-Jones, Richard A. Long, Elizabeth Martin, Elisabeth McPherson, Geneva Smitherman, and Ross Winterowd.

3. According to Parks (2000), Elisabeth McPherson wrote this in a letter dated November 15 to Richard Riel Jr.

4. Lederman's (1969) report was cited in the extensive bibliography accompanying the *Students' Right* background statement.

5. Skinner et al. (2001), *Reagan in His Own Hand*, is an edited volume of the handwritten texts of Ronald Reagan. Reagan used many abbreviations in his drafts.

6. Nancy Reagan read the address at the taping.

7. However, as Baron (1990) points out, the decision in *Lau v. Nichols* never guaranteed the language rights of the students.

8. For Reynolds's record on civil rights enforcement, see Lipsitz (1998). Lipsitz notes that Reynolds filed "only two housing discrimination suits in his twenty months in office, a distinct drop from the average of thirty-two cases a year filed during the Nixon and Ford presidencies" (p. 31).

9. Because the Philippines had colony status, these acts didn't apply to Filipinos until they were divested of their status as nationals in 1934 (Ancheta, 1998, p. 27).

10. This quotation from Hall was read during the hearings over the McCarran/Walter Act (see *Hearings*, 1952, p. 1839).

11. John F. Kennedy, then a Massachusetts representative, and Henry Cabot Lodge Jr., then a Massachusetts senator, both spoke out at this hearing against the racism of the national origins quotas.

12. See Lowe (1996) and Eng (2001) for a discussion of the various exclusion and restriction laws leading to immigrant "bachelor" communities. These scholars note that immigration law was gendering as much as racializing.

13. The title of the report, *Whom We Shall Welcome,* is taken from the words of George Washington in 1783, printed on the inside cover of the volume:

> The bosom of America is open to receive not only the Opulent and Respectable stranger, but the oppressed and persecuted of all Nations and Religions; whom we shall welcome to a participation of all our rights and privileges, if by decency and propriety of conduct they appear to merit the enjoyment.

We might note that African Americans were not in 1783 deemed meritorious of that enjoyment, regardless of decency or propriety.

14. Smitherman (1999) cites Thomas Farrell's (1983) "IQ and Standard English" in the pages of *College Composition and Communication* as an exemplar of cognitive-deficit theories of literacy achievement.

5. Literacy and Racial Justice in Practice: High School X

1. See Kozol (1982) for a discussion of the movement toward alternatives in public education.

2. Alex Haley's *The Autobiography of Malcolm X* makes use of these names to structure the story of Malcolm X.

3. All names are pseudonyms.

4. Although not tracked, some students might be encouraged into Lyla's Academic Study Skills Class.

5. I have attempted to indicate where racial identifications of others have been mine by adding "appearing." Where students have identified themselves by race, I have noted that as well.

6. The present mission statement of HSX expresses this interest in community:

> The mission of [High School X] is to create a harassment-free learning environment where all people, regardless of previous academic performance, family background, socio-economic status, beliefs and abilities, appearance, race, gender or sexual orientation, are respected. It is a school where all students are able to feel safe and are encour-

aged to take academic and social risks. Expectations for achievement are high and learning is viewed as life long. Curriculum and personalized instruction are multicultural as well as challenging. A strong sense of community exists in which students are asked to participate in school decision-making. Fundamental to the school's philosophy are viewing the student as a whole person and strengthening the connection between the student, family and community.

7. HSX also requires students to meet all state requirements in terms of credit hours but is creative in balancing its own requirements with the state. HSX I and II, for example, can be taken for either social studies or English credit.

8. The course description for New Visions reads: "Work for the course will be both academic—studying theories of learning and school reform—and practical: undertaking projects to make [HSX] as good as it can be."

9. This observation was made by David Gregory to the entire staff of HSX during the School Improvement staff meeting at the beginning of the term.

10. The ellipses indicate that the groups studied change from quarter to quarter.

11. Unfortunately, there was too little time to complete the assignment and discuss it in class that hour, so a discussion on the accomplishments of the civil rights movement did not occur.

12. I do not know the exact author of these passages.

13. For discussion of gender constraints on data collection, see Heath (1983) and Cintron (1997). Cintron and Heath both acknowledged that collecting data about members of the opposite sex proved difficult.

14. HSX I was certainly a much larger class than the HSX II class I observed, which had generally eleven to thirteen students in it.

15. Prospective students must attend their home school for at least a semester before applying to HSX. Students go through an interview process before being admitted. There are approximately 150 HSX students at any given time and approximately three hundred on a waiting list to attend. Those students who seem most at risk and most able to be served by HSX are admitted first. During the quarter I observed HSX, there were forty-five new students.

16. This incident represents perhaps one of the greatest and least easily measured differences between High School X and traditional schools. High School X takes it for granted that students have sometimes overwhelming family problems and seeks as much as possible to accommodate students in difficult circumstances. As Michelle Fine (1991) points out, the traditional public school does not generally accommodate students with family problems; such students are often purged from the school (p. 77).

17. Lenny wasn't there the day he was asked to describe himself; he was able to see how others described themselves, however, because in one of the early bonding games, the teacher passed around a sheet of paper with the descriptions and required students to ask each other which one corresponded to them.

18. This requirement to teach sixth graders, a recent addition to the requirements of the course, made HSX I a service learning course. HSX was a national demonstration site for service learning in 1996, and many courses had recently introduced a service learning component. Not all the staff considered the move of the school toward service learning appropriate; there was much debate on the topic at the staff meeting I attended at the beginning of the fall 1996 quarter.

19. Casey remarked later in the education unit that the traditional school on the west side (the one Don came from) was segregated within itself, keeping White students in honors courses on the lower floors and Black students in lower-tracked classes on the upper floors.

20. Casey had told the students that this wouldn't be the most demanding class they'd ever take, that it was designed to be a success experience from the very beginning. The lack of critical discussion of the students' efforts, then, is related to the school's retention goals.

21. Gilyard (1996), however, suggests that examining the unquestioning acceptance of the authority of *The Autobiography of Malcolm X* would be a good topic for discussion.

22. When I asked Lyla if other African American students besides Lenny treated her differently from the White staff, she said:

> It's funny, because I was talking to [Casey] about that the other day, and I get it both ways. I guess I have it both ways. I'll get what you just saw with [Lenny] and with many other students as well. . . . Also just in general, in terms of whether they're acting out or climbing over the desk and chairs and so forth, I find that with my students of color, I will garner more respect in terms of that. But on the other hand, when they are ready to act out and be naughty, I can get it in a more forceful way than the other teachers too.

Conclusion: The Politics of Learning after *Brown*

1. See E. Stevens (1988).

2. For an explicit version of this argument, see Patterson (2001).

3. See Wilgoren (2001).

4. This phrase was used by President George W. Bush as he argued for standardized testing of public school students and is mentioned in official literature for the No Child Left Behind Act.

5. The debate between phonics and whole language approaches to reading appears to be a debate over the content of instruction, but little is said even in these debates over what students should be reading, and why.

6. For example, see Barton (1994b).

✦ REFERENCES

Adams, D. W. (1988). Fundamental considerations: The deep meaning of Native American schooling, 1880–1900. *Harvard Educational Review, 58*(1), 1–28.

Amsterdam, A., & Bruner, J. (2000). *Minding the law.* Cambridge, MA: Harvard University Press.

Ancheta, A. (1998). *Race, rights, and the Asian American experience.* New Brunswick: Rutgers University Press.

Anderson, B. (1991). *Imagined communities: Reflections on the origins and spread of nationalism.* London: Verso.

Anderson, J. D. (1988). *The education of Blacks in the South, 1860–1935.* Chapel Hill: University of North Carolina Press.

Ball, A. (1992). Cultural preference and the expository writing of African-American adolescents. *Written Communication, 9,* 501–532.

Ball, H. (2000). *The* Bakke *case: Race, education, and affirmative action.* Lawrence: University Press of Kansas.

Baron, D. (1990). *The English-only question.* New Haven, CT: Yale University Press.

Barton, D. (1994a). *Literacy: An ecology of the written language.* Cambridge, MA: Blackwell Publishers.

Barton, D. (Ed.). (1994b). *Sustaining local literacies.* Reading, UK: Education for Development.

Battling against attrition. (Spring 2001). *The Newsletter of the University of Wisconsin–Madison School of Education,* p. 14.

Bell, D. (1980a). *Brown* and the interest-convergence dilemma. In D. Bell (Ed.), *Shades of* Brown: *New perspectives on school desegregation* (pp. 90–107). New York: Teachers College Press.

Bell, D. (Ed.). (1980b). *Shades of* Brown: *New perspectives on school desegregation.* New York: Teachers College Press.

Bell, D. (1987). *And we are not saved: The elusive quest for racial justice.* New York: Basic Books, Inc.

Bell, D. (1992a). *Faces at the bottom of the well.* New York: Basic Books, Inc.

Bell, D. (1992b). *Race, racism and American law* (2nd ed.). Boston: Little, Brown & Company.

Bell, D. (1994). *Confronting authority: Reflections of an ardent protester.* Boston: Beacon Press.

Bell, D. (1995a). *Address.* Wisconsin Union Theater, Madison, Wisconsin.

Bell, D. (1995b). Who's afraid of critical race theory. *University of Illinois Law Review, 4,* 893–910.

Bernstein, B. (1971). *Class, codes and control* (Vol. 1). London: Routledge & Kegan Paul.

Bernstein, B. (1975). *Class, codes and control* (Vol. 3). London: Routledge & Kegan Paul.

Brandt, D. (2001). *Literacy in American lives.* New York: Cambridge University Press.

Bridging the color line: The power of African-American reparations to redirect America's future. (2002). *Harvard Law Review, 115,* 1689–1712.

Brief for Petitioner in Support of Certiorari, Washington v. Davis, 512 F.2d 956 (D.C. Cir. 1975), *petition for cert. filed,* 44 U.S.L.W. 3035 (U.S. May 28, 1975) (No. 74–1492), cert. granted, 423 U.S. 820 (1975).

Brodkey, L. (1996). *Writing permitted in designated areas only.* Minneapolis: University of Minnesota Press.

Brown, C. M., III. (1999). *The quest to define collegiate desegregation: Black colleges Title VI compliance, and post-Adams litigation.* Westport, CT: Bergin & Garvey.

Brown, M. E. (1999). *Shapers of the great debate on immigration: A biographical dictionary.* Westport, CT: Greenwood Press.

Brown v. Board of Education I, 347 U.S. 483 (1954).

Brown v. Board of Education II, 349 U.S. 294 (1955).

Brown v. Board of Education of Topeka, Shawnee County, Kansas, 98 F. Supp. 797 (1951).

Brumley, C. (1957, December 17). Segregation costs. *The Wall Street Journal,* p. A1.

Carter, D. (1996). *From George Wallace to Newt Gingrich: Race in the conservative counter-revolution, 1963–1994.* Baton Rouge: Louisiana State University Press.

Carter, R. (1980). A reassessment of *Brown v. Board of Education.* In D. Bell (Ed.), *Shades of* Brown: *New perspectives on school desegregation* (pp. 21–28). New York: Teachers College Press.

Cintron, R. (1997). *Angel's Town: Chero ways, gang life, and rhetorics of the everyday.* Boston: Beacon Press.

Clark, K. B. (1950). *Effect of prejudice and discrimination on personality development.* Paper presented at the Midcentury White House Conference on Children and Youth: Washington, DC.

Clifford, J. (1986). On ethnographic allegory. In J. Clifford & G. Marcus (Eds.), *Writing culture: The poetics and politics of ethnography* (pp. 98–121). Berkeley: University of California Press.

Complete oral arguments of the Supreme Court of the United States: A Retrospective 1969 term through 1979 term. 1980. Frederick, MD: University Publications of America.

Conley, D. (1999). *Being Black, living in the red: Race, wealth, and social policy in America.* Berkeley: University of California Press.

Cook-Gumperz, J. (Ed.). (1986). *The social construction of literacy.* New York: Cambridge University Press.

Cornelius, J. D. (1991). *When I can read my title clear.* Columbia: University of South Carolina Press.

Crenshaw, K. (1988). Race, reform and retrenchment: Transformation and legitimation in antidiscrimination law. *Harvard Law Review, 101,* 1331–1387.

Crenshaw, K., Gotanda, N., Peller, G., & Thomas, K. (Eds). (1995). *Critical race theory: The key writings that formed the movement.* New York: The New Press.

Cunningham, W. (1991, April 1). UT excellence began with constitution. *On Campus* (University of Texas), p. 2.

Daniell, B. (1999). Narratives of literacy: Connecting composition to culture. *College Composition and Communication, 50,* 393–410.

Dean, T. (1989). Multicultural classrooms, monocultural teachers. *College Composition and Communication, 40,* 23–37.

Delgado, R. (1984). The imperial scholar: Reflections on a review of civil rights literature. *University of Pennsylvania Law Review, 132,* 561–578.

Delgado, R. (Ed.). (1995a). *Critical race theory: The cutting edge.* Philadelphia: Temple University Press.

Delgado, R. (1995b). *The Rodrigo chronicles.* New York: New York University Press.

Delgado, R., & Stefancic, J. (1993). Critical race theory: An annotated bibliography. *Virginia Law Review, 79,* 461–516.

Delgado, R., & Stefancic, J. (2000). California's racial history and constitutional rationales for race-conscious decision making in higher education. *UCLA Law Review, 47,* 1521–1614.

Delpit, L. (1988). The silenced dialogue: Power and pedagogy in educating other people's children. *Harvard Educational Review, 58*(3), 280–298.

Dorsey, P. (1992). Women's autobiography and the hermeneutics of conversion. *A-B/Autobiography Studies, 8*(1), 72–90.

Douglas, D. (1994). The quest for freedom in the post-*Brown* south: Desegregation and white self-interest. *Chicago-Kent Law Review, 70,* 689–755.

Douglas, D. (1995). *Reading, writing, and race: The desegregation of the Charlotte schools.* Charlotte: The University of North Carolina Press.

Dressman, M. (1999). On the use and misuse of research evidence: Decoding two states' reading initiatives. *Reading Research Quarterly, 34*(3), 258–285.

Dreyfuss, J., & Lawrence, C. (1979). *The* Bakke *case: The politics of inequality.* New York: Harcourt Brace Jovanovich.

Dudziak, M. L. (1995/1988). Desegregation as Cold War imperative. In R. Delgado (Ed.), *Critical race theory the cutting edge* (pp. 110–121). Philadelphia: Temple University Press.

Eng, D. (2001). *Racial castration: Managing masculinity in Asian America.* Durham, NC: Duke University Press.

Ewald, H. R., & Wallace, D. (1994). Exploring agency in classroom discourse or, Should David have told his story? *College Composition and Communication, 45,* 342–368.

Ex parte Shahid, 205 F. 812 (E.D.S.C. 1913).

Faigley, L. (1992). *Fragments of rationality: Postmodernity and the subject of composition.* Pittsburgh: University of Pittsburgh Press.

Farrell, T. J. (1983). IQ and standard English. *College Composition and Communication, 34,* 470–484.

Fine, M. (1991). *Framing dropouts: Notes on the politics of an urban public high school.* Albany: State University of New York Press.

Foster, M. (1997). *Black teachers on teaching.* New York: New Press.

Fox, T. (1990). Basic writing as cultural conflict. *Journal of Education, 172,* 65–83.

Freedman, S. W., & Calfee, R. (1984). Understanding and comprehending. *Written Communication, 1,* 459–490.

Freeman, A. D. (1980). School desegregation law: Promise, contradiction, rationalization. In D. Bell (Ed.), *Shades of* Brown: *New perspectives on school desegregation* (pp. 70–89). New York: Teachers College Press.

Freeman, A. D. (1995/1978). Legitimizing racial discrimination through antidiscrimination law: A critical review of Supreme Court Doctrine. In K. Crenshaw, N. Gotanda, G. Peller, & K. Thomas (Eds.), *Critical race theory: The key writings that formed the movement* (pp. 29–46). New York: The New Press.

Friedman, L. (Ed.). (1969). *Argument: The oral argument before the Supreme Court in* Brown v. Board of Education of Topeka. *1952–1955.* New York: Chelsea House Publishers.

Gabel, P., & Kennedy, D. (1984). Roll over Beethoven. *Stanford Law Review, 36,* 1–55.

Gilroy, P. (1994). *Small acts: Thoughts on the politics of Black culture*. London: Serpent's Tail.

Gilyard, K. (1996). *Let's flip the script: An African American discourse on language, literature and learning*. Detroit: Wayne State University Press.

Goldberg, S. (1992, September). Who's afraid of Derrick Bell? A conversation on Harvard, storytelling and the meaning of color. *ABA Journal*, pp. 56–58.

Goldman, J. (Ed.). (1999). *The Supreme Court's greatest hits* [CD-ROM]. Evanston, IL: Northwestern University Press.

Goldman, J. (Ed.). (2002). *The OYEZ Project* [On-line]. Available: http://oyez.nwu.edu/cases/.cgi?command=show&case_id=434.

Goody, J., & Watt, I. (1988/1968). Consequences of literacy. In E. Kintgen, B. Kroll, & M. Rose (Eds.), *Perspectives on literacy* (pp. 3–27). Carbondale: Southern Illinois University Press.

Gormley, K. (1997). *Archibald Cox: Conscience of a nation*. Reading, MA: Addison-Wesley.

Graff, H. (1979). *The literacy myth: Literacy and social structure in the nineteenth-century city*. New York: Academic Press.

Graff, H. J. (1995). *The labyrinths of literacy: Reflections on literacy past and present*. Pittsburgh: University of Pittsburgh Press.

Griggs v. Duke Power Co., 401 U.S. 424 (1971).

Guinier, L., Fine, M., Balin, J., Bartow, A., & Stachel, D. L. (1994). Becoming gentlemen: Women's experiences at one ivy league law school. *University of Pennsylvania Law Review, 143*, 1–110.

Haley, A. (1999). *The Autobiography of Malcolm X*. New York: Ballantine Books.

Hanchard, M. (1996). Cultural politics and Black public intellectuals. *Social Text, 48*(14), 95–108.

Hanifin, P. (1978, November 3). Did Blacks lose the *Brown* case? *Harvard Law Record, 67*(7), 3, 14.

Harris, C. (1993). Whiteness as property. *Harvard Law Review, 106*, 1707–1791.

Harris, V., & Willis, A. (1997). Expanding the boundaries: A reaction to the First-Grade Studies. *Reading Research Quarterly, 32*(4), 439–445.

Hearings before the Committee on Immigration and Naturalization. (1924). Europe as an emigrant-exporting continent and the United States as an immigrant-receiving nation. 68th Congress.

Hearings before the United States President's Commission on Immigration and Naturalization. (1952). 82nd Congress.

Heath, S. B. Papers. Dacus Library. Winthrop University, Rock Hill, South Carolina.

Heath, S. B. (1983). *Ways with words*. Cambridge, Eng.: Cambridge University Press.

Heath, S. B. (1993). The madness(es) of reading and writing ethnography. *Anthropology and Education Quarterly, 24,* 256–268.

Henley, N., & Kramarae, C. (1991). Gender, power, and miscommunication. In N. Coupland, H. Giles, & J. Wiemann (Eds.), *"Miscommunication" and problematic talk* (pp. 18–43). Newbury Park, CA: Sage.

Herrnstein, R., & Murray, C. (1994). *The bell curve: Intelligence and class structure in American life.* New York: The Free Press.

Holme, J. (2002). Buying homes, buying schools: School choice and the social construction of school quality. *Harvard Educational Review, 72,* 177–205.

Horner, B., & Lu, M-Z. (1999). *Representing the "Other": Basic writers and the teaching of basic writing.* Urbana, IL: NCTE Press.

Hymes, D. (1968). The ethnography of speaking. In J. Fishman (Ed.), *Readings in the sociology of language* (pp. 99–138). The Hague, The Netherlands: Mouton & Co.

Hymes, D. (1977). *Foundations of sociolinguistics: An ethnographic approach.* London: Tavistock.

In re Najour 174 F. 735 (N.D.Ga. 1909).

Jackson, S., & Solís, J. (1995). Introduction: Resisting zones of comfort in multiculturalism. In S. Jackson & J. Solís (Eds.), *Beyond comfort zones in multiculturalism* (pp. 1–16). Westport, CT: Begin & Garvey.

Jacobson, M. F. (1999). *Whiteness of a different color: European immigrants and the alchemy of race.* Cambridge, MA: Harvard University Press.

Jinks, C. (1997). Essays in refusal: Pre-theoretical commitments in postmodern anthropology and critical race theory. *Yale Law Journal, 107,* 499.

Jorgensen, D. (1989). Participant observation: A methodology for human studies. Newbury, CA: Sage.

Jost, K. (1991, July). Up close and personal. *ABA Journal,* pp. 97–98.

Keane, A. (1908). *The world's peoples: A popular account of their bodily and mental characters, beliefs, traditions, political, and social institutions.* London: Hutchinson & Co.

Kelly, E. (1968). Murder of the American dream. *College Composition and Communication, 19,* 106–108.

Kintgen, E., Kroll, B., & Rose, M. (1988). *Perspectives on literacy.* Carbondale: Southern Illinois University Press.

Kleinfield, N. R. (2002, June 2). The elderly man and the sea? Test sanitizes literary texts. *The New York Times,* p. B1.

Kozol, J. (1982). *Alternative schools: A guide for educators and parents.* New York: Continuum.

Kozol, J. (1991). *Savage inequalities: Children in America's schools.* New York: Crown.

Kurland, P., & Casper, G. (Eds.). (1978). *Landmark briefs and arguments of the Supreme Court of the United States: Constitutional law* (1977 term supplement, Vol. 100). Washington, DC: University Publications of America.

Labov, W. (1972). *Language in the inner city.* Philadelphia: University of Pennsylvania Press.

Ladson-Billings, G., & Tate, W. (1995). Toward a critical race theory of education. *Teachers College Record, 97*(1), 47–68.

Lamos, S. (2000). Basic writing, CUNY, and "mainstreaming": (De)-racialization reconsidered. *Journal of Basic Writing, 19*(2), 22–43.

Lassiter v. Northampton Election Bd., 360 U.S. 45 (1959).

Lau v. Nichols, 414 U.S. 563 (1974).

Lawrence, C. R. (1980). "One more river to cross"—Recognizing the real injury in *Brown:* A prerequisite to shaping new remedies. In D. Bell (Ed.), *Shades of* Brown: *New perspectives on school desegregation* (pp. 48–69). New York: Teachers College Press.

Lawrence, C. R. I. (1987, January). The id, the ego, and equal protection: Reckoning with unconscious racism. *Stanford Law Review, 39*, 317–388.

Lederman, M. J. (1969). Hip language and urban college English. *College Composition and Communication, 20*, 204–214.

Lipsitz, G. (1998). *The possessive investment in whiteness: How white people profit from identity politics.* Pittsburgh: Temple University Press.

Litwack, L. (1986). *"Blues falling down like hail": The ordeal of Black Freedom.* In Robert H. Abzug & Stephen E. Maizlish (Eds.), *New perspectives on race and slavery in America: Essays in honor of Kenneth M. Stamp.* Lexington: University of Kentucky Press.

Litwack, L. (1998). *Trouble in mind: Black southerners in the age of Jim Crow.* New York: Alfred A. Knopf.

López, I. H. (1996). *White by law: The legal construction of race.* New York: New York University Press.

Lowe, L. (1996). *Immigrant acts: On Asian American cultural politics.* Durham, NC: Duke University Press.

Lunsford, A., Moglen, H., & Slevin, J. (Eds). (1990). *The right to literacy.* New York: Modern Language Association.

MacLeod, J. (1991). *Minds stayed on freedom: The civil rights struggle in the rural South, an oral history.* San Francisco: Westview Press.

Malcolm X. (1992/1970). *By any means necessary.* New York: Pathfinder.

Marable, M. (2001). Racism and reparations. *Rethinking schools: An Urban Educational Journal, 16*(1). http://www.rethinkingschools.org/Archives/16–01/Rep161.htm. Accessed 7/11/02.

Matsuda, M. (1987). Looking to the bottom. *Harvard Critical Race-Critical Law Review, 461*, 322–399.

Matsuda, M. (1996). *Where is your body?* Boston: Beacon Press.

McIntosh, P. (1990). White privilege: Unpacking the invisible knapsack. *Independent Schools, 49,* 31–36.

Minda, G. (1995). *Postmodern legal movements: Law and jurisprudence at century's end.* New York: New York University Press.

Moses, R. (2001). *Radical Equations.* Boston: Beacon Press.

Muhammad, E. (1973). *The fall of America.* Chicago: Muhammad's Temple of Islam No. 2.

Muse, B. (1964). *Ten years of prelude: The story of integration since the Supreme Court's 1954 decision.* New York: Viking Press.

Musgrave, M. (1971). Failing minority students: Class, caste, and racial bias in American colleges. *College Composition and Communication, 22,* 24–29.

Nadel, M. (1978). Supreme Court raps gavel: *Bakke. Harvard Law Record, 65*(2), 4, 6.

Nystrand, M. (in press). Janet Emig, Frank Smith, and the new discourse about writing and reading, or How writing and reading came to be cognitive processes in 1971. In M. Nystrand & J. Duffy (Eds.), *Towards a rhetoric of everyday life: New directions in research on writing, text, and discourse.* Madison: University of Wisconsin Press.

Omi, M., & Winant, H. (1994). *Racial formation in the United States: From the 1960s to the 1980s* (2nd ed.). New York: Routledge.

Parks, S. (2000). *Class politics: The movement for Students' Right to Their Own Language.* Urbana, IL: NCTE Press.

Patterson, J. T. (2001). Brown v. Board of Education: *A civil rights milestone and its troubled legacy.* New York: Oxford University Press.

Petition of NAACP. (1978). Regents of the University of California v. Bakke, 438 U.S. 265.

Plessy v. Ferguson, 163 U.S. 537 (1896).

Pratt, M. L. (1987). Linguistic utopias. In N. Faub (Ed.), *The linguistics of writing* (pp. 48–66). Manchester, UK: Manchester University Press.

Prendergast, C. (1998). Race: The absent presence in composition studies. *College Composition and Communication, 50,* 36–53.

Regents of the University of California v. Bakke, 438 U.S. 265 (1978).

Resource unit on respecting differences for kindergarten. (1974). Author unknown. In S. B. Heath Papers. Dacus Library. Winthrop University, Rock Hill, South Carolina.

Rieder, J. (1991, October 21). Tawana and the professor. *The New Republic, 21,* 39–42.

Roediger, D. (1991). *The wages of whiteness: Race and the making of the American working class.* New York: Verso.

Royster, J. J. (2000). *Traces of a stream: Literacy and social change among African American women.* Pittsburgh: University of Pittsburgh Press.

Sahlins, M. (2000). *Historical metaphors and mythical realities: Structure in the early history of the Sandwich Islands Kingdom*. Ann Arbor: The University of Michigan Press.

Saville-Troike, M. (1982). *The Ethnography of communication: An introduction*. New York: Basic Blackwell.

Scribner, S., & Cole, M. (1988). Unpackaging literacy. In E. Kintgen, B. Kroll, & M. Rose (Eds.), *Perspectives on literacy* (pp. 57–70). Carbondale: Southern Illinois University Press. (Original work published 1981).

Selmi, M. (1999). The life of *Bakke:* An affirmative action retrospective. *Georgetown Law Journal, 87*(4), 981–1022.

Senate Report 290. (1896). 54th Congress, 1st Session, pp. 22, 23.

Severino, C. (1992). Where the cultures of basic writers and academia intersect: Cultivating the common ground. *Journal of Basic Writing, 11,* 4–15.

Sirc, G. (1994). *The Autobiography of Malcolm X* as a basic writing text. *Journal of Basic Writing, 13,* 50–77.

Skinner, K., Anderson, A., & Anderson, M. (2001). *Reagan in his own hand: The writings of Ronald Reagan that reveal his revolutionary vision for America*. New York: Free Press.

Smitherman, G. (1977). *Talkin' and testifyin'*. Boston: Houghton.

Smitherman, G. (1999). Shaping controversies—CCCC's role in the struggle for language rights. *College Composition and Communication, 50*(3), 349–372.

Stack, C. (1974). *All our kin*. New York: Basic Books.

Sternglass, M. (1974). Dialect features in the compositions of black and white college students: The same or different. *College Composition and Communication, 25,* 259–263.

Stevens, E. (1988). *Literacy, law, and social order*. De Kalb: Northern Illinois University Press.

Stevens, J. P. (personal communication, December 19, 1977). Thurgood Marshall Papers, Library of Congress, Box 204, Folder 3.

Street, B. (1984). *Literacy in theory and in practice*. Cambridge, Eng.: Cambridge University Press.

Students' right to their own language. (1974). *College Composition and Communication, 25,* 1–32.

Swann v. Charlotte-Mecklenberg Board of Education, 402 U.S. 1 (1971).

Thernstrom, A. (1992, November 16). Almost ad nauseam. *National Review,* 58–59.

Tucker, W. (1994). *The science and politics of racial research*. Chicago: University of Illinois Press.

Tushnet, M. (1994). *Making civil rights law: Thurgood Marshall and the Supreme Court, 1936–1961*. New York: Oxford University Press.

United States v. Cartozian, 6 F.2d 919 (D. Or. 1925).

United States v. Fairfield County School District, South Carolina, and A. L. Goff, Civil Action No. 70–608 (filed August 18, 1970).

Villanueva, V. (1998). Maybe a colony: And still another critique of the comp community. *Journal of Advanced Composition, 17,* 183–187.

Walker, E. V. S. (1993). Caswell County Training School, 1933–1969: Relationships between community and school. *Harvard Educational Review, 63*(2), 161–182.

Washington v. Davis, 426 U.S. 229 (1976).

Whitman, M. (1993). *Removing a badge of slavery: The record of* Brown v. Board of Education. New York: Markus Wiener.

Whom we shall welcome: Report of the President's Commission on Immigration and Naturalization. (1953). Washington, DC: U.S. Government Printing Office.

Wiener, J. (1989, September 4). Law profs fight the power. *The Nation,* 246–248.

Wilgoren, J. (2001, January 23). Bush to launch federal education plan. *The New York Times,* p. A1.

Williams, P. (1991). *The alchemy of race and rights.* Cambridge, MA: Harvard University Press.

Williams, P. (1992). A rare case study of muleheadedness and men. In T. Morrison (Ed.), *Race-ing justice, engendering power: Essays on Anita Hill, Clarence Thomas and the social construction of reality* (pp. 159–171). New York: Pantheon Books.

Williams, P. (1995). *The rooster's egg: On the persistence of prejudice.* Cambridge, MA: Harvard University Press.

Williams, P. (1996, April 29). Notes from a small world. *The New Yorker,* 87–92.

Williams, P. (1997). *Seeing a color-blind future: The paradox of race.* New York: Farrar, Straus & Giroux.

Willis, A. I. (1995). Reading the world of school literacy: Contextualizing the experience of a young African American male. *Harvard Educational Review, 65*(1), 30–49.

Woodward, C. V. (1974). *The strange career of Jim Crow.* New York: Oxford University Press.

Yamamoto, E. (1999). *Interracial justice: Conflict and reconciliation in post–civil rights America.* New York: New York University Press.

Zak, F. (1990). Exclusively positive responses to student writing. *Journal of Basic Writing, 9,* 40–53.

Zelman v. Simmons-Harris, 537 U.S. 639 (2002).

Zeni, J., & Thomas, J. (1990). Suburban African-American basic writing, grades 7–12: A text analysis. *Journal of Basic Writing, 9,* 15–39.

✦ INDEX

Till, Emmett, ix–x
tokenism, 49, 55
Topeka, Kan., 27
Trackton, 59–60, 66, 74–76, 86, 171; people of, 63–64, 68, 78, 81, 85, 87–88, 92. See also *Ways with Words*
Truman, Harry S., 14, 113
Tushnet, Mark V., 22, 183n. 8

United States v. Cartozian, 113
universities, literacy and racial prejudice in, 95–100
University of California. See *Regents of the University of California, The, v. Bakke*
University of Minnesota, 98
University of North Carolina at Charlotte, 80
University of Texas, 3, 99–100, 103

values, cultural, 9–10, 13–14, 43, 171–72
Villanueva, Victor, 56
Virginia, 23

Wallace, David L., 98, 99
War on Poverty, 9
Washington Post, 30
Washington v. Davis, x, 19, 28–30, 32, 35, 43
Ways with Words (Heath), xii, 12–13, 58–94, 169, 171; on community, 72–76, 91; on institution of segregation, 62–64; on levels of communication, 87–91; people in, 59,

81–84; on race and class, 64; 78–80, 85–86; on relationship of context to language, 70–71, 80, 82, 89, 92; researching, 58, 61, 68–69, 71, 76–77; on rights, 91–92; on stereotypes, 66–67; on taboos, 65, 90–91; use of stories in, 59–60
wealth, gaps in, 175. *See also* economy
White, Byron R., 39
White identity, 7–8, 10, 12, 14, 18, 78–80; through immigration, 101–2, 111–13; privileging of, 13, 19–20, 25, 52, 57; in real estate, 40–41. *See also* race
"White Privilege: Unpacking the Invisible Knapsack" (McIntosh), 130
White property, literacy as, 7–8, 11–12, 20, 53, 111, 166–67; backlash to, 100; economics of, 34
Whom We Shall Welcome (Commission on Immigration and Naturalization), 115–16, 184n.13
Williams, Patricia, 40–41, 45–46, 51–56, 153–54, 182n. 5
Wilson, Elizabeth, 115
Wilson, Woodrow, 108
Winant, Harold, 106, 118
Winthrop University, 61, 65–66, 80, 83
workers, students as future, xii–xiii

Yamamoto, Erik, 176

Zak, F., 118
Zelman v. Simmons-Harris, 173–74
Zeni, J., 118

Catherine Prendergast is an associate professor of English at the University of Illinois at Urbana-Champaign. Her articles have appeared in *Harvard Educational Review, Written Communication, College Composition and Communication,* and *JAC.* She received the 1999 Richard Braddock Award from the Conference on College Composition and Communication for her article "Race: The Absent Presence in Composition Studies."